AMERICA'S
CONTINUING
STORY

AMERICA'S CONTINUING STORY

An Introduction to Serial Fiction, 1850–1900

Michael Lund

 Wayne State University Press   Detroit

Library of Congress Cataloging-in-Publication Data

Lund, Michael, 1945–
    America's continuing story : an introduction to serial
fiction, 1850–1900 / Michael Lund.
        p.   cm.
    Includes bibliographical references (p.   ) and index.
    ISBN 0–8143–2401–0 (alk. paper)
    1. American fiction—19th century—History and criticism.
2. Serialized fiction—United States—History and criticism.
3. Literature publishing—United States—History—19th
century.   4. Authors and readers—United States—
History—19th century.   5. Serialized fiction—United
States—Bibliography.   6. American fiction—19th century—
Bibliography.   I. Title.
PS374.S446L8   1992
813'.4009—dc20   92-18953

Designer: Mary Primeau

FOR MEREDITH LUND AND JOHN LUND

Contents

Preface

I have been inspired to write this book for teachers as much as for literary critics. Since I began advocating the teaching of long novels in parts, as they were originally published, many teachers, especially in high schools, have asked me for information about specific titles: Were they serialized? In what magazines? Where were the parts' divisions? This last question was especially crucial for anyone who wished to read a novel in installments for a particular class. Although we can seldom copy exactly the reading schedules of historical audiences, teachers of novels in parts today still want to organize the reading assignments for students in units that include one, two, or more of the original installments. (I have included a fuller description of the practice and rewards of teaching serially in an appendix to the introduction.) J. Don Vann has provided the standard reference guide to British fiction of the nineteenth century, but nothing that I know of is available for teachers of American literature. So, in response to a very specific need, I embarked on this project.

Like most scholarly projects, the scope of this one quickly outran my original design. Searching for fiction published serially in the United States, I soon found more titles than I could possibly handle in a single work and signs of more titles in the distance lured me on in exploration. In the process of seeing my field expand beyond the limits of chronology, genre, mode, and style, I came to consider as well the critical implications of what I was finding. Installment issue and parts reading, it seemed to me, determined the primary shape of literary experience in America from 1850 to 1900. But the effects of this format and its reception did not seem adequately acknowledged in scholarship, particularly in assessments of how major works achieved their places in our cultural history. So a critical introduction to this work began to grow as rapidly as the listing of serial titles, which had been intended as the body of the study.

I hope, then, that I am offering here something for both critics and teachers: an explanation of audience reception in nineteenth-century America and a guide to parts publication from 1850 to 1900. Neither element can be said to be complete or inclusive, for I have drawn limits around this study that must be, as explained in the pages that follow, arbitrary. Still, I hope that this much of a potentially larger study will answer some of the needs that compelled me to begin in the first place.

Acknowledgments

I wish to thank the Virginia Foundation for the Humanities and Public Policy, which funded a one-semester residence at the Virginia Center for the Humanities in the spring of 1989. The initial phases of this project were completed at that time. I am also happy to acknowledge Longwood College's sabbatical program, which allowed me to draft much of this book in the fall of 1990.

Lowell Frye of Hampden-Sydney College read an early version of the manuscript, and his incisive questioning of many points greatly improved later versions. I am grateful to all my colleagues in the Department of English, Philosophy, and Modern Languages at Longwood College who offered encouragement and advice in the course of my work. Ellery Sedgwick in particular read the complete work and not only noted inconsistencies and shortcomings but provided valuable direction in my final revisions. Linda K. Hughes of Texas Christian University gave me some helpful hints for the appendix about teaching. A special note of gratitude goes to Beth Camillo, who worked with me in the last stages of production, checking documentation and refining my argument. I also wish to thank the staff at Wayne State University Press, especially Kathy Wildfong and Arthur Evans, for their support of the project.

INTRODUCTION

UNITS OF LITERARY HISTORY

Literary history in America has been built around individual names, titles, and dates, such as the years in which significant works of fiction by major writers were published: Herman Melville's *Bartleby the Scrivener* (1853), Oliver Wendell Holmes's *Else Venner* (1861), Bret Harte's *Gabriel Conroy* (1876), Mark Twain's *Huckleberry Finn* (1885), Henry James's *Tragic Muse* (1890), William Dean Howells's *Their Silver Wedding Journey* (1899). Authors, works, and years in sequence have been used to outline a development of genre, patterns of influence, and the emergence of culture. Moving from point *A* along a line through other points *B*, *C*, and *D*, we define our literary heritage, both the past through which we have traveled and the present we occupy. (See, for example, the structure of such works as Callow and Reilly's *Guide to American Literature*, Kirby's *American Fiction to 1900*, and Rogal's *A Chronological Outline of American Literature*.)

Yet such discrete dates, names, and titles mask much of the actual literary experience of America in the second half of the last century, for most of the fiction published in those decades appeared first in one of a number of installment formats. The reading of these works, rather than being concentrated in single moments (the dates of volume editions), was spread out over many months' time. As Richard H. Brodhead notes, this was "a century in which most literary reading was done in magazines" (471). As these continuing stories appeared serially in daily, weekly, or monthly periodicals, their impact on America's consciousness was gradual, enduring, and open-ended rather than immediate, dramatic, and clearly delimited. Melville's classic tale, for example, first appeared in the November and December 1853 issues of *Putnam's Magazine*. Holmes's groundbreaking novel was initially issued under the title *The Professor's Story* from January 1860 to April 1861 in the *Atlantic Monthly*. Ten installments in *Scribner's Monthly*, beginning with the November 1875 number, made up Harte's popular story. Three parts of

Mark Twain's classic—"An Adventure with Huckleberry Finn: With an Account of the Famous Grangerford-Shepherdson Feud," "Jim's Investments and King Sollermun," and "Royalty on the Mississippi"—were published in successive issues of *Century* magazine (December 1884–February 1885). James's *Tragic Muse* ran in the *Atlantic Monthly* from January 1889 through May 1890. And Howells's late novel, actually a sequel to *Their Wedding Journey* (July–December 1871), graced the pages of *Harper's New Monthly Magazine* for the twelve issues of 1899.

The date of the volume edition that usually followed a serial run, then, often did not mark the first appearance of a work on the American literary scene; that publication event was for serials the culmination of a process begun many months earlier, during which story and characters took their fundamental hold on the nation's memory. *Huckleberry Finn* did not spring full-blown into America's consciousness on 1 March 1885; but this central work in the canon emerged slowly over time in the 1880s, as literate citizens became aware of a new voice in their midst that described their national character in different prominent forums, the pages of periodicals and, later, the individual volume.

Publication in one of the major periodicals of the time meant that a work received notice: reviewers and subscribers read in installments and told others about continuing stories that had captured their interest. Booth Tarkington, as a boy in Indiana, eagerly waited for the mail to bring each installment of Howells's *The Rise of Silas Lapham* as it came out in *Century Magazine*. When he learned that Silas had gotten drunk at a dinner party in the April 1885 installment, Tarkington wept. At about the same time, a public library refused to stock the completed *Huckleberry Finn*, and *The Literary World* saw this step as a necessary antidote to the powerful effect of periodical publication: "We are glad to see that the recommendation to this sort of literature by its publication in the *Century* has received a check" (Mott 4:130). The serial form was the mode of issue for much of the major writing not only of Mark Twain but of Caroline Chesebro', George Cable, Rebecca Harding Davis, Edward Eggleston, Harold Frederic, Joel Chandler Harris, William Dean Howells, Henry James, Mary Noailles Murfree, Harriet Prescott Spofford, Harriet Beecher Stowe, Constance Fenimore Woolson, and others.

Of course, most of these novelists did later issue their completed works in volume form. The reception of these volumes, however, was inevitably shaped by response to the serial versions that had preceded them, as was the case for *Uncle Tom's Cabin*. Much has been written about the storm caused at home and abroad by Harriet Beecher Stowe's tale after it appeared in volume form on 2 March 1852. However, Gamaliel Bailey, editor of the *National Era*, in which Stowe's classic text was serialized from 5 June 1851 to 1 April 1852, placed installment publication at the base of this intense national interest. In an 1853 letter (later published in the June 1866 *Atlantic Monthly)* Bailey explained how the work was originally intended to be brief but grew in the writing:

> Some time in the summer [Harriet Beecher Stowe] wrote me that she was going to write me a story about "How a Man became a Thing." It would occupy a few numbers of the Era, in chapters. She did not suppose or dream that it would expand to a novel, nor did I. She changed the title to "Uncle Tom's Cabin," and commenced it in August. I read two or three of the first chapters, to see that everything was going on right, and read no more then. (748)

Very soon, however, this new novel had an excited, growing audience:

> She proceeded,—the story grew,—it seemed to have no end,— everybody talked of it. I thought the mails were never so irregular, for none of my subscribers was willing to lose a single number of the Era while the story was going on. . . . Of the hundreds of letters received weekly, renewing subscriptions or sending new ones, there was scarcely one that did not contain some cordial reference to Uncle Tom. (748)

Such growth in text and audience was characteristic of successful serials in nineteenth-century America and England; and the volume publication of Stowe's tale is best seen as one more phase in the development of a national phenomenon.

Bailey's reference to "hundreds" of letters suggests a substantial readership among nineteenth-century Americans for the *Era*, and an argument he subsequently made regarding payment to the author also underscores the importance of this serial version in the history of *Uncle Tom's Cabin*. Bailey noted that, because the novel had gone on longer than anticipated, he had paid Mrs. Stowe two hundred dollars more than the one hundred he had originally offered. As the work neared completion of its installment run, he wished to settle their account. In his view, the serialized novel had, during the nine months it was appearing before volume publication, created the larger audience the book would receive: "[M]y large circulation had served," he wrote, "as a tremendous advertisement for the work, which was now about to be published separately." Thus, he concluded, he "ought not to pay for it so much if these circumstances had not existed" (749). He then asked Mrs. Stowe to determine what was appropriate: "She named one hundred dollars more; this I immediately remitted" (749).

This process of generating an audience through serial publication had first been accomplished by Charles Dickens in *The Pickwick Papers* (April 1836–November 1837), a model bestseller of the new industrial age, where improvements in printing technology and the appearance of a genuine mass audience encouraged new modes of literary production (Feltes 1–17). An American analogy to Dickens's masterpiece, Stowe's novel took advantage of an extensive new readership for a particular kind of fiction; and its success in book form came in large part because audience expectation had already been created by the serial version. Readers of the *National Era* spread the word, and those who had not been subscribers were ready not simply to pay for a volume edition after 1852 but also to find for themselves the excitement and pleasure experienced by others in reading the serial *Uncle Tom's Cabin* from 5 June 1851 to 1 April 1852. James West has reported an instance in which the serial version of a novel had a negative effect on the reception of a twentieth-century novel: F. Scott Fitzgerald serialized *Tender Is the Night* (1934) in four installments of *Scribner's*, and he "was convinced that most reviewers of *Tender* had read it as a serial and that they had gotten a negative first impression of the book in that medium" (108). To understand any serial novel's place in our literary history, then, we should start with the core of periodical readers and the response created by first publication.

Serial versions of nineteenth-century American classics like *Uncle Tom's Cabin* are sometimes wholly ignored in accounts of literary history, and the exact nature of these texts is often simplified. Novels did not at first exist in an autonomous, pure state between two hard covers, as do current library editions and textbooks; instead, each installment of a work was spread out in the pages of a magazine along with many different articles on diverse subjects. For instance, in the same issue with Melville's first installment of *Bartleby the Scrivener* in the November 1853 *Putnam's Magazine* appeared a Maine travelogue entitled "A Moosehead Journal: Addressed to Edelmann Storg at the Bagni di Lucca"; scholarly reviews including "The Works of William Hamilton" (a contemporary philosopher), "Mr. Collier's Folio Shakespeare of 1632:—Its Most Plausible MS. Corrections," and "Characters in Bleak House"; a humorous social commentary, "The Potiphurs in Paris: A Letter from Miss Caroline Pettitoes to Mrs. Settem Downe"; three poems, "Odensee," "The Crucifix," and "Inscriptions for the Back of a Bank-Note"; a learned article, "Cassiterology: A Discourse on Tin"; informative pieces including "The Pacific Railroad and How It Is to be Built" and "The Life of a Dog"; the fourth number in "Reminiscences of an Ex-Jesuit"; and chapters 10 and 11 of the novel *Wensley*. And, of course, many other magazines, with their own serials and other offerings, competed for readership at the same time as the November 1853 *Putnam's*, creating a rich context that surrounded and shaped the individual texts.

Since installment novels often appeared anonymously within the larger framework of their specific periodicals, they were recognized as "*Scribner's* current serial" or the "tale running in *Atlantic Monthly*"; author and work were not at the time of first publication so discrete as an entry in a modern bibliography might suggest. Even when authorship was acknowledged (the more frequent practice in the last quarter of the century), the exact limits of a single work of art were still not absolute. Individual authors were often defined by their reputations, and any new effort was seen within the context of previous publication. In its review of James's first collection of short fiction, *The Passionate Pilgrim and Other Stories*, the April 1875 *Atlantic* assumed its readers already understood the author's work: "Mr. Henry

James, Jr., has so long been a writer of magazine stories, that most readers will realize with surprise the fact that he now presents them for the first time in book form. He has already made his public" (490).

Some monthlies featured illustrations with their fiction, an element of the works' original form almost universally ignored in the paperback editions teachers use in the classroom today, as well as in the books scholars refer to in their writing. *Scribner's Monthly* frequently claimed in the middle decades of this period that it owed much of its success to the quality of its illustrations (see, for instance, "Topics of the Time" in June 1881: 303). Scholars have only begun to explore how increasingly sophisticated engravings directed readers' attention toward specific elements of novels in their first appearance. Also missing even from the standard library copy of nineteenth-century periodicals are the advertisements that took up their share of space in individual numbers of most magazines. Binders and librarians later made the judgment that such advertisements were not relevant to the literary material of a journal; but such expressions of cultual values might well alter our understanding of why and how certain titles were responded to in their first publications.

The lengthy publication schedule of a major work allowed other publications to influence its reception, and each week or month before another issue of the periodical appeared, events in the real world could affect response to the fictional worlds. Sometimes reviewers in other periodicals shaped interest in a continuing story, as happened with James's *Daisy Miller*, a work influential in establishing the author's reputation both in and outside America. The story first appeared in the June and July 1878 *Cornhill*, a British periodical with a substantial circulation in America. The October *Harper's* explained how the first part received attention in England because it was thought to be written by a newcomer to the trade: "In its notice of the first part, the *Spectator*, struck by the singular felicity of an unknown hand, suspects the name of the author to be fictitious" (779). Their interest stimulated by the initial installment of *Daisy Miller, The Spectator* and its readers were prepared to pay special attention to the next part. That paper concluded, after the story's final installment was read, that the author "ought to do something very considerable in the way of a character novel. It is nearly impossible to exaggerate his quality of touch, so light, yet leaving such a definite impress" (*Harper's* 780).

At other times, the larger background of current events might determine response, especially when a periodical placed articles on world events in the same issue as the ongoing serial installments. In the first three months of 1899, for instance, when George Washington Cable issued *The Entomologist* in three parts for *Scribner's Magazine*, Theodore Roosevelt's account of the Spanish-American war also ran in the same periodical under the title "The Rough Riders." The excitement of the factual account might have muted response to the tame subject suggested by Cable's title. The Civil War, similarly, provided an important background to all fiction appearing during the period 1861–65. For much of the second half of the century, *Harper's* carried a detailed summary of current events in each number under the title "Monthly Record." The potential influence of such records of current events on specific literary works offers rich material for historians and literary critics interested in tracing the origin of an author's or a specific work's reputation. Donald Pease takes such analyses one step further by showing how the context of original publication *and* the context of later critical study inevitably shape literary understanding. His *Visionary Compacts: American Renaissance Writings in Cultural Context* explains, for example, how the Cold War era of the 1950s reversed nineteenth-century perspectives on the characters in Melville's *Moby Dick* (235–75).

Not only could discussions of current events frame individual works of art in their original installment format, but works of fiction sometimes functioned almost as direct commentary on other titles. When Mark Twain was serializing *Pudd'nhead Wilson* in *Century* in 1893–94, for instance, a story by Kate Chopin, "A No-Account Creole," appeared on neighboring pages of the same magazine in January 1894 and took up some remarkably similar themes. While Twain's novel was exploring with dizzying switches and reversals the ways in which cultural types define and distort individual identities, Chopin juxtaposed the proper, successful Wallace Offdean with Placide Santien, the "no-account Creole" of her story's title. The two men become rivals for property and for the love of beautiful, young Euphrasie Manton. Chopin's story pursued with subtle modulation the question of who would win Euphrasie and inherit control of the Natchitoches property, raising one man's chances one moment, dashing them the next. For readers of *Century* in the first months of 1894, the issues of caste and class in Southern society presented by Chopin echoed and reverberated in Twain's on-going novel, and vice versa. America's literary history at this time and throughout the second half of the nineteenth century was being shaped not by single texts in isolation but by multiple texts that overlapped and interpreted each other.

The lengthy temporal contexts that defined Twain's *Pudd'-nhead Wilson* and other installment works of the period suggest that literary history in the nineteenth century could be reckoned by months rather than years. Because we have arranged literary chronologies by years, however, significant elements of America's literary experience have been omitted or overlooked in the traditional record. Richard Ludwig and Clifford Nault, for instance, assert that the aim of their *Annals of American Literature* is "to show what books people were likely to be reading at any time [from 1602–1983], and with what rivals a candidate for literary fame had to reckon" (v); yet they admit to using "the date of the book, not that of the serial or magazine, publication" (vi) in their guide.

America's story from 1850 to 1900 was very much a continuing story, one told and received in parts over extended time. To understand that story, our literary tradition, it is important to recover the installment texts readers held in their hands for those years and to identify the contexts that fit between and around many serial parts. Although in *Reading in America* Cathy Davidson refers to the volume publication of books, her caution to literary historians applies to the study of periodicals and the fiction that appeared on their pages: "Those interested in the history of books must . . . be sensitive to the 'material embodiment' of books and to the material reason for that embodiment. Yet such 'mundane realities' are often ignored by literary critics who for the most part have been trained to explicate complex meanings in subtle texts, texts that until recently came pack-

story. According to *A Literary History of the United States* (Spiller et al.), "Before the establishment of *Harper's Monthly* (1850), few American novels were serialized. By that date Cooper had serialized one of his last romances, the other major writers none. But by 1870 almost all recognized novelists were selling their work first to magazines" (520). To begin making the elements of that tradition more available, I include here the serial publication history of nearly three hundred works by more than seventy authors. Works that first appeared in more than a single installment are listed, even if they might now be termed short stories or novellas. (The titles of such multipart works are distinguished from single-number stories here by being italicized instead of appearing within quotation marks.) For the original reading audience, such works were assimilated in parts over extended periods, and the meanings they assumed in their original appearance were affected by that installment format. Both the structure of the individual installment and the gap between parts influenced the ways in which works were perceived and interpreted, the ways in which literary history was created.

The case of Melville's *Bartleby* can serve to demonstrate briefly both of these principles. The story broke in *Putnam's Magazine* at the point where the narrator was attempting to rid himself of the reluctant copier by simply "assuming" Bartleby would leave the premises of his law office. The installment concluded with the narrator's realization that Bartleby might not accept his employer's assumptions: "He was more a man of preferences than assumptions" (557). In the first part of the story that appeared in the November *Putnam's,* Bartleby was an unusual individual who strained convention, which was embodied by the narrator; but he did not seem to be radical or deranged or diabolical. Melville's original audience lived with this unusual but understandable character for an entire month, November 1853. The structure of the first part of *Bartleby* was thematically important, since its form underscored one vision of the central character, one version of the narrator's ethical crisis.

When the second part of Melville's story appeared (December 1853), a new, more difficult Bartleby appeared: the narrator was "thunderstruck," like a man killed by "summer lightning" (609), when he found his copier had not vacated the premises.

The audience's awareness of a change—Bartleby, a man who had only irritated the narrator's sense of propriety, becoming a man who explodes ordinary frames of reference—would have been heightened by the story's installment structure. Those reading the work all at once will be more likely to blur the division of the story into two phases, particularly if, as in most modern editions, it is not marked even by so little as an extra space between paragraphs. Readers of one complete text find that Bartleby's history follows a single trajectory toward a tragic conclusion, whereas the original installments suggested a two-stage progression in his life's story after he came to work for the narrator. The gap between installments was significant because it insisted readers take time to fix a specific vision of Bartleby in their minds, then pause before considering a second portrait of this central character. And reading Bartleby's later life as divided into two distinct stages would suggest conclusions about the pyschological and philosophical implications of the story that differ from those conveyed in one continuous, uninterrupted text.

Modern readers are, in fact, seldom told about how this original audience was made to engage Melville's seminal text, or how other readers had to take in nineteenth-century works published serially in periodicals. The editors of *The Norton Anthology of American Literature* (Nina Baym et al.), for instance, use the *Putnam's* text of *Bartleby;* but they do not tell their readers where the division between parts occurred, a crucial element of the story's original form. Similarly, Michael Gilmore's recent, perceptive account concludes that *Bartleby* flows from Melville's suspicion "that the effort to free literature from its alliance with social and economic power is an exercise in futility" (145); but he does not refer to the periodical structure that shaped the author's own words. My aim here is to encourage the recovery of the original form of many nineteenth-century works and to assert that this form was an important element of meaning for original audiences. (In *The Victorian Serial*, Linda K. Hughes and I provide numerous, extended discussions of how installment issue shaped the reception and interpretation of major works of literature in nineteenth-century England.)

Because there were so many serial works and so many periodicals in the period 1850–1900, not all installment titles are included in this work. Writers whose reputations endured into the twentieth century, however, generally appeared in what Frank Luther Mott calls the "quality" monthlies, such as *The Atlantic Monthly, Century, Harper's Monthly,* and *Scribner's;* therefore, I have focused my search for serial titles on such magazines, though I have also reviewed *The Galaxy, Graham's, Knickerbocker, Lippincott's, Munsey's, Putnam's,* and *McClure's.* The reign of the "quality" magazines is generally said to have begun in 1850 with the founding of *Harper's* (Mott 2:3) and the *Knickerbocker's* loss of prominence (Mott 1:611). Their control of literary production began to decline significantly during the 1890s, so I have bracketed my study between the years 1850 and 1900.

This is not to say that installment works appearing in other monthlies or in the weeklies and dailies during this time are unimportant in literary history. Indeed, given the changing critical climate of our time, works first published in the *New York Ledger* or *The Saturday Evening Post* can be expected to take new, important places in our scholarship by the end of this century. Sacvan Bercovitch notes that scholars are becoming "increasingly uncomfortable about the restrictions inherent in the consensus that shaped our concept of American literary history: specifically the consensus on the meaning of the term *literary* that involved the legitimation of a certain canon, and the consensus on the term *history* that was legitimated by a certain vision of America" ("Introduction" vii). Jane Tompkins in *Sensational Designs* announces a methodology appropriate to a broader definition of the canon and to the present study: "Because I want to understand what gave these [popular] novels force for their initial readers, it seemed important to recreate, as sympathetically as possible, the context from which they sprang" (xiii). And Annette Kolodny has wisely urged "designing a literary history around the question of why texts do or do not 'have power in the world' at any given historical moment" (305).

Serialization, of course, did not begin or end precisely at the boundary dates I have chosen for this study. Edgar Allan Poe, for instance, published *The Narrative of Arthur Gorden Pym* in numbers of the 1837–38 *Southern Literary Messenger.* And, if we were to include novels published in more than one volume as serials, we could trace the origin of the genre back to the beginnings of American fiction. H. H. Brackenridge, for instance, published the first two parts of his picaresque novel *Modern Chivalry* in 1792, a third part in 1793, a fourth in 1797, a revised edition in 1805, and a final version in 1815. As John Seelye notes, Charles Brockden Brown's *Arthur Mervyn* was issued in two parts in 1799 and 1800 (179–80). And William Gilmore Simms wrote a seven-volume series about the American Revolution beginning with *The Yemassee* in 1835. While some might object to linking serial fiction in magazines with multivolume publication and older traditions of interrupted storytelling, this connection did occur to nineteenth-century readers (see, for instance, the essay from *The Galaxy*, Appendix A).

The first decades of the twentieth century also saw a continuation of installment texts by such major writers as Edith Wharton and Ernest Hemingway. Lesser known authors also serialized work in periodicals ranging from the still widely read *Scribner's Magazine* to literary reviews of very limited circulations. Beginning an account of America's continuing story at 1850 does, however, underscore an important moment in literary history: the emergence of a truly national audience. Richard H. Brodhead writes: "The minute circulations achieved for Hawthorne's *Twice-Told Tales* (1837), Poe's *Tales of the Grotesque and Arabesque* (1839), and Thoreau's *A Week on the Concord and Merrimack Rivers* (1849) illustrate the fact that American writing of the earlier nineteenth century is a virtually *undistributed* literature"(468). With the development of the major literary periodicals in the 1850s, American literature achieved a nationwide distribution.

In the pages that follow, I list the titles of works serialized by significant writers in major American periodicals, the chapters that appeared in individual issues, and the page numbers of the magazine for each installment. Where a break in installments did not match chapter divisions, and in short works that are now generally reprinted as single units, I have indicated by quotations the last passage of one part and the initial passage of the next. J. Don Vann has already produced a similar book on British fiction (*Victorian Novels in Serial*). The goal of such work is not only to provide the basic facts of serial publication but also to insist on the temporal framework of literary reception in the nineteenth century.

The decision to focus on works published in American periodicals does result in the omission of some important works here, such as James's *Daisy Miller,* which first appeared in the British *Cornhill.* And, to make matters even more difficult, this strategy results in the inclusion of a number of works by British authors, since they tended to dominate American periodicals early in this period. Yet this study pays particular attention to the American audience as well as to American authors, to those readers of serial fiction in this country from 1850 to 1900 whose response to serial texts generated literary history. And one consistent way to determine what was being read on this side of the Atlantic is to identify the periodicals produced within the U. S. borders.

The criterion of American production is appropriate in another way for defining literary culture at this time. These were, after all, the decades in which a former British colony completed the establishment of its own national literature; and the evolution of a native magazine industry was one central element of the larger cultural movement, a point I explore in more detail later in this introduction. The serial works that achieved publication in the major American periodicals, then, constitute units in a central tradition.

One revealing feature of this serial tradition is the number of women authors. Nina Baym has noted that by 1840 "women and young people increasingly formed the chief audience for imaginative literature in nineteenth-century America. The publisher had to find and cultivate authors who could write for them" ("Rise" 289–90). Susan Coultrap-McQuin reports: "By 1872 women wrote nearly three-quarters of all the novels published" (2). And Richard H. Brodhead asserts: "In fact the official literary culture of the Gilded Age was much less closed than its detractors make out" (472). The decades after 1850 saw a deliberate attempt by editors and publishers to include women writers in their magazines, although a countermovement gained increasing strength toward the century's end (Baym, "Rise" 290–91). Ann Douglas refers to "the dominance women

26

writers exercised over the field of fiction in the 1880s" (96), but Susan Coultrap-McQuin reminds us that "writing as a career choice was generally limited at mid-century to white, Protestant, middle-class women (there were exceptions, of course)— women of the same race, class, and economic background as those men who were the predominant spokespersons of Victorianism" (21). Still, she concludes of these major women writers: "Although they had to conform to certain magazine requirements, such as the length of a serial installment, on the whole these women planned and wrote what they wished, not what publishers and editors told them to write" (196).

Great popular successes by writers like Susan Warner, Harriet Beecher Stowe, and Mrs. E.D.E.N. Southworth made the compelling argument that women authors deserved space in the nation's publishing industry. In addition, adherence to the egalitarian principles inherent in the abolitionist movement and the Civil War encouraged women to write and men to take their work seriously. Foreign examples like that of George Eliot also helped change some prejudices. The serial works by women writers outside the "quality" monthlies were prodigious; and a full picture of serial literature in America will need to add to works listed here hundreds of titles from the dailies and weeklies, as well as from the magazines (*Godey's, The Ladies Companion, Peterson's Magazine*) directed specifically at female readers. The inclusion of such works in the canon must alter significantly our sense of the American literary tradition.

The serial or periodical text is treated as authoritative here since a primary interest is to define the times when specific titles were first available to a general readership. This practice digresses from traditional scholarly practice, whereby critics have tried to identify as authoritative the last version of a work whose shape was clearly governed by the author. Robert Milder has pointed out one case for which that method is problematic: "[Herman] Melville was still interpolating, deleting, and refining passages [in *Billy Budd*] when he died [in 1888], leaving behind a chronologically complete manuscript in such disarray that a reliable *Billy Budd* would not appear until the Hayford-Sealts edition of 1962, long after *Billy Budd* criticism had taken its shape" (446). Other major works of American literature, like *Pudd'nhead Wilson* and *The Red Badge of Courage*, possess equally complex textual histories, as Hershel Parker has shown. The customary method of establishing a reliable text in such cases derives from a definition of literary history based on the authors' achievements, whereas the approach being used here asserts that literature becomes significant in cultural history when it gains an audience. And that process in nineteenth-century America usually began with a serial text that preceded and shaped response to subsequent texts, as happened with *Uncle Tom's Cabin*. Unfortunately, then, some texts sitting on library shelves and others being used in classrooms are distanced from the serial texts I propose as deserving the attention of scholars and teachers.

While responses to the volume editions of these works were consistently predetermined by initial serial reading experiences, the sense of a completed novel was sometimes still seen as distinctive. A February 1887 *Atlantic* article entitled "Recent Novels by Women" observed: "In literature as in life, judgment is on wholes, and the reader who has followed a serial story like [Mary Noailles Murfree's] *In the Clouds* through its successive parts is very likely, when the end is reached, to revise his judgment, and to precipitate a decision which has been held in suspense" (265). This magazine also specifically suggested that there were two primary centers of interest in James's *Tragic Muse*, one more prevalent in the serial version, another in the volume form. In September 1890, four months after the novel had finished its installment run, the editors commented: "we make the assertion with confidence that if, after reading the novel as it has been appearing in The Atlantic, with delight in the brilliancy of the group of portraits which it presents, they now take up the two comely volumes in which the serial is gathered, their attention will be held by what may be called the spiritual plot of the tale" (419). While modern critics have tended to value this "spiritual" plot over the "brilliancy of the group of portraits," a complete literary history must include both aspects of James's, and his contemporaries', work.

AUTHORIAL INTENTIONS

Whoever the author, the exact relationship of a nineteenth-century serial text to subsequent volume publication (and later, revised editions) was often complex; and it is not feasible to include here the complete textual history of every title. Scholars concerned with authorial intention, then, may find the information presented in this guide inconclusive. The serial text most often does represent the first form by which a work of literature gained the attention of a significant audience; yet the pressure to meet publication deadlines and the existence of editorial constraints may have made these texts less reflective of the author's ideal than did later editions. Indeed, if authors had more control over volume editions and more time to prepare them, those later versions would seem to represent the preferred texts for an account of literary history.

James West has outlined an authorial practice that had been established by the end of the nineteenth century:

> A dependable writer whose work was in demand could often contract for serial rights on the basis of a manuscript that was only about one-fourth complete. If an editor liked the finished chapters and the accompanying synopsis of the rest of the story, the magazine would buy the serial rights for a stated figure, payable in installments. An advance of perhaps one-third of the money would be made initially. The author lived on these funds while composing subsequent chapters and collected further checks as later chapters were delivered against specific deadlines. Often the early chapters were running in the magazine before the final chapters had been composed. When these last chapters were delivered, the author received the remainder of the money and was free to begin revising the novel for book publication. (107–8)

In this description the pressures of time and economy seem significant for determining literary production. However, the practice of revising an original installment text for subsequent publication in volume form was not common among nineteenth-century authors. These first book editions often appeared right at the end of, or sometimes even one month before, the last periodical part. The volume edition was thus being prepared at the same time the installment issue was appearing, and both texts were often based upon a single manuscript copy. Further, though this was an age when authors might earn their living by writing, most were engaged in a number of projects simultaneously and did not have time for detailed revision between serial and first-volume edition. (Christopher P. Wilson has noted, "the general consensus in the 1870s was that average pay scales had been still far too low to provide many writers with a steady income" [6].) Thus, any extensive reworking of an individual title more often occurred some time after both the serial and first-volume edition had been completed, when a collected or new edition was being prepared.

So widespread was the practice of publishing serially in periodicals that most aspiring and established writers had an installment structure in mind from the first stages of composition. Henry James wrote William Dean Howells on 2 January 1888 that, though he did not like to read in installments, he composed within that form: "how little the habit of writing in the serial form encourages one to read in that odious way, which so many simple folk, thank heaven, think the best" (134). Many of James's early magazine stories were designed for periodical publication and appeared in neat two- or three-part structures, with installments often labeled "Part One" and the title of the whole followed by the phrase "In Two Parts." *Poor Richard* (1867) and *Gabrielle de Bergerac* (1869) were issued in three parts. *A Passionate Pilgrim, in Two Parts* and *Guest's Confession, in Two Parts* appeared in 1871 and 1872 respectively; *Adina* and *Eugene Pickering* were published over two months in 1874. W. D. Howells similarly worked within the given structure of periodical issue. His *A Day's Pleasure* appeared in the July, August, and September 1870 *Atlantic Monthly*. The three parts of this story were entitled "I—The Morning," "II—The Afternoon," and "III—The Evening."

James and Howells, then, composed their early stories and novels to fit the existing patterns of periodical issue, making the most of the standard form by which authors reached their public in these times. A common practice is reflected in John K. Reeves's account of W. D. Howells's composition of *Their Wedding Journey*. This was Howells's first published long fiction; and Reeves makes clear that he composed it in installments, referring to his manuscript as a "serial" that he anticipated publishing in *The Atlantic* (xiii). James wrote to Howells on 28 May 1876 about his work in progress, *The American*: "I shall be very glad to do my best to divide my story so that it will make twelve numbers" (47). Of course, in practice James often found his fiction at the manuscript stage taking its own rather than the magazine's form. Still, the assumption that novels would be composed for a specific serial format seems widespread even late in the century, as can be seen in a work by artist-turned-novelist George du Maurier, a writer whom James promoted. *The Martian* (October 1896–July 1897) was divided not into chapters but into ten parts, each almost exactly the same length and each making up one installment in the magazine.

Because of the cordial relationship that generally existed between author and periodical editor in the last century, the requirements of parts structure were often seen as an extension of natural or inevitable limits and guidelines. Robert Underwood Johnson explains in *Remembered Yesterdays* that authors acknowledged editorial structuring of their work: "Both [Richard Watson] Gilder and I in those early days received many letters from authors of note in appreciation of helpful suggestions that we had given them. . . . Of course there were many writers with whom such editing and criticism was not necessary, but I could cite a dozen instances of persons who enjoy a large reputation for fiction in which the sympathetic criticism was gratefully received and followed" (114). S. S. McClure similarly insisted that Robert Louis Stevenson, like others in the top class of writers, did not waste time and energy over minor questions of style and format:

> Stevenson had no copy of the story [*The Black Arrow*], but he sent to England and got the files of *Henderson's Weekly* which contained the story, and sent them to me. I read the story, and told him that I would take it if he would let me omit the first five

chapters. He readily consented to this. Like all writers of the first rank, he was perfectly amiable about changes and condensations, and was not handicapped by the superstition that his copy was divine revelation and that his words were sacrosanct. I never knew a really great writer who cherished his phrases or was afraid of losing a few of them. First-rate men always have plenty more. (186).

Of course, these men are speaking as editors, and the frustration expressed by authors in letters to friends and other writers suggests that we cannot accept this testimony without reservations.

The nineteenth-century publishing practice of featuring British serials in American magazines also suggests that authors allowed (or were unable to prevent) editorial alterations of their texts. Although many of these Victorian classics were printed from advance sheets sent directly from England, their form in New World periodicals often differed from the original. Not only were spelling and usage generally made to conform to American standards, but installment structure was often altered to fit a periodical's requirements of space. Anthony Trollope's remarkable ability to write parts of equal length, for instance, led in England to balanced serial issue of his major works. *The Eustace Diamonds,* for example, appeared as twenty symmetrical, four-chapter installments, one per month, in the *Fortnightly Review* (July 1871 through February 1873 [Vann 153]). The American publication of the same title, however, occurred in seventeen monthly issues of *The Galaxy* (September 1871 through January 1873), with individual numbers containing anywhere from three to seven chapters. Eight parts were made up of four chapters each, but none of those matched any four-chapter unit in the British version.

Trollope was such a master of installment structure that, as Mary Hamer writes, in 1866 he was prepared to organize the manuscript of *The Last Chronicles of Barset* so that it could later be divided by his British editor, George Smith, into *either* "thirty four-chapter numbers" *or* "twenty six-chapter numbers" (148). (It eventually appeared in thirty-two weekly parts in England but was not picked up, so far as I can determine, by an American magazine.) Still, it seems unlikely that Trollope's scheme for *The Eustace Diamonds* was so flexible as to allow for the eccentric structure provided by *The Galaxy*. Also affecting response to this Trollope novel in America would have been the special context of *The Galaxy*'s other features during the months of its serialization. On neighboring pages with the variously sized installments of *The Eustace Diamonds* in 1872–73, for example, were parts of General G. A. Custer's serialized autobiography, *My Life on the Plains*. Rebecca Harding Davis also must have faced changes in the planned parts structure of her *Waiting for the Verdict*. When this novel began appearing, *The Galaxy* was coming out bi-weekly; but in May 1867 that periodical switched to monthly issue, calling for longer installments of Davis's text.

Another case of altered format involved George Eliot's fiction; and here it is possible to see how different structures generated different meanings, almost surely straying from what the author had intended. With the first chapters of her *Romola* in the August 1862 *Harper's New Monthly Magazine*, the editors immediately directed their readers' attention toward a feature of special interest to Americans: "The opening scenes are laid in Florence, in the year of the discovery of America by Columbus" (cover). This concern with national history and identity would have been sharpened and intensified by the many references in *Harper's* to the American Civil War. In August they recommended a paper, "South Carolina Nullifiers," and "the biographical sketch of John P. Kennedy" to "those who wish to study the inception and progress of the present struggle in which we are engaged" (cover).

Harper's shaping of George Eliot's text for an American audience was further evident in the parts division. The British monthly *Cornhill* issued *Romola* in fourteen parts. In America the same novel appeared (some months delayed) in fifteen numbers. The American parts structure of *Romola* was especially significant as the early numbers departed from their British models. While the initial installment was identical in each magazine, the second, third, and fourth *Cornhill* installments were rearranged to make four different parts in *Harper's*. Since a serial's success depended greatly on initial reaction, this regrouping of chapters could well have affected the American response to George Eliot's complete novel.

Linda K. Hughes and I have argued that each of the *Cornhill* installments presented a complete phase in *Romola*'s history:

> In general, serial readers found themselves completing an installment of the novel at the same time as the characters completed a sequence of related actions in the plot. Furthermore, because the story's chronological time usually passed within installments rather than between them, the end of each installment was often a pivotal moment in the plot, a turning point in the causal sequence of events that presented Eliot's moral vision. (81)

For instance, in the *Cornhill* text the second installment ended with chapter 10, at the moment Tito learns that Baldassarre "is alive but a slave for whom ransom is required . . . inaugurating a new phase in Tito's life" (Hughes and Lund 87)

The *Harper's* version of *Romola*, however, ended its second installment on a more positive note about Tito's future. The September 1862 part concluded with chapter 8, not chapter 10: here Tito has just glimpsed a "sweet round blue-eyed face under a white hood" (97), that is, the young girl Tessa, who will become his mistress. Tito's prospects for employment and romance, in fact, are great at this moment in the novel; only in chapters 9 and 10 (published in October 1862, along with chapters 11 and 12) did the readers of *Harper's* learn the extent of Tito's debts to Baldassarre and of the older man's appearance as a slave in Florence. Because the conclusion was such a strategic point at which understanding of an installment took place, American readers of September 1862 had a different idea of where events were headed than did George Eliot's British audience in the early numbers of *Romola*.

A similar shift in emphasis was accomplished in the arrangement of the *Cornhill*'s third number by *Harper's*. The British version again emphasized the complex net of selfishness that would doom Tito; chapter 14 concluded the third installment (September 1862) with Tito's pretending to marry Tessa and an ominous foreshadowing by the narrator: "There was no possible attitude of mind, no scheme of action by which the uprooting of all his newly-planted hope could be made otherwise than painful" (318). More than the "pain" in Tito's future, the *Harp-*

er's text emphasized hope as a final note in its third installment of the novel. The American text for October 1862 concluded with chapter 12, as Tito is inspired to a higher love of Romola: he "hoped" that events would free him from the "danger of being disgraced before her" (685).

Harper's editors continued to direct reaction to this novel while it was in the middle of serialization. They felt compelled, for instance, to insist that *Romola* had become more interesting than had earlier been anticipated. In December 1862, at the fifth part of the novel's fifteen-month run, the editors said: "When [*Romola*] began, a few months since, we spoke of the difficulty of writing a novel of Italian life nearly four hundred years ago, but this difficulty has disappeared in the profound interest and power of the story" (135). The magazine went on to give a detailed analysis of the characters and situation in the novel, hoping that it would bring readers to, or back to, a novel that had not been holding its audience. Whatever the author's original intentions about her tale of Florentine life at the time Columbus sailed for the New World, then, American editors later shaped the work's reception.

American response to George Eliot was additionally influenced by other features of the context *Harper's* magazine provided for *Romola*. In the 1 July 1862 issue, the editors noted: "Mr. Thackeray's 'Philip' approaches its close. The publishers are happy to announce that it will be followed, commencing probably in the next Number, by a New Novel, by the Author of 'Adam Bede,' 'The Mill on the Floss,' and 'Silas Marner' " (cover). Although the text was printed "with the Original Illustrations, from early sheets, furnished in advance of its publication in England," the drawings were sometimes placed in different parts of the text from those selected by *Cornhill*. Full-page illustrations (such as the first installment's "The Blind Scholar and His Daughter") generally preceded all text in each month's *Cornhill*. *Harper's*, however, often placed such illustrations within the text, close to the corresponding narration of the scene. "The Blind Scholar and His Daughter," for instance, was four-fifths of the way through *Harper's* August 1862 installment (on page 399, where the text ran from page 380 to page 404). Placing illustrations at the start of the text would tend to direct reader interest forward, toward specific scenes; delaying those illustrations until the pictured scene was narrated, however, might allow for more attention to other elements. And, whereas *Cornhill* gave George Eliot's new novel the prime position at the beginning of each monthly issue, *Harper's* generally placed chapters of *Romola* in the middle section of its number. Also framing the early chapters of George Eliot's tale in *Harper's* were parts of Trollope's *Orley Farm* (issued in separate monthly parts in England) and Mrs. Dinah Maria Mulock Craik's serial, *Mistress and Maid: A Household Story.*

The editors' explanation of the magazine's complete contents in September further suggested that George Eliot's readers in America were to place themselves within a specific context:

> The materials in the hands of the Publishers of HARPER'S MAGA-ZINE were never more abundant and valuable than at present. Tales, Essays, and Poems; Voyages, Travels, and Explorations, in every part of the world, papers upon Natural History, Popular Science, Literature, Arts and Manufacturers . . . The Editorial Departments will include notes and comments upon the topics of the day at home and abroad; a condensed summary of the current history of the times; with anecdotes and facetiae. Illustrations will be profusely given whenever they can add to the value or interest of the papers. (cover)

In this issue were articles on ironclad vessels, buffalo, smoke, and St. Luke's Hospital. In October 1862 *Harper's* readers saw *Romola* next to "The Pioneers of Kentucky," "A Monthly Concert at Tampa Bay," "The New England Confederacy," and "The English in India." Those who were reading George Eliot's novel in America, then, created a specific meaning for it within a framework established by the host periodical.

Although such cases involve a work already out of the author's hands, other instances reveal that editors and readers could alter authorial intentions even before the work arrived at the publisher. Authors accustomed to working in the serial mode of magazine publication were capable of making changes as they wrote, both when audiences seemed to want them and when the author's concept of the work itself had changed. Hershel Parker observes, for instance, that "characterizations" in some novels by Henry James "go in different directions at different points of the same story" (112). This occurred, Parker explains, "in some novels which were serialized during composition. Critics insist that James changed his characterization of Miss Birdseye in mid-composition of *The Bostonians*, for instance; and beyond question he changed the status of Fleda Vetch as orphan during the serialization of *Spoils*" (112–3). While writers probably made major changes rarely in works-in-progress, the methods of serial composition did allow for response to new ideas provided by readers or by the author's own continued creation process. (See also the *Galaxy* essay in Appendix A.) No later critical effort is likely to recover in full the author's original intention, even in the relatively rare case when all documents of the publication process can be examined. What we can establish with some certainty in most cases, however, is what an original American audience found in its hands at the time of a work's first appearance.

FRINGES OF THE SERIAL CANON

There are other works which might have been included in the category of "America's continuing stories" from 1850 to 1900. A working definition for "serial" is "a continuing story over an extended time with enforced interruptions" (Hughes and Lund 2). Although the great number of serial novels in nineteenth-century America appeared in periodicals, other formats also existed. Copying the major mode of Dickens in England, some writers published novels in separate parts. The June 1854 *Putnam's Magazine*, for instance, referred to Paul Creyton's *Martin Merrivale, his Mark*, issued fortnightly by Phillips, Sampson, and Co. The multivolumed histories, studies, and biographies—such as Washington Irving's five-volume *Life of Washington* (1855–59) or Theodore Roosevelt's *Winning of the West* in four volumes (1889–96)—reinforced a national habit of reading in installments, of expecting stories to be continued at a later date. A sequel issued in a single volume might even be considered the second in a two-part serial. Many nineteenth-century authors followed a successful story with one involving the same characters and setting. In such cases as Mark Twain's *Tom Sawyer, Detective: As Told by Huck Finn* (itself serialized in the August and September 1896 *Harper's*), the appeal of known personalities and a recognized fictional past, both key elements in serial literature, were very much a part of the original audience's reading experience.

Indeed, the qualities of a familiar narrator and a returning set of characters might allow a number of unexpected works to be considered serials. James Russell Lowell's *The Bigelow Papers* appeared sporadically in the Boston *Courier, The Atlantic Monthly,* and elsewhere from 1846 to 1866. Oliver Wendell Holmes published chatty ongoing pieces (his *Breakfast Table* books, for instance) which, featuring both prose and poetry, shared essential traits with many serials. In the inaugural issue of *The Atlantic* (November 1857) Holmes even began decades of dialogue with his audience using words that assumed both the shared past and an anticipated future characteristic of serial literature: "I was just going to say, when I was interrupted . . . " (48) And his first work of fiction, *Elsie Venner* (volume publication, 1861), appeared first as a serial under the title *The Professor's Story* (January 1860–April 1861). He and the editors of *The Atlantic* knew that readers of his *Breakfast Table* columns would constitute an immediate audience for his latest work.

A number of biographical and autobiographical works also appeared in periodicals, and each presented a continuing story and fixed cast that gave it the skeletal structure of a serial. Even travelogues, standard magazine pieces for a young and growing nation, often were issued over many months' time and gained a regular readership. Robert Grant's writing provides another example of works that shared a continuing set of characters and a loose narrative structure but which perhaps are not technically "serials." Grant met considerable success with *The Reflections of a Married Man,* issued from March to June 1892 in *Scribner's Mag-*

azine, in which he tried to come to terms with the "new woman" of his age. More an essay than a work of fiction, perhaps, this continuing story still featured a returning set of characters and a consistent narrator. Its appeal was evident in the fact that Grant later published several related pieces, *The Opinions of a Philosopher,* from June to September 1893, and *Searchlight Letters,* from June to September 1899, both in *Scribner's Magazine.* Thus, the form of ongoing reflections mirrored or echoed the more recognized genre of the installment novel, which often had a later sequel.

So pervasive was the medium of installment issue in various forms that a number of poems were even published serially, though, as William Charvat points out, the long poem was generally "not suited to magazine publication" (102). Some eighteenth-century poets continued a British tradition of occasionally publishing poems a volume at a time. John Trumbull, one of the Connecticut Wits, for instance, issued *M'Fingal* in parts: one canto in 1775, a second in 1776, and the complete work of four cantos in 1782. This pattern was repeated by Longfellow when he published *Michael Angelo* in three 20 to 35-page parts in *The Atlantic Monthly* from January to March 1883. He also issued *Tales of a Wayside Inn* serially, though not in a periodical; three parts appeared separately in 1863, 1872, and 1874. And James Whitcomb Riley included the *Rubaiyat of Doc Sifers* in two parts for the November and December 1897 *Century.*

Although each of these works had a single, clearly focused subject, other loosely related poetic works were sometimes included in periodicals. Bayard Taylor, one of the Knickerbocker group, published nine short poems under the single title "Improvisations" in *Harper's* from August 1872 to January 1874. And the development of Whitman's *Leaves of Grass* from first edition in 1855 to a final version in 1892 should not be ignored; this work grew over time, and the individual editions might profitably be thought of as installments in a work comparable to Tennyson's masterpiece of the same period, *Idylls of the King* (1842–85). Even Emily Dickinson apparently thought of her short poems as organized into a loose parts structure. Wendy Martin notes: "Emily Dickinson sewed her poems into small packets that her sister Lavinia called *fascicles.* . . . With the recent publication of an edition of her poems that restores the original order of the fascicles, it is becoming increasingly clear that Dickinson's poems have thematic groupings, with each packet constituting a coherent narrative" (622).

As has already been noted, hundreds of domestic novels by women were serialized in popular ladies' magazines and are only now receiving a review by feminist scholars. James Playsted Wood notes that "the women's magazines, since their inception and publication on a large scale to huge circulations [after 1860], have published fiction of many kinds, some of it excellent" (124). The literature of minority authors also sometimes appeared in periodicals. The early African-American novel, Harriet Wilson's *Blake; or, The Huts of America*, for instance, was published in the *Anglo-African Magazine* (1859–60). And William Wells Brown's *Clotel* (first published in 1853 in England) was issued in sixteen parts in *The Weekly Anglo-African* (1 December 1860 to 16 March 1861) under the title of *Miralda; or the Beautiful Quadroon: A Romance of American Slavery, founded in Fact*. Henry Gates has speculated that there are many more important nineteenth-century novels lost in library archives: "We can only wonder how many other texts in the black woman's tradition have been lost to this generation of readers or remain unclassified or uncatalogued and, hence, unread" (xii). There was even an early German-American novel issued serially in 1853–54: *Cincinnati; oder, Geheimnisse des Westens* (Sollors 582).

Houston Baker has articulated a method for studying historical discourse that offers "revised readings of traditional texts" and "the laying bare, the surfacing and recognition, of myriad unofficial American histories" (169). Applying this perspective to the many bodies of serial literature in the last century allows us to conclude that, while the "quality" magazines dominated the national market and established the tradition of serial fiction that would shape literary history into the next century, other serial texts broadened and deepened America's continuing story in ways we are just beginning to uncover. (See Herbert F. Smith for a general survey of popular fiction in these years.)

At one point in his *The New Portfolio* (January 1885–July 1886 in *The Atlantic*) Oliver Wendell Holmes touched on the way all such ongoing literary works marked the passing of time in a story and in readers' lives: "The holder of the Portfolio closes it for the present month. He wishes to say a few words to his readers, before offering them some verses which have no connection with the narrative now in progress" (April 1885: 533–34). While Holmes presented here a major change of narrative, readers could bridge the two materials ("narrative now in progress" and "some verses") through the familiarity of this authorial voice. Holmes's presence, that is, created a framework not only for fictional events but also for the ongoing story of the readers' own lives.

In the digression that followed, furthermore, Holmes identified one of the most basic appeals of serial literature, the way in which continuing stories got bound up in the audience's everyday consciousness, becoming landmarks in their progression through life:

> If one could have before him a set of photographs taken annually, representing the same person as he or she appeared for thirty or forty or fifty years, it would be interesting to watch the gradual changes of aspect from the age of twenty, or even of thirty or forty, to that of threescore and ten. The face might be an uninteresting one; still, as sharing the inevitable changes wrought by time, it would be worth looking at as it passed through the curve of life,—the vital parabola, which betrays itself in the symbolic changes of the features. (534)

The pattern of any continuing work—serial novel or series of photographs or autobiographical reminiscences—resembles the universal "curve of life," the "vital parabola": it begins as a single unit, grows and matures over time, and arrives at a final, completed shape. The human interest in such "clocks" marking off the stages of development belongs both to the aging author and to the aging audience. Holmes concluded:

> The same kind of interest, without any assumption of merit to be found in [such records of time's passing], I would claim for a series of annual poems, beginning in middle life and continued to what many of my correspondents are pleased to remind me—as if I required to have the fact brought to my knowledge—is no longer youth. Here is the latest of a series of annual poems read

during the last thirty-four years. There seems to have been one interruption, but there may have been other poems not recorded or remembered. This, the latest poem of the series, was listened to by the scanty remnant of what was a large and brilliant circle of classmates and friends when the first of the long series was read before them, then in the flush of ardent manhood. (534)

Then followed Holmes's poem presented at a Harvard class reunion, for which "Our heads with frosted locks are white, / Our roofs are thatched with snow, / But red, in chilling winter's spite, / Our hearts and hearthstones glow" (534). Celebrating the feeling that has endured among his fellows, Holmes closed the poem: "Say that when Fancy closed her wings / And Passion quenched his fire, / Love, Love, still echoed from the strings / As from Anacreon's lyre!" (534). Both young and old subscribers could identify with these figures, the young seeing themselves at the beginning of such pilgrimages and older readers knowing that they were nearing the end.

Holmes's writing in *The Atlantic*, then, bound together audience and author into a community, represented here by the poet and his classmates. (He also extended this work's range by publishing *Songs of the Class of 1829* in multi-volume editions beginning in 1854.) Such ongoing stories were central to his culture, for shared experience over time built up a common past and a set of relationships that structured a national identity. In these formative years after the Civil War, readers of periodicals, the major literary and political forum of the age, came together to define a people. The lines between autobiography and fiction, between novel and journal, between installment fiction and ongoing correspondence were often less important than the larger unity of authors and audience.

Lesser known serials, popular novels by women overlooked or undervalued in the masculine literary establishment of the time, works traditionally classified as prose rather than fiction, and long installment poems blur the boundaries of the territory denoted as "serial fiction in periodicals, 1850–1900." Because the central interest in this study is the audience of general readers across America and their initial engagement at specific moments in time with texts that became significant components of our literary heritage, this study restricts itself primarily to serial fiction in the "quality" periodicals between 1850 and 1900. The field of installment works spreads out in time and space, however; the fringes created by these current limits deserve study and may, in fact, later become the core of a new, exciting literary tradition.

READING PERIODICALS

The number of authors and works of fiction included in this volume indicates that the continuing story was a primary form for writers during the period 1850–1900. These dates, titles, and names also suggest that the way in which America read its novels in the second half of the last centry was serially, in installments, as they appeared in the major literary periodicals of the day. Periodicals, of course, had provided one of the most important forums for public discourse in America from its earliest days. Benjamin Franklin published his Dogood essays in the *New England Courant* (1721–26), which, as Kenneth Silverman writes, was "the first American periodical with literary pretensions" (109). Political discussions, such as John Dickinson's *Letters from a Farmer in Pennsylvania* (1767–68), often appeared serially in newspapers during the revolutionary years. *The Federalist* began as letters to New York newspapers appearing over a six-month period. Works of a more literary than political nature, such as Emerson's early essays, also often appeared in installments in the first half of the nineteenth century. Irving and his circle found an identity in the *Knickerbocker Magazine* (1832–65); the Transcendentalists had their journal, *The Dial* (1840–44); and Southerners published in the *Southern Literary Messenger* (1834–64).

Certainly, the set of circumstances created by early nineteenth-century industrialization included a new, larger body of literate citizens as well as the technological means of production and distribution to supply this audience with reading material. Cathy Davidson notes: "Numerous historians have argued that the technological innovations of the early nineteenth century were as momentous as Gutenberg's invention of movable type, and that the increasing literacy, expanding mass education, and developing technologies that characterize this era constitute a veritable 'reading revolution' " (15). In its inaugural issue (January 1853), *Putnam's Magazine* explained the success of *Uncle Tom's Cabin* in precisely these terms: "Such a phenomenon as its present popularity could have happened only in the present wondrous age. It required all the aid of our new machinery to produce the phenomenon; our steam-presses, steam-ships, steam carriages, iron roads, electric telegraphs, and universal peace among the reading nations of the earth. But beyond all, it required the readers to consume the books" (98). And the December 1874 *Lippincott's Magazine* echoed *Putnam's* confidence in American expansion: "It is doubtless perfectly true that our industrial progress is unparalleled in history. Nowhere in foreign countries, as we travel over the highways and railways, do we pass the multitudes of thriving villages and prosperous country homes that we encounter from Maine to California" (769).

An expanding readership, cheaper paper, more efficient printing methods, rapid railroad distribution, and a developing economy provided the framework for a growing book market and an exploding magazine trade. This set of conditions continued at least to the end of century. The publisher of *Munsey's Magazine* wrote in January 1899: "I am going to repeat in substance what I said last month, namely, that I want to see the time come, and come speedily, when every family everywhere will make the magazine a part of its home life—not necessarily *Munsey's Magazine*, but some good magazine. This will mean more culture, broader information, better citizenship, and happier lives" (662).

Changes in the material world of the nineteenth century were generally matched by the psychological temper of the times. Americans, like their industrialized European cousins, the colonial powers, believed in expansion as a fundamental principle of their world. As Carolyn Porter notes, "Nothing signals more clearly the expansion and growing diversity of the public forum in Jacksonian America than the growth of periodical publishing" (351). So confident of their society's growth in general were Americans that metaphors of progress and development shaped their belief (and their prose) about the periodical industry, as this July 1879 *Harper's* comment showed: "If the reader happens to have the whole series of *Harper's New Monthly Magazine* from the beginning, and will compare this number, or that of last month, with which the new volume began, with the first number, which was published twenty-nine years ago, he will find that while the general superiority of this number is manifest and remarkable, it is the result of a natural and logical development, so that the present copious, ample, various, brilliant, and beautiful magazine is but the full flower which has opened from that bud" (298). Much earlier in the period, the March 1860 *Atlantic* similarly asserted an organic principle behind the development of periodicals in an article entitled "American Magazine Literature of the Last Century": "we are sometimes presented also with the earlier blossoms and the fresher odors of a rich and perennial growth of genius . . . crowded here as in a nursery, to be soon transplanted to other and more permanent abodes" (438).

The expansion of the book and magazine trade was a continual process throughout the second half of the century, as the March 1880 *Harper's* noted in an editorial comment: "It was recently said that the public is losing its interest in magazines. But it is curious that the decline of interest should be coincident with the publication of more and better and very much more costly magazines than ever before, and with a profusion and excellence of illustration which is producing a new school of engraving" (621). In January 1878 *Harper's* reprinted a statement by *Appleton's Journal,* which recognized "how old we are as a magazine-writing nation" (303). Thus, despite the economic downturns once every decade or so, the overall pattern for nineteenth-century American life was expansion; and literary production followed the same course.

The field of the monthly literary magazines grew steadily after the founding of *Harper's* in 1850, featuring expanding readership for established journals (national as opposed to regional) as well as the appearance of rival periodicals. At the heart of the success for these magazines was the serial novel. *Harper's* called the serial "essential to every periodical" (803) in May 1866; and *Scribner's Monthly* noted in November 1878: "In the success of a popular magazine, the serial novel has become a very important factor" (146; see also the *Galaxy* essay in Appendix A).

The April 1877 *Lippincott's Magazine* linked the new habit of reading serials with the development of a national railroad system, admitting that novelists controlled the "railroad train, in which our people are coming to live as the continental Europeans do in the theatre and the restaurant . . . only [their books] go abroad over the land and are read in motion . . . in all shapes and sizes, bound and unbound, cut up into installments and doled out through a certain or uncertain number of weeks or months" (512). Even at the end of the century, most important voices of society asserted that serial literature formed the backbone of significant magazines. *Century* commented in March 1897, "It is inconceivable to the casual reader how much literature of real and permanent value appears monthly in the magazines and reviews in the United States and England" (794). For readers throughout this half-century, such literature had its moral and social qualities, according to the December 1855 *Harper's:* "And, say what we will, a serial is good; a serial is very good. . . . A serial is strictly the growth of modern time, of an improved press, of a diffused education, of a universally reading nation" (127).

Before the 1850s, of course, much serial fiction read in America had been British, and English magazines had held a substantial share of the American market. One of the lines of development over these decades, then, was the increasing influence of American periodicals, first at home and then abroad. By February 1881, for instance, *Harper's* could announce that it was now invading foreign markets: "the Magazine will be published henceforth simultaneously in England, where there is no native periodical of the same general character" (304). This magazine and others were successful in England, a fact explained as unsurprising by a May 1881 *Scribner's Monthly* article, "American Magazines in England": "America, with her fifty millions of people, is the country of readers, and, too, of intelligent readers" (146). *Harper's* made the same point much earlier, in December 1855: "The great fact about America is that we are a reading people. Foreigners see this and wonder; authors see it and rejoice" (127).

Harper's had begun its magazine life featuring serials by established British writers like Dickens, Charles Lever, and William Thackeray. A May 1870 comment in the "Editor's Literary Record" revealed the magazine's conviction that, so far at least, American writers were not meeting the standards of the Old World: "We are so weary of depending on England, France, and Germany for fiction, and so hungry for some genuine American romance, that we are not inclined to read very critically the three characteristic American novels which lie on our table, and which, owing perhaps to our national prejudice rather than to their own superior excellence, we take up first" (925). At the same time, *Lippincott's* explained that the decision to feature British writers like Anthony Trollope was a simple reflection of their audience's tastes: "The 'Vicar of Bullhampton' will end in our May number. The marked favor with which this agreeable story has been received by the public has induced the publishers to make arrangements with the author for another novel, to appear in serial form in *Lippincott's Magazine*" (March 1870: 343). By the end of the century, however, most of the fiction featured in *Harper's* was American in both authorship and subject. Other periodicals, like *The Atlantic* and *Putnam's*, had made it their goal with their first issues to feature native authors. *Scribner's Monthly* admitted in November 1878 that some magazines were still including foreign writers: "For many years the American public depended upon the British novel" (146). This magazine felt, however, "that it could do no better for its own countrymen and for American literature than to discard utterly the British novel and get the best American novel it could, to take its place" (147).

Throughout this fifty-year period, of course, not only good literature proliferated in magazines; the expansion of cheap fiction designed for a mass audience was also making itself felt, and was often seen as dangerous to the individual and society. In an April 1878 article entitled "What Our Boys Are Reading," *Scribner's Monthly* presented a picture of the entire nation's youth ensnared in "periodical literature for boys" (681). Such works "appear not only among the idle and vicious boys in great cities, but also among school-boys whose parents are careful about the influences brought to bear on their children" (681). Another sign that these stories were having a significant national effect was "the eagerness with which some of these papers were read, and the apparent familiarity with which they were discussed by a number of boys" (681). This writer concluded that such stories "can be easily obtained, and easily concealed" (685) by anyone.

Similarly concerned about the nature of literature offered to adults in such periodicals as *The New York Ledger, Saturday Night, Fireside Companion*, and others, the *Atlantic Monthly* observed in September 1879 that "story-paper literature" is "the greatest literary movement, in bulk, of the age" (383). For this "quality" periodical, the increasing number of magazines and newspapers was leading to two results: sensationalism and "an increase in the number of serial stories" (386). Such profusion threatened to entrap literary citizens: "Overlapping as [serials] do, a new one commencing as an old one finishes, how does the subscriber ever escape from their toils?" (386). Of course, some well-read citizens admitted that the problem might not be what others were reading, but how much that process occupied them. In the August 1885 *Century*, Eliot McCormick in "A Boy's Approach for Fiction" wrote: "Even if a boy does not incline to the dime novel or the weekly 'penny dreadful,' he is hardly less in danger from what we call the standard fiction, if he uses it— as too many do—without moderation" (650).

Even cheap, melodramatic, and sensational novels, however, were sometimes seen by educated Americans as signs of an improving national literature, a step for authors and, more importantly, for readers on the way toward serious cultural understanding. In July 1891 the *Atlantic Monthly* lamented the railway fiction available to travelers: "I should hardly like to confess how many coins of the realm I dissipated before learning the melancholy truth, that the seductive titles and cuts which form the *tours de force* of penny fiction bear but a feeble affinity to the tales themselves, which are like vials of skimmed milk, labeled absinth, but warranted to be wholly without flavor" (78). Still, this author believed that such works could and often did lead to a taste for "higher" literature in readers. A similar sentiment colored a much earlier *Edinburgh Review* discussion reprinted in the May 1853 *Harper's:* "If novels and romances, of which the tone is low, and the taste bad, and the colouring voluptuous, and the morality questionable, are among the subtlest and deadliest poisons cast forth into the world, those of a purer spirit and a higher tendency are, we honestly believe, among the most effective agencies of good" (77). Abstention from novel reading altogether became for some a sign of inexcusable ignorance. In an August 1879 piece, "On Novel Reading," *Lippincott's* claimed: "When I hear a person say that he or she has never read novels, I instantly decide that such a person is not worth cultivating as a friend" (254). The "quality" monthlies, of course, could always be counted on to provide acceptable reading material, as the August 1891 "Editor's Study" from *Harper's* explained. Expressing a concern about novels for sale at a train station newsstand, the editor concluded: "In the end, after lingering long and anxiously over this store of unwholesome sweets, the timid and fastidious Study ended by buying no novel at all. It bought several magazines, of the kind whose name is an absolute warrant of decency, to say the least; those novels all finally looked doubtful, if not indecent" (476).

Even in the later decades of the century, the quality monthlies held on to large readerships against the competition of newer, less expensive magazines thought to be pandering to the untrustworthy tastes of the lower classes. The December 1886 *Century* identified one of the strategies by which better magazines kept their readers: "The larger magazines of our day are evidently made up with a view of presenting such a variety of contents that every intelligent reader can, in each number, find something especially adapted to his or her taste" (318). Indeed, the variety of magazines seemed to many an extension of America's constitutional democracy, as *Harper's* observed in April 1860 about the typical popular magazine, "It is a monthly feast to which we all sit down: some older, some younger: of all denominations in religion, of every party in politics; but the fare is wholesome, and of a kind for which nobody can have a distaste" (704). Almost twenty-five years later the magazine was clearly operating under the same assumptions, as this comment from the December 1884 issue suggested: "In the warm glow of Christmas feeling, therefore—and we declare that it is no other glow, for the plum-pudding is not yet served, nor the hot spiced wine—this Magazine complacently regards itself as helping, in ever so small a way, the better understanding of the great family to which it belongs" (168).

Thus, America in the second half of the nineteenth century identified its own expanding and developing identity with a growing magazine trade and the continuing story that was one of its central, enduring features. When new periodicals appeared, they often expressed a heady optimism for the future shared by authors, editors, publishers, and readers. In its first year of issue *Lippincott's*, for example, repeatedly noted the "favor with which the enterprise [of its own publication] has been received, as well by the public as the critics" (July 1868:110). *The Galaxy* in its first years sounded the common theme of plenty for a growing nation: "Whatever the most liberal expenditure can procure and the largest hospitality to fresh, free, individual, natural, and original literary production invite, the readers of *The Galaxy* shall always have" (July 1871:148; see also the 1869 *Galaxy* essay in Appendix A). In its July 1880 "Editor's Easy Chair," *Harper's* expressed this faith that the future would only naturally produce a better nation with better magazines. When a contributor praised the magazine's having grown "better and better," hardly leaving room for improvement, the editor asserted, "but we know there will be [improvement], for the world moves, and so will the *Magazine*" (303).

Nina Baym has noted that writers for periodicals knew and reflected the values of their readers; thus, novel reviewing in such periodicals "was directed toward readers, was conducted in constant awareness of what people were reading, and was always trying to understand the reasons for public preferences. The reviews offer guidance and correction in a way that enables us to see what they thought they were guiding and correcting" (*Novels* 19). These professional writers, thus, often performed dual functions, reflecting and shaping cultural values. In attempting to characterize such national attitudes as a general belief in progress, then, I cite here editorial columns, specific articles, and letters to editors from many magazines. While the views of such writers cannot always be equated with those of the average reader, they still provide the best means available, the single largest store of material, for defining the attitudes of a general audience.

The comments of magazine writers are generally attributed here to the periodical in which they appeared, not to individuals, in part because material often appeared without identifying the author. In addition, however, this work locates literary history in the minds of readers as much as in the words of writers; thus attributions sometimes remain general, even when a specific author is now well known, because the great body of nineteenth-century readers understood these writers to be synonymous with certain periodicals. William Dean Howells, for instance, served as the voice of "The Editor's Study" in *Harper's* after 1886; but his words will sometimes be attributed to *Harper's* because the audience received them as representing that organ. This is not to suggest that editors who were also distinctive persons of letters did not contribute a significant body of work to the tradition. Nor am I attempting to disguise the fact that such voices had distinctive regional, class, and ideological affiliations that must qualify my attribution to them of a national identity. But I am proceeding under the assumption that, in the context of this particular study, their individual voices are often best understood in their public, institutional capacities.

THE SHAPE OF SERIAL FICTION

There was widespread agreement in the second half of the century that the best writers in America published their work first in periodicals and only later in volume form. At the beginning of the period, the June 1850 inaugural issue of *Harper's* asserted: "Periodicals enlist and absorb much of the literary talent, the creative genius, the scholarly accomplishment of the present age. The best writers, in all departments and in every nation, devote themselves mainly to the Reviews, Magazines, or Newspapers of the day" (1). *Scribner's Monthly* further explained in November 1878, "Now it is the second or third rate novelist who cannot get publication in a magazine, and is obliged to publish in a volume, and it is in the magazine that the best novelist always appears first" (146). *Harper's New Monthly Magazine* in January 1879 similarly insisted that authors in all professions sought space in periodicals to present their views: "Not only the chief poets and storytellers publish their works first in the magazine, but statesmen and divines, the leaders in science and philosophy, hasten to place upon its pages the latest thought and the most recent discovery" (306). *Century's* editors noted later, in January 1890, that their own magazine had received nine thousand manuscripts in the previous two years, a small measure of the desire authors had to appear in one of the major monthlies.

The most obvious advantage to authors' appearing in periodicals was the established audience they could reach. The March 1899 *Munsey's* explained: "Apropos of the serialization of novels, in these days of enormous magazine circulation, writers are particularly desirous of having their stories first appear in this form. Where the book itself may be considered as doing well if it sells ten thousand copies, the same tale, printed in one of the popular magazines, will carry its author's name to the ends of the earth" (978). John De Forest complained to W. D. Howells at one point that the "quality" magazines received so many manuscripts from first-rate writers that he feared "I shall be driven to volume publication, which at present is almost without profit" (quoted in Ballou 357; see also the *Galaxy* essay in Appendix A).

The recognized circulation of periodicals naturally gave great authority to editors; and *Harper's* admitted in October 1888 that magazine editors were "the real avenues to the public" (800) in American society. Michael Anesko writes that "the serial market" was the "key" to economic survival for men and women of letters in the nineteenth century: "Publishers themselves testified to it. 'It is impossible to make the books of most American authors pay, unless they are first published and acquire recognition through the columns of the magazines,' one publisher told a Congressional committee studying the question of international copyright in 1885. 'If it were not for that one saving opportunity of the great American magazines, which are now the leading ones of the world and have an international reputation and circulation,' he continued, 'American authorship would be at a still lower ebb than at present' " (168). The formats editors offered to writers, then, were the means of access to large readership and established reputation; and writers were encouraged to organize their tales in the traditional patterns.

Of course, it is difficult to be exact in counting readers, both of periodicals and of the novels being serialized in their pages. The practice of reading aloud, particularly in the home, meant that there was often more than one reader for each subscriber. In M. G. Snow's article, "A Gossip about Novels," in the April 1863 *Harper's*, readers were told that the serial novel is "one of the strongest bonds of social family enjoyment we possess" (695). And later in the same article the serial was termed "the proper form for the novel; for it so encourages sympathy of tastes in the family circle, and being short, [an individual installment] is usually read aloud" (695). Other situations also inspired multiple readership for each issue of a periodical, as the following letter from a Civil War soldier in Virginia suggested in the March 1863 *Harper's*: "We *sometimes* get hold of *Harper*, and then again we don't. When we do get a number it circulates through the camp until it is read all up" (568). And publishers offered special deals to increase circulation, as the January 1865 *Harper's* explained in listing its subscription rates: "But if the sly Public choose to unite in clubs of five subscribers they can send twenty dollars and receive six copies, giving them one extra copy every month, the disposition of which may profitably create a generous rivalry" (260).

An even more extensive readership was projected in an exchange of comments between editors and readers in the 1875 *Scribner's Monthly*. In its "Home and Society" section for May, *Scribner's* had responded to a query about what subscribers should do with their old magazines that were taking up space in the basement or attic. The editors began with a tongue-in-cheek recommendation to use the papers as "kindling," but then they went on, "We confess to being a little selfish in this matter of magazines; like the Rothschild, who gave guineas to beggars just for the fun of it, we give all the old magazines that we don't want to a certain bright little Irish girl, whom we happen to know, and who manifests the most amusing delight in their possession. Not only she, but her whole family of brothers and sisters, not to say fathers and mothers" (117).

The number of readers for each copy of the magazine was enlarged even more by "J. L." of Nashville, Tennessee, who responded to the earlier discussion in a 21 August 1875 letter (printed in the November 1875 issue). J. L. used the editors' term "burning" metaphorically to mean "reading" periodicals. After his family of eight (and a number of friends) had enjoyed single issues of a periodical, he explained, he "gave them to a young laboring man to show his wife and children, all of whom, he assures me, enjoyed the reading and illustrations hugely. After they had consumed the magazines they turned them over to a neighbor, who followed suit. These copies have now passed through ten families, and been read by about seventy people, and are amazingly well preserved, considering the burning they have had" (131). While we can hardly justify multiplying subscription figures by seventy to measure nineteenth-century audiences, it does seem reasonable to conclude that individual readers often shared their copies with relations and close friends, and then sometimes passed on their copies of magazines to others, discussing material of interest as they did so. Such a process deepened and intensified the involvement of popular serial novels with American society; and authors accepting the format of this established installment mode were finding their audiences.

As periodicals spread across the country and through social ranks, however, some worried that high standards for literary material would be lost in new, cheap magazines and newspapers and that the numbers of the marketplace would determine what was successful writing. *The Galaxy* issued a familiar complaint in August 1870 about the power of new media to shape public opinion: "Which is the more extraordinary, the rage for newspaper notoriety, or the willingness of newspapers to gratify it?" (270). Especially as the century drew to a close, established literary magazines increasingly called for rigorous criticism of works of art in order to avoid a deterioration of culture. In an article entitled "The Newspaper Side of Literature," for example, the May 1888 *Century* saw two kinds of newspapers and writers:

> It would be unfair to ignore the fact that some of our newspapers do exert the best literary influence on their readers, and conscientiously subordinate other features of their work to their duties as educators. But the typical modern newspaper, to meet the taste which it has created, must surrender whole columns to writers who aim only at being amusing, and often succeed only in being pert, slangy, or scandalous; and it must find or invent "news" items which have about as lofty an influence in the minds of readers as the wonders of the fair had on the mind of Moses Primrose. (151)

In general, writers and editors in the monthlies derided fiction appearing in weekly or daily periodicals, not unaware, of course, that such works represented competition for the fiction appearing in their own publications. In the March 1877 *Atlantic*, for instance, E. S. Nadal wrote about "Newspaper Literary Criticism." He concluded that "books of the hour" cannot be very good (312), even though they were often popular. For him, the socially responsible critic should point out the weaknesses of such fiction in order to warn less educated readers against ethical or moral dangers: "To write only what is good of a book is therefore bad for the critic; it is bad also for the public" (313). The authors of such merely popular fiction and the critics who failed to censure their work were ultimately controlled, according to writers like Nadal, by advertisers: "If newspapers are to be better conducted, therefore, it is the owners who must reform them" (317). Such statements underscore a natural desire of writers and editors closely associated with the "quality" magazines to hold their audience; and the effect on aspiring writers was to reinforce the formula for success already embodied in a certain kind of continuing story appearing in those periodicals.

A fear similar to Nadal's that the dominance of periodical writing could mean the loss of lasting literature was heard in the September 1892 *Harper's*. In this comment from the "Editor's Study" there was worry that continued expansion of the periodical press—weekly and daily papers in particular—would eventually render bound books extinct: "Must we all go to making scrap-books in order to preserve the good things that fly on the leaves of the winged press? Or will there remain enough lovers of literature in covers to warrant authors and publishers in gathering together from the daily, the weekly, and the monthly the writings that a modest vanity hopes were not born to die?" (639–640). The point was made more poetically two months later in the November 1892 *Harper's*: "Whoever helps to keep alive the respect for a book, for books as books, renders a great service in this time, when the feeling towards books is becoming like that towards newspapers—that they are to be rudely handled and cast aside when the news has been snatched out of them—or when regard for them is like that of a hungry man for oysters, who scoops out the soft parts and chucks away the shells, perhaps with pearls in them" (966). Thus, on the one hand, many Americans heralded the spread of serial fiction in periodicals as a triumph of their developing society, yet others at the same time feared the phenomenon might be a sign of weakening national character. This ongoing tension between the desire for a cohesive national identity and the freedom of individuals and regions within the country, of course, runs throughout American political and intellectual history.

That the pattern of expanding readership provided a model for aspiring and successful writers of all classes and kinds is evident in a Brander Matthews story, which appeared in the October 1891 *Century*. In this sentimental tale about authorship, "The Story of a Story," the importance of readers' expectations in determining the shape of fiction is underscored. Matthews, author of *Cheap Books and Good Books* (1888), was a central figure in the drive for the protection of authors' rights in the last quarter of the nineteenth century (Colby 15). Hence "The Story of a Story" insists that writers need recognition for their efforts and that readers deserve credit in the reception of literature. The story begins when a young, sickly writer mails off to "The Metropolis" his latest piece, "one of the best things you have ever done" (871), according to his wife. Matthew's narrative follows the course of the manuscript through the hands of editors, illustrator, printers, publisher, and critic, each of whom is interested in something tangential to the literary value of the young writer's effort. That the story has a special quality, however, is made evident when it becomes the only work besides the featured serial mentioned by the critic's review of the midsummer issue of "The Metropolis."

In a section of the story entitled "Two Young Readers," a young lawyer recommends the piece to a young lady; he had read the story while riding the train to visit her in the country. Because both are significantly moved by the story, he proposes marriage and she accepts him. Similarly, in the next section, "One Old Reader," an elderly woman riding through a grim urban environment is relieved to enter into the story's imagined world of fiction. When a scamp makes off with her copy of "The Metropolis," she is not angry but buys "another copy for the sake of the story she had read already" (876). Yet another reader, this time an engineer, one of "the pioneers of civilization in the new West" (876), passes on his copy of the magazine to a white man who serves as the single government representative to the "Indians" inhabiting a vast territory. That lonely figure is cheered by the story, which he also intends to read more than once.

Finally, an aspiring young boy in Buffalo reads the story to his mother, who had found a discarded copy of the magazine in her work cleaning a parlor car at the train station. Inspired by the story (and other things), the boy rises to become a respected lawyer and elected official. Seeing the tattered copy of "The Metropolis" in his desk drawer years later, he "read the story again, for perhaps the twentieth time; and he recognized again that it had been the inspiration of his life" (880). Although he then learns that the young author had died years ago, "a fortnight after his story had been printed" (880) in "The Metropolis," the lawyer sends a letter of appreciation to the widow, "and she thrilled with pleasure when she heard how her husband's last work had been as lamp to a man's feet" (880).

In this paradigm of nineteenth-century literary activity, readers multiply and lives are inspired or reinspired through the circulation of an established monthly magazine. The effects could have been even greater and more widespread had the author been healthy and able to continue his career, for the next step in his development was to have involved the writing of serials and their even larger, more powerfully affected audience. Well aware that the continuing story received the primary attention of reviewers and subscribers, the author had told his wife that the editors "spoke to me about writing a serial for them" (871). Readers' expectations, then, along with editors' strategies and reviewers' preferences, provided the model for an author's developing craft.

Of course, the lack of the highest artistic sympathy among many of "The Metropolis" staff members provides an undercurrent of irony, which might be said to indict the literary system of the day. Only the writer's wife understands fully his story's greatness; and the general readers of the magazine unconsciously, almost accidentally, receive the benefits of good literature. There is money to be made in this business, obviously, and a certain set of values—industry, persistence, optimism about the future—to be reinforced in the country at large. But throughout the world of Matthews's fiction the literary system generally works, despite some flaws: authors compose worthwhile works, editors recognize good literature, and readers' lives are beneficially affected.

The validity of a pattern is, of course, sometimes reinforced when it is satirized. Mark Twain inverted the notion of the benevolent, far-reaching effects of periodical literature in a brief story, "A Literary Nightmare," appearing in the February 1876 *Atlantic*. In this case readers are the victims rather than the determinants of literary form. Twain's narrator is "taken possession of" by a jingle designed to help a tram or bus conductor remember the different fares and tickets for passengers:

> "Conductor, when you receive a fare,
> Punch in the presence of the passenjare!
> A blue trip slip for an eight-cent fare,
> A buff trip slip for a six-cent fare,
> A pink trip slip for a three-cent fare,
> Punch in the presence of the passenjare!

Punch, brothers! punch with care!
Punch in the presence of the passenjare!"
(167)

The haunting rhyme would not leave the narrator's consciousness and in a few short days rendered him incapable of living a
normal, productive life. The one short piece of writing expanded to dominate his mind, driving out all other thoughts.
The only release from this "nightmare" was to pass on the jingle to another victim, a Rev. Mr. ——. That poor fellow similarly
became incompetent and was only saved by delivering the jingle to students at a neighboring university. They became part of
an increasing community of individuals deadened rather than
inspired by literature; and, of course, Twain's readers, who un-
suspectingly took in the rhyme as they read, at some point
might have seen how they had been included in that circle. Of
course, Twain's narrative is not to be taken literally; but his
story did explore the dark side of imaginative experience, the
ways in which some knowledge can be disabling. And the
spread of even worthless ideas through a culture underscored
his society's awareness of the power of literature to affect
audiences.

Patterns of growth, development, and change, then, were reinforced by theme and form in nineteenth-century American literature. Not only did works of fiction trigger chains of reaction
throughout audiences, but an individual writer's own seeds of
inspiration led to larger and larger creations. The author's development from writer of short stories to major serialist featured
in one of the "quality" monthlies governed the careers of real as
well as fictional writers. When Henry James proceeded from
short stories to his first short novel, *Watch and Ward,* in 1871, the
narrative was organized neatly for serial publication: two chapters each made up five separate parts; a part was a single
monthly installment. Then, for the full-length novel of 1875, *Roderick Hudson,* each issue of *The Atlantic* included a single chapter separately titled, generally by a name or place ("Rowland,"
"Roderick," "Rome," etc.).

Readers of the early James, then, received his fiction in small units over a long time, the short stories and novels in parts that appeared regularly in magazines. In February 1876 a discussion of *Roderick Hudson* in the *Atlantic* confirmed that many readers did not automatically read volume editions, having already followed serial stories to completion through their appearance in periodicals. *The Atlantic* had to urge re-reading of the text in volume form: "We think that even those who most admired the work while it was appearing in *The Atlantic* will be surprised to find how much still remains in its pages to impress, attract, and satisfy them; how much also which deserves renewed and careful consideration" (237). Later in the century James and other writers began to desire escape from the strict limitations of periodical issue. William Charvat refers to the "correspondence (most of it unpublished) in which [James and Howells] quarreled, sometimes bitterly with editors over problems of instalment publishing" (288). Their late novels sometimes strained at the serial form. While individual installments of James's *Tragic Muse* (1889), for instance, were almost exactly the same length, numerous parts divisions did not coincide with chapter endings.

Still, for most of the years in this study, the format of installment issue provided an acceptable medium of composition for writers of short and long fiction, at the same time that it answered the desires of audiences. The "Introductory" comments in the inaugural January 1853 issue of *Putnam's Magazine* expressed the belief that the periodical format, with its variety of subjects and styles, matched the nation's tastes: "A popular Magazine must amuse, interest and instruct, or the public will pass by upon the other side" (1). Nearer the end of the century, *Harper's* concluded in March 1890 that American authors had risen to the challenge of providing fit material for such standard magazines as *The Atlantic, Scribner's Magazine*, and *Century*: "In fine, we say in all seriousness, that in this new country, drunk with prosperity and besotted as it is with material ideals, the literary standard is as high as ever it was in the world; and that the literary performance is of an excellence which is only not conspicuous because it is so general" (647).

60

THE LIMITS OF SERIAL FICTION

Authors consciously adapted their material to fit the physical space of periodical publication, meeting such regular demands as *The Atlantic*'s preferred twenty-page length for each install-ment in a serial novel. Other constrictions on the form and content of their work also existed. *Harper's* "Easy Chair" wrote to a disgruntled younger author in January 1855 that it "has long ago renounced the writing of books, not because it disbelieved the honesty of publishers, but because it saw too plainly the dismal chances of a book-making career. A man who lives by the pen must make up his mind to compromise, and submit, and suffer, as in all other pursuits" (266). Ann Douglas has shrewdly traced some of the forces shaping nineteenth-century literature in *The Feminization of American Culture*, noting, for instance, that, "literature then, like television now, was in the early phase of intense self-consciousness characteristic of a new mass medium: the transaction between cultural buyer and seller, producer and consumer shaped both the content and the form" (9). Later in the century the July 1889 *Atlantic* explained how periodicals influenced fiction: "The exigencies of magazine life call for serial novels. . . . We suspect even that this serial mode has some influence upon a writer, and that he looks after the articulation of his work more carefully than he would if it were to appear in the first instance as a book" (122). Predict-ing that magazine publication of fiction would pass, as had the issuing of novels in separate parts, *The Atlantic* hoped for an ideal state when literature would be free of all external con-straints: "it is manifest that a work of art in literature ought to be quite independent of its mere mode of publication, and the final issue in book form certainly gives the reader a better opportu-nity of regarding it as a whole than when it was constantly in-terrupting itself" (122). Of course, as contemporary literary criticism is repeatedly showing us, a work "in book form" is no less "independent" of shaping contexts than is publication in parts, despite the latter's constant "interrupting" (see, for in-stance, Feltes 76–98).

61

Many limitations on the form of fiction, however, went unnoticed by writers and readers because they were such accepted principles of the world in which they lived. For instance, the conviction that both human and natural history followed forward-moving, chronological schemes was widespread. Warner Berthoff notes: "Decade by decade after 1860 both reasoned understanding and popular feeling moved forward in the United States under the coercions of a steady and prodigious growth—financial panic or depression in every decade between 1870 and 1910 hardly broke the ascending curve of it—in societal wealth, numbers, integration, and power" (483). And Brian Lee reminds us that after 1850 there remained "in American thought a strain of buoyant optimism and expectation that . . . had been almost thoroughly extinguished in Europe" (9). One of the more conspicuous harmonies of form and content in the period was the installment issue of *Nature's Serial Story* in *Harper's* from December 1883 through December 1884, for the belief that human efforts and natural phenomena inevitably build toward appropriate fulfillment underlay subject and form in this work. Copiously and elaborately illustrated, the narrative insisted on harmonies of growth in landscape and human life, even as it moved itself from a single initial installment toward the completed form of a full-length novel.

The principle governing events in *Nature's Serial Story* and its own literary form was established in the initial December 1883 number. The narrator described a country cottage:

> We propose to make a long visit at this old-fashioned homestead; we shall become the close friends of its inmates, and share in their family life. They will introduce us to some of their neighbors, and take us on many breezy drives and pleasant excursions, with which it is their custom to relieve their busy life. We shall take part in their rural labors, . . . and we shall learn how the ceaseless story of life, with its hopes and fears, its joys and sorrows, repeats itself in the quiet seclusion of a country home as truly as in the turmoil of the city. (45)

The ties of this rural community were to be copied in the links between author and readers, contributor and subscribers to this monthly periodical. The "ceaseless story of life" would be spelled out in the world of these characters and in the install-ment structure that provided an analogue of growth and development.

Readers further learned in the first installment of *Nature's Se-rial Story* that a country home, where the story was set, "has be-come a part of the landscape, like the trees that have grown up around it" (42); thus human and natural processes are inter-twined, governed by the same benevolent impulses. That this part was read in December only heightened the harmony of fic-tional and real worlds, of characters and audience: "It is now late December, and in contrast with its leafy retirement the old homestead stands out with a sharp distinctness in the white landscape; and yet its sober hue harmonizes with the dark boles of the trees and suggests that, like them, it is a natural growth of the soil, and quite as capable of clothing itself with foliage in the coming spring" (43). Acknowledging principles of decay and disruption primarily to provide rhetorical balance in such con-structions, the narrative supports a vision of the world in which magazine subscriber, novel reader, editor, and publisher all are carried forward together toward a happy resolution of tempo-rary difficulties.

While better writers did not romanticize their narratives to such a degree, they generally accepted the implied parallels among literary accomplishment, productive labor, and nature's pattern of a fall harvest following spring planting. In one of his early chapters of *The Autocrat at the Breakfast Table* in the *Atlantic Monthly*, for instance, Oliver Wendell Holmes gestured toward a harmony among human efforts in composition and natural laws: "The 'A[*tlantic*]' obeys the moon, and its LUNIVERSARY has come round again. I have gathered up some hasty notes of my remarks made since the last high tides, which I respectfully submit" (January 1858: 312; see also discussion of the "green" covers of Dickens's monthly parts in *The Galaxy* for January 1869 in Appendix A). Some authors, however, challenged the under-lying values of their society by rebelling against installment publication in magazines; but those who did, like Melville, of-ten failed in their lifetime to gain the larger audience of general readers. Refusing to accept the assumption that citizens of this

63

country shared common values, these authors were in turn excluded from the established publishing industry.

Still other writers could get away with attacks on conventional ideology. For the May 1878 *Atlantic* Mark Twain published a short piece entitled "About Magnanimous-Incident Literature." In this essay Twain presented a series of short anecdotes or fables, each exhibiting a moral lesson; but then he added a "sequel" to that narrative which undercut its point. In the first episode, for instance, a "benevolent physician" (616) repaired the broken leg of a poodle; when that dog the next day brought another injured animal to the man's office, the physician was reminded (as was the fable's reader) of the multiplying benefits of good deeds.

Twain's sequel, however, found the poor doctor faced with not just two, but soon four, and then eight injured dogs, and so forth until he finally encountered on his doorstep "a massed and far-reaching multitude of clamorous and beseeching dogs" (616). Exhausted by the demands now placed on him, the doctor went mad, was bitten by the very dog he had originally helped, and soon succumbed to "hydrophobia" (616). On his deathbed he advised his friends: "Beware of the books. They tell but half of the story. Whenever a poor wretch asks you for help, and you feel a doubt as to what result may flow from your benevolence, give yourself the benefit of the doubt and kill the applicant" (616). In Twain's account, then, sequels or additional installments (the "results" which "flow" from previous acts) did not reveal happy principles of a harmonious and ever-improving universe, but instead presented a pattern of corrupted or diseased processes breaking down well-meaning individuals.

Twain's inversion of convention took on a specifically literary quality in the second narrative, in which an established author assisted a "poor young beginner" (617) into print and affirmed the same principle of good coming from an effort to aid someone in need. Of course, in the sequel, the senior author found himself forced "to give daily counsel, daily encouragement [to the junior author]; he had to keep on procuring magazine acceptances, and then revamping manuscripts to make them presentable" (617). And worse, "the young aspirant . . . rode into sudden fame by describing the celebrated author's private life with such a caustic humor and such minuteness of blistering detail that the book sold a prodigious edition, and broke the celebrated author's heart with mortification" (617). The elder man died with the benevolent physician's words on his lips: "the books deceived me; they do not tell the whole story" (617). Thus, the accepted paradigm of literary effort (providing "the whole story") was reversed in Twain's account: giving more of the story, a central tenet of serial literature, destroyed the existing work of art rather than completing it. But, again, Twain's humor suggested the strength of society's commitment to principles of natural growth and development, a belief in the benevolent outcome of human striving thought to be visible in the larger industry of periodical publication. If Twain was right that literature involved a bitter battle for wealth and status, most readers in his day accepted the humor but not the accuracy of his conclusions.

Another principle of the American worldview that shaped installment literature in this period was evident in a sentimental June 1898 *Atlantic* piece, part of a regular section entitled "The Contributor's Club." Here a pair of elderly friends attempt to form "The Club of Old Stories" (854), a gathering of retired classmates who would meet "fortnightly, and dine and wine together" (855). A key to their association would be the telling of what a granddaughter terms "their century-old stories" (855). An encounter with a grandson provided the impetus for this organization, as one of the friends explained: "I was trying to make [my grandson] understand the advantages of a protective tariff, and he contested every point. Finally I asked him how it happened that he, who had lived so short a time, should know so much more than I about national affairs. And what do you think the young dog replied? *'Oh, I began where you left off!'* " (855). While the two oldtimers object to such presumption on the part of the younger generation, writers, editors, and readers of *The Atlantic* shared the belief that their knowledge built upon foundations established by their forefathers. And serial publication rested on the same principle, as readers added installment to installment in many continuing stories. Further, each generation of authors (Howells and the realists, for instance) believed they should go beyond the work of earlier writers

65

(sentimental idealists). It was, after all, an era of rapid progress, especially after the Civil War; and Americans saw all their efforts building toward greater achievements in the future at home and abroad.

The process of individual and national development, however, was generally seen as gradual or longterm; and installment fiction again matched this model for accomplishment by appearing in parts over long periods of time. If a great many of the short stories of this period took two or three months to be read by original audiences, installment novels generally ran about a year in the monthly periodicals. Readers did not expect, then, to gain instant mastery of literary material but rather anticipated a slow accumulation of experience and understanding over time. This principle of gradual learning was spelled out in relationship to a number of subjects in a June 1861 *Atlantic* article, "Concerning Things Slowly Learnt." The author said, "we are going, my friend, to have a little quiet talk," and asserted that the "truth is, a great many things are slowly learnt" (697). These things slowly learnt included not only difficult, complex subjects but fundamental, even simple elements of human nature—that a person "is of much less importance than he has been accustomed to think" (699), for instance. This single principle, variously considered, required the author to take the full sixteen pages of a standard periodical essay in his initial presentation; and even then he considered options for additional treatment (asking the editor for "forty or fifty pages" or continuing "my subject in a future number of the magazine" [710]). These authorial strategies of repeated or expanded explanation were necessary, according to this article, because some things are not learned quickly in single sittings by most readers; thus serial presentation is an appropriate form for learning.

Other accepted principles of American life in this period did create friction with writers as the century moved toward a close. There was, for instance, a traditional insistence on adherence to "human nature" as a requirement for fiction. The September 1878 *Scribner's Monthly* stated: "We simply say that art can never be effective in engaging the interests of those who study its works, if it strays from the natural fountains of feeling and life" (743). Yet who defined "nature" in such cases was a matter of considerable debate, particularly as the opposition between new schools of realism or naturalism and the established tradition of idealist literature intensified in the last decades of the century. The December 1878 *Scribner's Monthly* pointed out: "The question naturally arises whether sins against social purity are legitimate literary material" (297); and this writer thought such acts were appropriate in literature, but only if the depiction of vice left one "disgusted with it" (297).

Others writers felt that literature and related fields like journalism enjoyed distinct provinces and should not attempt to move beyond them. Adams Sherman Hill wrote in the September 1887 *Scribner's Magazine:* "At its best, journalism can never, in any of its forms, take the place of literature. It does not, as literature does, lift us out of the trivial interests and petty passions of daily life into a pure and invigorating air" (377). *The Atlantic's* December 1888 "Contributors' Club," under the title of "More Remarks on Realism," made a similar assertion: "The literary artist may not contradict the facts of observation, but surely he should transcend them if he is to give us the truth of human nature and life; for truth is a universal, and the actual fact of observation is always a particular, a part which exists only as related to other particulars or portions of the whole" (847). The "quality" monthlies in general adhered to this concept of high art, motivated in part by larger ideological concerns. As voices of the established literary and political order, they did not wish to exaggerate failures or ruptures in the social order in literature (though they did do so more openly in nonfiction writing). The morally and spiritually uplifting novel fit their definition of good art, directing readers toward apparently available solutions more than a need for action.

The established periodicals had called for accurate descriptions of the world in the middle of the century, when they were themselves getting started; but their aim in the 1880s and 1890s was to assert that readers did not need to remain trapped within the problems of everyday reality. The January 1858 *Atlantic* observed in its first year of existence that, although most contemporary novels were "far off" from "life and manners and motives," the form was earning respect: "In novels the most serious questions are really beginning to be discussed" (351). By the time of its fortieth anniversary issue, October 1897, however, the same magazine concluded: "amid all the changes of these forty years the magazine has tried not to forget the purpose of its early days,—to hold Literature above all other human interests, and to suffer no confusion of its ideals" (576). Some established writers blamed the novel late in the century for failing to rise to this higher calling of convincing readers that the "banal" can be transformed to the "ideal." In the June 1890 *Atlantic* Charles Dudley Warner wrote: "The novel, mediocre, banal, merely sensational, and worthless for any purpose of intellectual stimulus or elevation of the ideal, is thus encouraged in this age as it never was before. The making of novels has become a process of manufacture" (724)

Throughout the years 1850–1900 some writers expressed a concern that too rigid a pattern of serialization or too narrow a definition of subject matter could dampen creativity. In its May 1885 issue *Century Magazine* admitted that there was limited space for the work of many aspiring authors: "It behooves all concerned to see to it that the limitations of the popular periodical do not have a narrowing or flattening effect upon current literature; do not put our best writers into a sort of literary bondage; do not repress originality and individuality either of style or opinion" (164). The October 1885 *Atlantic* worried that installment issue did limit appreciation of certain authors, such as Mary Noailles Murfree, whose *Prophet of the Great Smokey Mountains* it was reviewing: "now that it appears in book form, how inadequate a serial reading is to a full perception of the merits of this remarkable book. . . . It is the substantial unity of design which excites our admiration, as we look again at a whole whose fragments we have found so full of individual life" (557).

The concern with "unity of design" evident in this *Atlantic* review did lead to a change of mode among writers, especially in the 1890s. Poe sounded this aesthetic ("unity of effect") in his 1842 review of Hawthorne's *Twice-told Tales;* however, it was not to the publication of fiction outside the pages of magazines that this movement led, but to an interest in the short story as fiction's most suitaitable genre. Indeed, as I will explain in more detail later in this introduction, the new form of a collection of related short stories seemed to emerge with the generation of writers who would produce their major work after 1900. In such collections, which were generally still published over a number of months in a specific periodical, each story remained self-contained and complete, even though its setting and cast of characters could be shared by companion stories. Novels in single-volume editions might also have lent themselves to aesthetic consistency, but the favorite mode of publication for long fiction throughout the nineteenth century continued to be the periodical serial.

SERIAL AUDIENCES

One of most important factors shaping periodical publication of fiction was the perceived existence of a known audience, the editors and publishers, subscribers and letter writers who responded directly to authors' continuing stories. Writers could be gratified by the sheer numbers of readers reached by their works. *Scribner's Monthly,* for instance, reported "a patronage crowding closely upon a hundred thousand" (146) in November 1878. And in November 1887 *Century* claimed that its authors enjoyed "the largest audience that was ever gathered about any periodical of its class printed in the English language" (160), more than a quarter of a million. Authors whose work was accepted by one of the major literary monthlies could be assured, then, that their latest efforts came to the homes of a large block of readers.

Authors and editors could be impressed not only with the great numbers represented by their audience but also by individual readers who made themselves known, usually through letters. Some writers tended to address such readers rhetorically, keeping periodical subscribers at a distance. Elizabeth Stuart Phelps, for instance, asked her audience to read about their right *not* to read in the December 1895 installment of *Chapters from a Life,* which was appearing in *McClure's Magazine:* "If *you* will care to hear such chapters as may select themselves from the story of the story-teller,—you have the oldest right to choose, and I, the happy will to please you if I can" (49). A few writers spoke directly to readers or reviewers who had commented on their work. During the months that *The Rise of Silas Lapham* was appearing in *Century,* for instance, William Dean Howells was criticized for allowing an anachronism in his text. In the January 1885 issue of *Century,* when the novel was at its third installment, the author acknowledged the "newspaper paragraph" making the charge of inaccuracy and then responded: "I discharge my whole duty to reality in giving, as well as I can, the complexion of the period of which I write" (477). Thus, Howells said, he

> would make bold to use a type-writer in 1875, when it had only come into the market in 1874; and if an electric light threw a more impressive glare upon certain aspects of life than the ordinary gas-burner, I should have no hesitation in anticipating the inventions of Mr. Edison several months. . . . For it is the effect of contemporaneousness that is to be given, and the general truth is sometimes better than the specific fact. (477)

Not only did Howells, then, pay attention to what was being written about his novel as it appeared serially, he responded directly to one reader's complaint, continuing a dialogue between author and audience that was characteristic of serial literature. And such dialogue tended to move writer and reader closer ideologically, further solidifying the system of literary production dominated by the "quality" magazines.

Although public responses by authors during a novel's serialization were rare, writers were nevertheless influenced by reviews and letters from readers. The returns of famous fictional characters such as Natty Bumpo in *The Pathfinder* (1840), last seen in *The Prairie* (1827), and Sherlock Holmes, after his apparent death in "The Adventures of the Final Problem" (December 1893), were certainly inspired in part by popular demand. Publishers also advised authors during serialization of changes that would be appropriate for their particular audiences. Kenneth S.

Lynn reports that the *Century*'s editor in 1884, Richard Watson Gilder, discovered in page proofs for the April installment of *The Rise of Silas Lapham* that a character used the word "dynamite" in a discussion of elegant Boston houses. Alarmed by recent outbreaks of urban violence, the editor immediately wrote William Dean Howells, asking him to change the wording; and the author complied (279–80).

Editors and publishers more often than authors addressed their readers directly in response to specific inquiries. When *Madeleine Schaeffer* incurred a three-month delay in its serial appearance, *Harper's* explained through the "Editor's Easy Chair" for September 1862, "The numerous friends of 'Madeleine Schaeffer,' who have written to us to know of the success of her school in Charleston, whether she married, and if so whom, are informed that the story will be resumed in the next number of the magazine" (567). Readers made their presence felt not only when there was an unexpected break in the publication schedule, but also at the beginning of new serials, as *Scribner's Monthly* noted in a January 1879 comment about James's *The Europeans:* this novel had been "received with marked favor when the first chapters made their appearance in 'The Altantic' " the previous year (447). Not only did the "quality" monthlies refer to novels appearing in parts in rival periodicals, but less prestigious or less specifically literary magazines and newspapers also gave brief notices of ongoing stories. The weekly periodical *Nation*, for instance, published regular reviews of the monthly magazines, frequently commenting on serials and often establishing a line of interest in a specific work that would become characteristic of other, later reviews.

Publishers naturally tried to anticipate or prompt response to works not yet appearing through careful announcement or even advertisement. *Harper's* stated in its December 1855 "Literary Notices" column that Dickens would soon begin parts publication of a new novel: "The plan and purport of Dickens's 'Little Dorrit' is kept a profound secret" (118); the first number appeared in the January 1856 issue of the same magazine. When many editors concluded around 1870 that native rather than foreign serials would better serve their readerships, they often stressed the American authorship of a work soon to appear in their pages. *The Galaxy* noted in July 1870 with the last chapters of Charles Reade's *Put Yourself in His Place* that a "new novel, of English and American life, by Justin McCarthy, will be begun in the September Number of THE GALAXY" (132). And in February 1896, during intense competition between established "quality" periodicals and new, cheaper magazines, *McClure's* drew attention in a column entitled "Magazine Notes" to Anthony Hope's forthcoming serial, which "begins in our April number. It is a spirited story of adventure. It is his first novel since 'The Prisoner of Zenda,' and has even more action than that splendid story" (304).

Editors also sometimes attempted to direct reaction to a novel while it was in the middle of serialization. *Harper's* made an energetic attempt to persuade readers of the value of Thackeray's *The Newcomes* in the middle of its serial run. Admitting in July 1854 that "many of our readers are not yet interested in the fortunes of that 'most respectable family' " (259), the editors argued that this novel "makes its impression, like life, silently and unsuspectedly" (259). Responding to more specific complaints that *The Newcomes* mocked religion, *Harper's* proposed to prove the author "just, generous, thoughtful, and humane, with only the natural human and kindly feeling of a human heart, which smiles with pity in the midst of its sighing over the sickly glare of gilded goodness" (260). The magazine then printed a long passage from Thackeray's installment in the April magazine number, a "description of the performance of family prayers" (260).

When Thackeray later seemed to be critical of America in an early number of *The Virginians, Harper's* found it necessary to defend the author and itself for publishing his work. The novel had begun appearing in December 1857, and in March of the next year *Harper's* printed a letter from a subscriber in Newark angry about Thackeray's depiction of George Washington: "Do you know that legions, who have been the ardent admirers of *Harper* feel, just now, 'largely aggrieved' because Thackeray is writing about the Americans, holding up in a ridiculous light the *most honorable name* our country can boast[?]" (558). Thus accused of being anti-American, the magazine offered a lengthy explanation of Thackeray's art, saying that up "to the present point of the story," Washington had appeared as "a young, dignified gentleman" (559). *Harper's* insisted that what Americans should require is a fair, not idealized, portrait of this national hero: "What we want is, that Washington should be represented, not as the miraculous founder of a nation, but as a simple Republican citizen" (559).

Obviously, however, this public debate continued, for *Harper's* admitted three months later, in June 1858, "The discussion of the treatment of Washington in 'The Virginians' has by no means died away. The Easy Chair constantly sees fresh attacks and defenses—a perpetual skirmishing all along the line" (123). The magazine repeated its basic defense that Thackeray was presenting a balanced portrait of Washington and then tried to turn attention to other parts of the novel, the reappearance of familiar characters from earlier Thackeray works and a noteworthy emphasis on character over plot. This tactic did not succeed, however, and in the next month (July 1858), the editors admitted, "In the March Number of the Magazine the Easy Chair tried to show that Thackeray had not unjustly represented the youth of Washington. It has received a great many public and private replies to what it said" (268). The magazine then printed portions of a letter from someone it identified as "California" and used the opportunity to continue a defense of its own position.

One additional effort to appease its offended readers might have been the inclusion of a nonfiction article on George Washington along with the continuing text of *The Virginians*. Entitled "Washington at Morristown: During the Winters of 1776–77 & 1779–80," this February 1859 piece might have helped some readers understand that the magazine admired the founder of their country, even if one of its contributors failed to respect adequately the audience's patriotic sentiments. In June 1859, however, the editors were still feeling compelled to justify their inclusion of a British work in an American periodical: "In some of the earlier chapters there were allusions to Washington that were not read with favor by Washington's countrymen; and yet we earnestly advise every body to read those chapters again in the volume when it appears, that they may see, in a cooler moment, how much mistaken they were in supposing that the spirit of the author in speaking of Washington was not perfectly loyal and honorable" (124). In such ongoing exchanges with editors and readers during a novel's serialization, then, authors encountered immediate and specific reactions to their stories. (I explain in *Reading Thackeray* [59–78] how the author of *Pendennis* made specific responses in subsequent installments of his text to editorial comments about early numbers of his ongoing serial.)

As happened in the case of Thackeray's *The Virginians*, despite the efforts of *Harper's* editors, reaction to the serial version could dominate reviews of the whole when it was published as a volume. The *Atlantic* began its review of Holmes's *Elsie Venner* in April 1861 with this admission: "There is no need of our analyzing 'Elsie Venner,' for all our readers know it as well as we do" (511). The novel had appeared in this magazine under the title of *The Professor's Story* from January 1860 to April 1861. *Harper's* similarly referred to James's *Tragic Muse* in September 1890: "As we think back over our year's pleasure in the story (for we will own we read it serially as it was first printed), we have a rather dismaying sense of its manifold excellence; dismaying, that is, for a reviewer still haunted by the ghost of the duty of cataloguing a book's merits" (641). Reviewers who wrote about completed novels in the monthly periodicals, then, had often read the novel in parts as it was appearing and used that reading as the basis for their criticism.

Even though reviewers and readers ended up following a number of novels simultaneously in the regular periodicals, there seemed to be no confusion of stories in their minds. *Harper's* explained in January 1858 that a literary magazine like theirs, with its many ongoing stories, "is like a banquet in a colossal palace. From every quarter throng the guests, and from every side the good things are gathered to feed them. And the great company constantly increases" (270). Even much later in the century, when the number of daily, weekly, and monthly periodicals was multiplying rapidly, readers followed a number of novels appearing simultaneously. A typical "contemporary reader" was briefly described in the November 1893 *Scribner's Magazine* as someone who enjoyed a wealth of opportunity: "Such an amount of reading is offered him now for two cents that he feels that he cannot afford to take in less than two or three newspapers, and the magazines are so cheap and so admirable that he must read one or two of them every month" (659). And central to those magazines was still installment fiction: "If he reads the best of what is in the magazines he will read most of the best new fiction before it gets between covers, and will supplement usefully the current information that he gets from the newspapers" (660).

While the audience's role in these ongoing literary events was usually thought of in terms of emotional or intellectual response, sometimes even more was suggested. In the July 1865 *Atlantic* story "Ellen," by Rebecca Harding Davis, author, publisher, and reader all appeared as major actors in the world of the characters. Since the work was first published during the troubled time of the Civil War, when real happenings tended to dwarf fictional events, the curious sliding of the story from fiction toward reality was not inappropriate. Certainly, the story was first read when old myths like a benevolent agrarian society were being broken down and new frames of reference such as national unity were established. How much of the story was based on real events in some senses did not matter, for the way in which readers were encencouraged to respond to the work in the *Atlantic* underscored a nineteenth-century idea of an actual audience.

Davis began with an acknowledgment of the publishers as living, real persons: "If the publishers of the 'Atlantic' will permit me, I should like to tell a little incident, growing out of the War, which came under my notice in the summer of 1861" (22). Admitting that the story was incomplete, the narrator identified the "principal reason for telling it at all,—in the hope, slight enough, it is true, that some chance reader may be able to supply to me what is wanting" (22). Readers were then implicitly encouraged at the beginning of the story to add to what was characterized as "only a simple story," the "bald facts" (22) offered by the narrator. And at the end, the narrator would turn even more directly to the audience for the completion of the tale, for action in the realm of the story's characters.

Asserting that "true names of persons and places, and the dates also, as nearly as I can recollect them" (22) were being used, the narrator traced in "Ellen" the history of a Michigan family, "named Carrol, or Carryl" (22–23), through the Civil War years. As "the States one by one seceded" (24), so were members of Ellen's family taken away by sickness and calamity until only her mother, one brother, and Ellen were left. Although they had kept "far off" from the war, "this country of the manhunters" (24), eventually Ellen's brother Joe was drawn into the fighting. *Atlantic* readers, of course, were similarly drawn closer to the troubles of the Carrol family as Davis's story proceeded in *The Atlantic*. Joe's enlisting led to the mother's death; and Ellen, struggling with mental and emotional collapse, began a lifelong effort to find her brother again.

Although a number of strangers (including the governor of Ohio) tried to help Ellen in her search, she never fully recovered from a "long-suspended brain-fever" (33). In Wheeling, West Virginia, the story's narrator saw Ellen and heard her story, or at least this much of it. After Ellen disappeared again, still looking for her brother, thought to be "in the wilds of the Virginia border in active service" (33), the narrator concluded: "My story ends here. We never could trace her, though no effort was left untried. I confess that this [story in *The Altantic*] is one [effort to find her], though almost hopeless. Yet I thought that some chance reader might be able to finish the story for me" (34). Thus, periodical readers were drawn into a fictional world, which in the end appeared to be their own world. Had they known anything about such a victim of the national conflict (and, certainly, many did), action in the story's realm was possible: they might have written to the magazine; or, in broader terms, they could simply have responded with more understanding to victims of war or personal suffering after reading this work.

The connections among author, publisher, and reader, then, were at times direct and compelling in the second half of the nineteenth century. Audiences of fiction were citizens of the same country as authors, editors, and publishers, having the power and sometimes the obligation to act. Not simply an abstract formulation, a "dear reader" never seen or heard, these readers had a major, indisputable role in shaping the real and the literary histories of their nation.

READING IN INSTALLMENTS

The audience that subscribed to American periodicals received more each month than specific texts by particular authors. *Harper's* January 1886 "Editor's Easy Chair" explained how the association of readers and writers established a community: "Now a magazine is something of a club. . . . Here the poets sing, and the travellers tell their wonderful tales, and the novelist lays upon us his magic spell, and the naturalist reveals his beautiful secrets, and the mysteries of mechanics are made plain by the inventor, and the world's general progress is noted by the 'intelligent gentleman' who hides his name but not his wisdom. They all meet in the spacious common hall, and the murmur of their voices is very musical" (316). Created in the regular meeting of author and readers, historical and fictional figures, editors and advertisers were communities that endured in time and through space, across the vast continent of a new country and over the centuries of an English cultural tradition.

Barbara Sicherman's recent study of the reading habits of one "late-Victorian upper-middle-class, mainly female family" (202)—the Hamiltons of Fort Wayne, Indiana—presents a pattern of communal literary experience typical for America in the nineteenth century: "Chief among these [family reading] practices was reading aloud, which for the Hamiltons was a pleasurable and a lifelong habit. Most such occasions were informal and structured by circumstance. There might be two participants or several; texts as well as readers might alternate. At times reading aloud was a duty as well as a pleasure: parents read to children, older siblings to younger ones, adult daughters to their mothers, women to invalids. Above all, reading aloud was social" (206). Editors and publishers of magazines often seemed to have such family gatherings in mind when they addressed or described their readership. Philadelphia's *Lippincott's Magazine* was clearly trying to generate a sense of the national family when addressing the readership of its inaugural issue in January 1868: "Dating from the City of Brotherly Love, with hatred to none and with charity to all, we desire to occupy the historical and geographical position of Philadelphia, as the common ground where all who love the union (and none others) can meet, and discuss materials relating to Literature, Science, and Education, in harmony and good fellowship" (114).

The sense of community could be triggered by the familiar cover of the monthly magazine, by regular sections where editors addressed their readers, in a recognized style of illustration, or whenever familiar authors began or resumed their narratives. Robert Underwood Johnson admits that such features were central to the continued success of nineteenth-century magazines: "I am inclined to think that more readers of magazines and even of newspapers are retained by regular well-sustained and varied departments than by 'body articles' and that therefore it is perilous to relinquish such features" (134). The loss of one such attraction was crucial to the history of New York's *Galaxy*. In March 1871 the editors wrote: "The friends of Mr. Clemens (Mark Twain) will share our regret that the sudden and alarming illness of his wife deprives us this month of his usual contribution to 'The Galaxy' " (478). In April Twain announced an end to his "Memoranda," a monthly feature of the magazine. The deaths of two family members, he said, made it impossible for him to write "humorous" entries (615). In fact, he concluded, "I shall write but little for periodicals hereafter" (615). Although in the next month, May 1871, "The Galaxy Club-Room" took the space formerly occupied by Twain's "Memoranda," a central, irreplaceable voice of the magazine had been lost.

The identity and continuity of a periodical's audience, then, were reinforced when readers heard familiar voices; and new works by well known serial novelists seemed especially to draw the interest of magazine subscribers. In the "Editor's Easy Chair" of February 1861, for instance, *Harper's* explained the pleasure of anticipation when it issued the first number of Thackeray's *The Adventures of Philip*: "the true policy is to begin the [serial] story with the first number, and read it regularly every month. In this way you establish not only the pleasantest relations with the author himself, but with all who are reading the tale" (414–15). Indeed, the simple arrival of the newest issue could invigorate a set of social relationships. In an Octo-ber 1864 *Atlantic* work, "Paul Jones and Denis Duval," readers were reminded of how a new story's appearance provided a sudden focus:

> Ingham and his wife have a habit of coming in to spend the evening with us, unless we go there, or unless we both go to Hal-iburton's, or unless there is something better to do elsewhere.
>
> We talk, or we play besique, or Mrs. Haliburton sings, or we sit on the stoup and hear the crickets sing; but when there is a new Trollope or Thackeray,—alas, there will never be another new Thackeray! [he died in December, 1863]—all else has always been set aside till we have read that aloud. (493)

In 1864 Americans were reading Thackeray's *Denis Duval* and Trollope's *Small House at Allington* in *Harper's*. Thus, as in this brief account, the physical presence of the magazine ordered in-dividuals and groups.

Although periodicals may not always have inspired a literal rearrangement of families or friends, most readers still imagi-natively saw themselves in new relationships. Joel Chandler Harris guided his readers toward such revision in the headnote to *Nights with Uncle Remus*, which appeared in three install-ments of *Century* from July to September 1883: "To give a cue to the imagination of the reader, it may be necessary to state that the stories related in this paper are supposed to be told to a little boy on a Southern plantation, before the war, by an old family servant" (340). Similarly, in a brief, evocative preface to her se-ries *Balcony Stories* in the December 1892 *Century*, New Orleans writer Grace King offered readers—particularly women—a chance to gather with friends, sharing private thoughts and feelings:

> There is much of life passed on the balcony in a country where the summer unrolls in six moon-lengths, and where the nights have to come with a double endowment of vastness and splendor to compensate for the tedious, sun-parched days.
>
> And in that country the women love to sit and talk together of summer nights, on balconies, in their vague, loose, white gar-ments,—men are not balcony sitters,—with their sleeping chil-dren within easy hearing, the stars breaking the cool darkness,

or the moon making a show of light—oh, such a discreet show of light!—through the vines. (279)

King's invocation recalled the ancient storytelling situation of hunters gathering around the campfire with women and children to hear of brave deeds. Indeed, with this invitation to join those sitting on the balcony, King invoked one of the most enduring qualities of oral storytelling and serial literature, the comradeship of writers and readers who, journeying together through life, routinely take time out to rest, recall the past, and prepare for the future.

There had been for several decades in America a broad, deep audience for the domestic subjects announced in King's preface. These subjects and related themes announced a new shape to the European literary tradition, as Richard H. Brodhead reminds us: "[The] mid-nineteenth-century conjunction of women's writing and a middle-class domestic audience is an event of central importance in American literary history, understood as the history of literature's whole life in the social world. This conjunction helped establish both the circle of readers and the reading tastes and habits by which the great bulk of literary production was consumed in later nineteenth-century America" (469). Ann Douglas explores in more detail the purpose of such writing by women—"to propagate the potentially matriarchal virtues of nurture, generosity, and acceptance; to create the 'culture of the feelings' that John Stuart Mill was to find during the same period in Wordsworth" (11).

King's preface also suggested how important the link to larger worlds provided by literature might have been for many readers in the last century: "in those long-moon countries, life is open and accessible, and romances seem to be furnished real and gratis" (279). Such small-town, outdoor moments were becoming more attractive in these times. Because it was harder to establish and maintain social relationships in a new, rapidly growing, urban industrial society, many recalled nostalgically the village life of the past. If individuals desired social connections in a city environment, they would often have to make them through the new media of magazines. In such an open territory, all had space to tell their own stories:

Each woman has a different way of picking up and relating her stories, as each one selects different pieces, and has a personal way of playing them on the piano.

Each story *is* different, or appears so to her; each has some unique and peculiar pathos in it. And so she dramatizes and inflects it, trying to make the point visible to her apparent also to her hearers. Sometimes the pathos and interest to the hearers lie only in this—that the relater has observed it, and gathered it, and finds it worth telling. For do we not gather what we have not, and is not our own lacking our one motive? (279–80)

The repeated comings together of many storytellers and listeners—balcony-sitters or periodical audience—provided opportunities to gather value from the tales of others and to invest meaning in one's own stories.

In long works such as serial novels (King's series appeared over an eleven-month period), readers had time to review their own stories and place them in relation to the author's fictions. Serial literature provided not only the expanded time of issue but the clear gaps between installments, the thirty days between numbers of the magazine, during which subscribers could shape and refine their responses to what they had read. King's text asserts that the children overhearing "balcony stories" from their bedrooms are given a similar opportunity: "memory makes stores for the future, and germs are sown, out of which the slow, clambering vine of thought issues, one day, to decorate or hide, as it may be, the structures or ruins of life" (280).

A December 1855 *Harper's* "Editor's Easy Chair" explained in some detail this anticipation readers felt at the experience to come with any serial: "There seems to be as much real interest in the announcement of a new novel by Dickens or Thackeray as there could have been in Scott's day. It is the rap of a friend at the door when Dickens announces a new book. The heart leaps like a girl at her lover's footstep, and quickly, cries, 'Come in!' He does come in, and how we laugh and cry!" (127). In its May 1856 "Editor's Easy Chair," *Harper's* advised its subscribers to read in parts rather than attempt a whole novel all at once: "When it is printed altogether at the end of twenty months, it is such a huge volume, or pair of volumes, that many a reader is repelled who could have easily mastered the whole by short spells of reading every month" (848). Of course, the magazine was also soliciting subscribers in such observations, discouraging the purchase of books in volume form.

In addition to the promise of future pleasures, the December 1855 article in *Harper's* praised the long time of involvement for nineteenth-century serials:

> Readers who complain of serials have not learned the first wish of an epicure—a long, long throat. It is the serial which lengthens the throat so that the feast lasts a year or two years. You taste it all the way down. You return to it. You have time to look back, to look over. As in life, you can sit, as the number ends, as you sit when the door closes, and muse upon what follows. Your fancy goes on and draws the beautiful result. Or your fancy steals out and returns to you in tears. (128)

For this audience, reading in installments encouraged a more thorough, more lasting involvement with any story, as readers took active roles in the literary experience. And the story was seen to move directly and forcefully into the lives of readers, according to the May 1856 essay: "Remember how it enriches your life for a year to bear about in your heart, unsolved, the riddle of these destinies" (849).

A final appreciation of the serial form in the December 1855 *Harper's* essay involved the belief that contemporaray authors used their highest skills in this genre: "Each number is intended to end where it ends, and no longer, as in old times, to pause upon a moment of horror, just as the robber was tumbling through the window, or, more breathlessly, just as Adolphus Augustus was going down upon his knee—'to be continued.' Now, every number has a certain kind of completeness" (128; see also the *Galaxy* essay in Appendix A). The May 1856 *Harper's* linked the skill of the writer to a similarly conscientious effort by the reader: "Remember that if you read it as it is written you have time to follow each delicate hint, to brood over each hidden excellence" (849). The same point was made twenty-five years later in the November 1882 *Atlantic:*

> It must be counted in favor of the serial publication of a novel that the author is enabled to secure a certain momentum of interest

on the part of his readers, correspondent to the momentum of his story; and if his power lies in a strong conception of character, which he must discover by a multitude of minute touches, then he is more than ever favored by the slow process of monthly publication. Time is given for the steady sinking of the story into the minds of readers, until the conclusion, which has been the author's from the beginning, becomes at last, and only at last, inevitable to them. (709–10)

Readers, thus, were encouraged by editors to use the built-in pauses of serial publication and its expanded time frame to study more closely what happened in the text.

The order inspired by periodicals in nineteenth-century life was temporal as well as spatial: that is, installment fiction and other serial writing bound together people in many different regions of the country, and it connnected inhabitants of the present with voices from the past in ongoing relationships. The sense of a tradition embodied in periodical publication was evident in the *Atlantic*'s reference to its own serialization of Hawthorne's *Septimus Felton*. The posthumous publication of this work began in January 1872, and in the "Recent Literature" section of the same issue the editors commented on how the past was being brought to life in the present: "out of his eternal absense and silence comes this wise, sad, beautiful story, a souvenir inestimably precious. . . . A posthumous work by Hawthorne must come before the world just as he left it; and the sympathetic reader will not enjoy this the less because of slight defects which the last touches of that exquisite hand would have repaired" (107).

Reaching more across space than time was a favorite kind of magazine series from 1850 to 1900, the nonfiction traveler's account of different states or sections of the country, often accompanied by illustration and maps, which placed distant and foreign regions within the national consciousness. Studies in parts of classical mythology, European and American history, world geography, and natural science also appeared regularly in periodicals, as editors sought to educate the citizens of a growing and prosperous democracy. Magazines even printed famous poems from the English literary tradition for an audience that did not have the resources to purchase volume editions, as *Harper's* explained in March 1878: "It has always been a good habit of *Harper's Magazine* occasionally to lead off a number with some of the standard English minor poems, beautifully illustrated, as in the holiday issue of this season, when it published Milton's 'Ode on the Nativity.' There are thousands of readers who would most highly enjoy such a poem, but who would never think of exploring a volume of Milton to find it" (622). Thus, novels and other features appearing in installments over many months' time slowly wove together—often with overlappings of genre, voice, and purpose—the fabric of a developing culture.

One figure whose work reached into a variety of fields and whose voice created a sense of community and tradition almost single-handedly was Oliver Wendell Holmes. His lifespan nearly matched the century's (1809–94), and he wrote for important magazines from the early 1830s into the 1890s. His numerous series in *The Atlantic*, a magazine he also helped found, made him a familiar household presence for several generations. In a January 1890 preface, "To the Reader," for one of his later works, *Over the Teacups*, Holmes noted that the regular return of a familiar voice was often welcome: "I think there are many among [his readers who subscribe to *The Atlantic*] who would rather listen to an old voice they are used to than to a new one of better quality, even if the 'childish treble' should betray itself now and then in the tones of the over-tired organ" (111). Naturally, Holmes's argument was self-serving to some extent: "I confess that there is something very agreeable to me in renewing my relations with the readers of this magazine"; he would enjoy reaching "the children, or the grandchildren" of his first readers (112). But the audience too had much to gain in the reappearance of a familiar figure, as was evident in the mail Holmes was receiving:

> I received congratulations on reaching my eightieth birthday, not only from our circle of Teacups, but from friends, near and distant, in large numbers. I tried to acknowledge these kindly missives with the aid of a most intelligent secretary; but I fear that there were gifts not thanked for, and tokens of good-will not

recognized. . . . I was grateful for every such mark of esteem; even for the telegram from an unknown friend in a distant land, for which I cheerfully paid the considerable charge which the sender knew it would give me pleasure to disburse for such an expression of friendly feeling. (113)

Appearing regularly, then, on the same pages of this magazine which itself traveled throughout the country and around much of the globe, periodical readers and authors continued to fix themselves in reassuring, enduring relationships.

Other benefits for readers derived from their engagement with periodical texts; and, again, some of the most enduring were not specific to any particular work but were intrinsic to the mode of installment issue. Charlotte Porter in her contribution ("The Serial Story") to an "Open Letters" feature of *Century* magazine in September 1885 articulated some of the benefits of reading slowly over an extended time. Pointing out that the "continued story is a literary product characteristic of our time" (812), Porter claimed such fiction as part of a natural development in the novel genre: "The flavor of the component parts of the novel is more distinctly appreciated when it is served up in a series of judiciously related courses. The hungry curiosity to follow the events, discover the plot, and swallow the book whole, which belonged to the world's younger days and long nights of novel-reading, is turned into the discriminating attention of a patient public, whose interest in the story does not preclude the study of underlying problems presented in a life-like and artistic way" (812; see also the *Galaxy* essay in Appendix A). The virtues of patience, concentrated attention, and a desire to see beneath the surface, according to Porter, characterized the installment reading experience. Porter also claimed that the audience's engagement with novels published in periodicals encouraged them to enter more fully into other lives: "Characters enlivened from the inside will make a story live in a reader's interest during a year of monthly magazines and beyond 'Finis,' more surely and clearly than the most cunningly contrived mock motions of petty puppets jerked about in a vain search for the unexpected" (812).

Porter went on to argue that composing novels in parts could place healthy demands on the artist, requiring attention to the

85

moral of a story at every point. Although the writer's intent should not be stated didactically, Porter felt concentration on each part of a work could infuse meaning more deeply into the whole. Then, in an interesting extension of her argument, Porter stated that the techniques fostered by the serial novel were helping develop more believable female characters in American literature: "The transfer of the author's attention from the story about his characters to the representation of the life within them has revealed the individuality of the heroine, and developed an altogether new estimate of woman's moral value" (812). In a fitting conclusion to her argument about the serial form, Porter foresaw many more stories being continued into the future and the genre of installment fiction itself evolving: "The development of [the heroine's] personal responsibility, expanding in contact with world-old customs, still powerful though waning, and with others stronger still that must forever live,—her spiritual growth and undetermined influence,—suggest lines of present and absorbing interest fit to be continued in serial novels yet unwritten" (813).

This sense of finding oneself in the midst of meaningful long stories—individual novels, the development of the genre, the movement of personal and communal history—was also one of the appealing qualities of nineteenth-century periodical literature. A December 1859 *Harper's* identified this feature of slow growth over time surrounding the individual in a celebration of its twentieth volume. Aware that it had to maintain a "constant adaptation to the demand of the time," the magazine was ready for a new phase in its development: "All hands are now piped to weigh anchor for a fresh voyage. Passengers may be very sure that if they have liked the ship hitherto they will like her none the less hereafter. May she long sail before favoring gales upon calm seas—the fortunate and triumphant *Great Eastern* of magazines!" (126). Although the magazine was speaking metaphorically here, many of the virtues of travel—anticipation, fellowship, discovery, arrival—were found in serial fiction. Each new work promised readers that they would undertake a journey, which would shape their lives in the months to come, putting them in the midst of a meaningful process. *Harper's* stated in its February 1861 issue: "Well, the curtain is now about to draw again, and we are to meet old friends and to make new ones. What a power and privilege a great and favorite novelist has! The world hears the preparatory ahem of his voice in the announcement, and leans back to listen, sure of its delight. . . . Already we are all friends of Pip and the moon-faced blacksmith [from Dickens's *Great Expectations,* then running in *Harper's Weekly*]; and before spring has opened the violets we shall be friends of [Thackeray's] Philip, and more than ever friends of Philip's father" (415).

For nineteenth-century audiences reading in parts was a distinctive experience that did not occur in isolation from other events. It was a process that extended over time and insisted on regular pauses. Futhermore, serial reading was a social act as well as a private one, for subscribers to magazines joined editors and reviewers in discussing, in print and in person, their ongoing stories. One writer for the *Knickerbocker,* for instance, demonstrated the intertextuality of nineteenth-century reading when he offered in the July 1860 issue his own conclusion to Hawthorne's *The Marble Faun.* Noting that many had been dissatisfied with or confused by the final chapters of Hawthorne's recently published tale, he explained: "Therefore, I for one have ventured on a guess, leaving to others full liberty to write different conclusions if they choose" (65). Although *The Marble Faun* was not issued in installments, the expanding number of periodicals in America provided a forum and a pattern for the publication of responses to fiction. And these magazines had a clear interest in arguing for the openness allowed by serialization. The number of magazine subscribers and the periodicals' continued ability to feature major writers suggest that installment reading appealed to fundamental needs of the time. *Harper's* argued, for instance, that serialization provided a necessary intimacy among readers and characters, insisting in December 1858 that a serial story should be read,

> as it is written, from month to month—sitting if you please, with a friendly circle who began with you, who know all the people in the book—who follow their fortunes as we hang upon the careers of real persons—who speculate, and wonder, and plan— who sympathize, and regret, and condemn; and who justly take

87

> a deeper interest in many of the characters than in many acquaintances, because they know them better—not to say because they are better worth knowing. (125–26)

The mixing of real and fictional realms in this passage—a "friendly circle" and "people in the book," "fortunes" and "careers," "characters" and "acquaintences"—was also characteristic of nineteenth-century serial literary experience. Reacting to imagined events as if they had happened in a neighboring community or in the recent past, readers were in a sense transported into the world of the fiction. And when they were the subject of such lively sessions, characters from the fiction were brought directly into the lives of the audience.

In fact, the form of installment fiction seemed especially suited to realism, the central mode of the era. In a September 1874 *Atlantic* article, "The Novel and Its Future," G. P. Lathrop termed "realism" a technique "essential to the best dramatic novel-writing" (321). He then defined one of its principal functions: "Realism sets itself at work to consider characters and events which are apparently the most ordinary and uninteresting, in order to extract from these their full value and true meaning" (321; see also the *Galaxy* essay in Appendix A) Since the lives of these readers were almost by definition "ordinary and uninteresting," yet full of "value and true meaning," they belonged in the world of the realistic novel. They acted as participants in the most basic plots of such novels, at the same time that they lived outside the fiction, as spectators. Readers moved each month into their continuing stories, forgetting for the time specific features of their own world; yet when the latest installment was over, they moved back out of the fiction and into the context of everyday life. The realistic mode made these repeated transitions almost seamless and allowed serial literature in periodicals to take a central place in American cultural history.

The principle of consistency in a magazine's content was sometimes revealed in editorial policy as well as in authorial style. In a May 1875 *Lippincott's* article called "Seasonable Reading," for instance, C. H. recalled: "I once wrote for a monthly magazine an out-door paper—a summer study . . . and timed the production of it so that it should appear in winter" (644).

The writer was arguing that winter would be the time when such a piece was needed, not summer when the magazine's readers would have the essay's subject (summer) itself. C. H.'s editor, however, held the piece for a summer number, following a different theory of context, that there should be continuity or harmony between periodical and reality. And the editor of *Lippincott's* agreed with his counterpart in the earlier situation, making his comment in a note appended to C. H.'s article.

Another frequently appreciated feature of serial reading related to realism was its property of continually opening toward a new, desired future, just as Americans found their own country expanding across new frontiers. The June 1886 *Atlantic* referred to a parade of new novels and was glad to find many of them by American writers: "We have long been used to the spectacle of English novelists turning out their work with all the regularity and punctuality of a machine in good running order. . . . It is only now, however, that one may count with equal confidence upon the home supply, and through the agency of the monthly magazine one may have his James, or his Crawford, or his Howells, year in and year out" (850). Even when one novel drew to a close, the magazine in which it was appearing offered another fictional world just in the future, the next number. Oliver Wendell Holmes, one of the symbols of that creative potential in nineteenth-century literary production, made this point in December 1885 at the close of one installment of *The New Portfolio*, appearing in the *Atlantic*.

Already a senior figure on the literary landscape, and having produced a remarkable number of written works, Holmes realized that he could be "perhaps presumptuous" to imply that he would appear in future issues of this periodical: "I am reminded from time to time by the correspondents who ask a certain small favor of me that, as I can only expect to be with my surviving contemporaries a very little while longer, they would be much obliged if I would hurry up my answer before it is too late" (847). Even so, Holmes went on, he was reluctant to say that his work had *no* future: "How do I know that I shall have a chance to open [this work] again? How do I know that anybody will want it to be opened a second time?" (847). Reviewing a number of reasons to think of ending this enterprise, and others to inspire continuing it, Holmes finally concluded by suggesting an unlimited potential for the future:

> The Records of the Pansophian Society contain a considerable number of essays, poems, stories, and hints capable of being expanded into presentable dimensions. In the mean time I will say with Prospero, addressing my old readers, and my new ones, if such I have,—
>
> > "If you ou be pleased, retire into my cell
> > And there repose: a turn or two I'll walk,
> > To still my beating mind."
>
> When it has got quiet I may take up the New Portfolio again, and consider whether it is worth while to open it. (847)

And, of course, *The New Portfolio* was opened again, fifteen times, in fact, through the next eighteen months, because authors and audiences of the time demanded it.

SERIAL CONTEXTS

Rather than functioning as little endings, signs of the termination of processes, the breaks between installments in nineteenth-century literature suggested continuity for their audience. Old stories ended so that new ones, which could be recognized as continuations of the old ones, could begin. The enforced pauses in serial publication also determined specific elements of meaning in many literary texts, for in that space between numbers readers reflected about the continuing stories, experienced more of their own lives, and read other literary and nonliterary texts. Because our modern editions and classroom textbooks generally ignore or collapse these gaps, creating continuous, uninterrupted texts, we have lost sight of the role of such pauses in American literary history.

One of the most important contexts that fitted around the parts of an individual work, for instance, was other fiction appearing in the same months, both the works included in that magazine and those issued in rival publications. The December 1855 *Harper's* alluded to the rich offering of fiction in American periodicals, even though at that time most serials were being written by European authors: "When Bulwer, and Dickens, and Thackeray, and how many French people, are writing stories and memoirs, how are they all to be compassed? Easily, in the serial. You breakfast on Thackeray, you dine on Dickens, you tea and toast on Bulwer" (127). Because readers were engaged with a number of texts at once, most literary activity was structured across time as well as through time. One way, in fact, to organize bibliographical information about serial publication would be to list works and parts of works published each month from January 1850 to December 1899, giving a cross-sectional view of literary history. David Reynolds, among others, has recently argued for the importance of recovering such contextual frameworks: he attempts to "reconstruct as completely as possible the socioliterary milieu of literary works through the exploration of a broad array of forgotten social and imaginative texts, paving the way for responsible reinterpretations of canonized works and making possible the rediscovery of lost literature" (561).

Sometimes an author's work provided its own larger context for interpretation, as in the cases of prolific writers like William Dean Howells and Henry James. *Harper's* pointed out in its October 1888 "Editor's Study," for instance, that James's work was appearing in a number of different forums simultaneously:

> their [editors'] recent unanimity in presenting simultaneously some of the best work of Mr. James' life in the way of short stories indicates the existence of an interest in all he does, which is doubtless the true measure of his popularity. With 'The Aspern Papers' in *The Atlantic*, 'The Liar' in *The Century*, 'A London Life' in *Scribner's*, and 'Louisa Pallant' and 'Two Countries' in *Harper's*, pretty much all at once, the effect was like an artist's exhibition. One turned from one masterpiece to another, making his comparisons, and delighted to find that the stories helped rather than hurt one another, and that their accidental massing enhanced his pleasure in them. (800)

Modern critics have lamented such overlapping of stories (and, ironically, James criticized Trollope for beginning one serial novel before another had completed its run). Although reading many texts at one time might seem to violate the principle of "organic unity" in art, nineteenth-century audiences could see such situations as enriching rather than confusing their literary experience. According to *Harper's*, individual texts "helped" and "enchanced" others when they were read concurrently.

While critics have studied how works in one writer's canon influenced each other, much less work has been done on how authors' careers were shaped by the magazines in which their work appeared. *Harper's*, for instance, asserted a union of magazine and novel when it observed in December 1858 that the "Editor's Easy Chair" and Thackeray's *The Virginians* "appear in the same uniform" (125). Writers might benefit serendipitously from a periodical's enjoying a sudden, new popularity. Especially later in the century, when the "quality" monthlies were being challenged by new, less expensive magazines with more extensive advertising, the sales of individual periodicals could fluctuate substantially from month to month. W. H. Bishop noted in the September 1879 *Atlantic* this "fierce rivalry between numerous competitors" (386) beginning in the magazine trade. In December 1893 the six-month old *McClure's Magazine* secured the American publication of Arthur Conan Doyle's "The Adventures of the Final Problem: The Last Episode in the Life of Sherlock Holmes." Taking advantage of the intense interest in the Sherlock Holmes stories, *McClure's* generated an audience for *The Ebb Tide* by Robert Louis Stevenson and Lloyd Osborne, which began serialization in *McClure's* in February 1894.

Readers lured to a specific periodical because it was featuring one well-known author might discover a new voice in the same issue. The serial appearance of Constance Cary Harrison's *An Errant Wooing*, for instance, was accompanied in *Century* by several Kate Chopin stories. The novel ran from December 1894 through May 1895; Chopin published her story "Azelie" in the December issue and "Regret" in May 1895. Regular readers of the periodical would have been encouraged to discover a second writer, then, simply because her work was on the neighboring pages to a first. Further, such readers would have had these works by two women writers in their minds at the same times, and their reaction to one could have been shaped by concerns in the other.

Novels published in parts in America at this time also were shaped by reaction to British fiction. George Eliot's *Daniel Deronda*, for instance, ran in eight issues of *Harper's* beginning in February 1876, at which point the magazine anticipated a wide involvement in this continuing story: "It is long since any tale has been published that aroused so deep and universal an interest as *Middlemarch*; and as the author is in the fullness of her powers, there is no doubt that the story by her which begins in this number of the Magazine will have the same remarkable and subtle charm" (461). *The Atlantic* began serializing Henry James's *The American* in June of the same year; so these two novels from different countries were read in overlapping fashion by many in 1876. James was certainly reading George Eliot's novel in those months, as he published his influential review, "Daniel Deronda: A Conversation," in the December 1876 *Atantic*.

The audience for both these writers had additional texts in mind during these same months. *The Atlantic* reviewed in its August 1876 issue Anthony Trollope's *The Prime Minister*, which had been published in eight monthly parts from November 1875 through June 1876. While *The Atlantic* complained that Trollope's story seemed to them an unsuccessful mixture of two plots, a love story and a political tale, their own readers were assimilating at the same time a number of separate narratives by different authors simultaneously. *Harper's* more openly admitted that the style of reading in these years involved multiple texts enjoyed concurrently. In June 1876 the "Editor's Easy Chair" explained: "There are two or three books of great interest recently published or publishing, and among them the novel of *Daniel Deronda*, which it is the good fortune of this Magazine to present to American readers" (144). *Deronda* was halfway through its eight-part publication, and *Harper's* provided here a fairly detailed analysis of its characters and style to date.

The context surrounding the individual parts of novels like Henry James's *The American* included nonfiction as well as the other fiction of George Eliot and Trollope. Because realism was the major mode for so many of these authors, the boundaries of any single work of art were difficult to discern. In its August 1882 "Editor's Literary Record," *Harper's* admitted that its audience might easily lose sight of the distinction between fictional and real worlds: "Although the reader of Miss Woolson's *Anne* knows that it is a novel, and may have been incited to read it because he knew it to be one, yet while he is engaged in reading it the thought that it is a *fiction* never enters his mind to disturb the genuine human interest he takes in its characters, and especially in its central figure the heroine" (478). The other side of this principle, that accurate pictures of reality often resembled novels, was expressed by *Harper's* September 1886 "Editor's Study": "It is an interesting proof of the intimate hold which fiction has taken upon life that when we wish to praise a true story we say that it reads like a novel" (642). Since periodical readers could not always know whether a subject was fictional or real, all the material in a periodical could blend together into one larger record of experience. *Harper's* felt in December 1855 that the "serial novel has the great advantage of drawing the author back to nature" (128); thus, in its view, serial fiction tended toward realism as opposed to romance. In such situations texts and contexts began to merge, and the meaning for a literary work's original audience was determined by much more than is usually available to modern readers using later volume editions.

Since many writers in this new age themselves produced both fiction and nonfiction, magazine audiences had additional reasons not to isolate literature from other prose. In February and March 1894, for instance, Joel Chandler Harris, certainly familiar by this date for his "Uncle Remus" stories, published a two-part account, "The Sea Island Hurricanes," in *Scribner's Magazine*. The first installment was entitled "The Devastation," the second "The Relief." Subscribers were not told by the periodical whether this work was factual or imagined, literature or journalism. Similarly, many journalistic pieces about Japan and the Caribbean by Lafcadio Hearn in the 1890s featured techniques traditionally associated with fiction; and he too wrote novels as well as nonfiction. So readers found themselves adding new pictures to their known world through the fiction and journalism of magazines; and from both genres they created larger contexts within which to understand themselves and the next literary texts they would encounter.

A regular topic in the periodicals that featured serial fiction was the business of writing, printing, and distributing literature; and here context and text in literary experience were even more intricately interwoven. One subject running throughout this period, for instance, was the question of copyright, particularly as an international issue. Nina Baym notes: "There was a problem with copyright [in the nineteenth century] that has not been adequately appreciated in a literary historical mode that deals only with the context of ideas" (*Novels* 23). Such issues as the nature of private property, the transaction of goods and services, or the relationship of capital to production were explored not only *in* works of fiction but also *by* the material texts themselves, which were produced and distributed within the larger social system.

Pirated editions of foreign authors made up much of American publishing throughout the nineteenth century, and other countries in turn were often reluctant to respect the rights of authors from the United States. In special articles on the issue, but also in the regular sections through which editors addressed their audiences, members of the profession of letters argued for a clearer delineation of the writer's ownership of his or her work. *Scribner's Monthly's* May 1880 section, "Topics of the Time," made a frequently heard remark: "We assume and assert that there is such a thing as literary property" (147). (See also the August 1868 *Atlantic's* "Ideal Property," 167–73.) The January 1872 *Lippincott's*, on the other hand, did not see copyright as such a simple matter: "The question [of literary or intellectual property] is a greater one than any international copyright can settle, for it concerns the proper relation of the literary man, the thinker, the artist, the scientist to society, and the just appreciation and valuation which should be placed upon their contributions to the common stock of the world's knowledge" (122).

The sense that literature was important enough to be considered property with more than one potential owner underscored its value in society. Many asked what sorts of this commodity ought to be published in periodicals. As *Harper's* commented in

April 1887, "novels are now so fully accepted by every one pretending to cultivated taste—and they really form the whole intellectual life of such immense numbers of people" (824); thus, who was paid to write fiction and who decided what kinds of novels ought to be published were significant social questions. *Scribner's* stated a central element of this culture's ideology in March 1878: "the supreme uses of fiction [involve] the organization into attractive, artistic forms of the most valuable truths as they relate to the characters and lives and histories of men" (735). Since readers could profit from reading novels, gaining "valuable truths," fiction was directly related to personal lives; and the shape of the individual's life helped form the context within which the work was read. Alfred Arden, therefore, concluded in a December 1883 "Open Letters" section of *Century:* "people should feel individually bound to encourage those novelists who seem to aim for and reach the highest standard of literary art by the simplest, most obvious course—by purchasing their books" (315).

Such convictions that literature had value and that individuals should weigh well the quality of the books they were buying sometimes became intangled in a debate about didacticism in art. Novels of purpose clearly served a social end but were frequently less compelling than other fiction. The "Topics of the Time" in *Scribner's Monthly* for September 1878 stated that attempting to preach a lesson often made art wooden: "goodness in the hands of a literary man must not be of the type that is formed by creeds and institutions, if he would make it interesting" (743). On the other hand, *Scribner's Monthly* argued for the novel of purpose in its August 1880 "Topics of the Time": "The man who denies to art any kind of service to humanity which it can perform is either a fool or a trifler" (630). Later in the century, an August 1891 *Scribner's Magazine* "Point of View" lamented novels written about "a question of the day": "Such novels are not likely to survive the discussion or disturbance that gave them birth" (261). Yet *Scribner's Magazine* also complained in August 1897 that Americans were giving "too many really 'trumpery concoctions' the benefit of the tradition of good fiction" (389). The requirement that a novel's worth to individuals and to the larger social whole be evident, then, as well as an insistence that fiction be enjoyable, formed an important context for any work's reception.

As the number of literate citizens and magazines increased through the century, a new class of writer emerged, the literary critic, to take on the question of what works society ought to condone and what works it should reject through the operation of its free-market system. Scholarly reviews of new and re-printed works of literature took up considerable space in each monthly issue of the "quality" magazines. And the role of the critic was frequently debated, the more established periodicals calling for careful judgment, which, they felt, would vindicate their own editorial principles. *Harper's* observed in its August 1896 "Editor's Study": "what writing or literary production needs in this country now, more than in any other, is criticism—cool, discriminating, relentless criticism" (476). Insomuch as readers began to function as critics, their evaluation of each work became increasingly rigorous. The June 1894 *Scribner's Magazine* noted the high standards of readers at that time: "To be a good reader is a vocation by itself, and one which writers habitually and enviously admire" (789). The magazine went on to praise those who made judgments while reading and thus were never "the gentle reader" who simply "reads books for the promotion of his own happiness, and if he likes them knows it and is cheerfully ready to say so" (789). Arguments about the aims of literature and the achievements of specific writers, then, surrounded each serial novel and often became a part of its meaning for that first audience.

If literature was of value to society, those who disseminated it had cultural and economic power. *Lippincott's*, for instance, noted in September 1874 the importance of distribution for all commercial publishing. Discussing W. H. Smith's use of the railroad in England, the magazine stated: "Even the newspaper magnates of the *Times* and the *Telegraph* have to 'kotoo' to these great people, who are the principal dispensers of their wares" (389). Magazine editors similarly exercised power in deciding which works were selected for distribution. Many essays in this period discussed the process of submitting manuscripts and the principles of editorial acceptance and rejection. Because this was an era in which writing became a profession, some people questioned the rules that were said to govern the industry. Disgruntled would-be authors complained that work obviously inferior to their own had received preferential treatment from publishers and magazine staffs. From the middle of the century magazines asserted, however, that they were flooded with submissions and were forced to make judgments about what could be included in their pages. The September 1855 "Editor's Table" in the *Knickerbocker,* in an article entitled "A Necessary Word to New Correspondents," asserted flatly: "We are never waiting for matter of any kind. A year's supply, at the very least, is always waiting for us" (310) Periodicals spent many columns explaining and defending what appeared in their pages (see, for instance, *The Atlantic*'s April 1862 "Letter to a Young Contributor"; *Harper's* September 1868 "Editor's Easy Chair"; and *Lippincott's* November 1880 "A Sermon to Literary Aspirants"). Again, since these letters to editors and magazine responses all appeared on pages next to stories in each periodical, a complex context determined the audience's reception of any text.

In the January 1893 *Harper's New Monthly Magazine,* Elizabeth Stuart Phelps published a story, "The Rejected Manuscript," which took up directly these issues of authorship and editorial practice. Like Brander Matthews's "The Story of a Story" (discussed earlier), this sentimental tale challenged the system of literary production near the turn of the century; but the work resolved its conflicts with an idealized vision of the American publisher, a *deus ex machina* who sets all to right in the end.

Phelps's story linked changing evaluations of literary effort to larger social developments, as its setting was a "fattening suburb" (282) of Boston. Cantelope Corner's most distinguished resident was "Mr. W. H. T. Wire, vaguely understood to be 'in electricity' "(283). To this new environment, both "rural" and "urban" (284), came Aristotle Demosthenes Hathorpe, a failed scholar, "an old-time student without modern 'go' "(282); his wife, an author of "poetry and love-stories" (284); and two children. Both Mr. and Mrs. Hathorpe belong to an earlier world, in which their talents would have been appreciated, he as perhaps "the pastor of a colonial parish, or the scholastic of a medieval controversy" (283). Drawing on this old tradition for metaphor, Phelps explains that Hathorpe is "a vellum volume out of print" (283).

His wife, the story's heroine, enjoyed an upper-class background; "the scorn of 'trade' was in her blood" (289), and in her youth "all the new magazines" (284–85) came regularly to her house. Drawing on that past, she had earned "excellent sales" (286) with a first novel, *A Platonic Friendship;* but that success in the literary world came without understanding of the market that purchased her novel: "She had written the book as naturally as she had fallen in love. She had accepted her success as simply as she sang to her babies. . . . She had, in fact, sold her copyright for a trifling sum" (286). In addition, her crushing duties as wife and mother, which have become "second nature" to her, have forced her almost to forget her "first nature" (284), which, presumably, includes her creative genius. In the new world, where the "punctuality" of the train schedule is "a duty" (282), these two Hathorpes seemed doomed to failure.

The world of Cantelope Corner, which ought to appreciate scholar and author, is shown to be ignorant of their special gifts and trials. The grocer, for instance, says: "Literary folks are darn hard up—Lord knows why, poor devils. But I never got a bad debt out of one of "em yet" (283). Phelps apparently felt her readers in *Harper's* needed to be instructed as well in the fate of "the literary class" (286) in the 1890s. "The Rejected Manuscript" includes, for instance, a long passage lamenting the destruction caused in an author's life by the arrival of "proof-sheets":

> The essentially modern imagination might call them the electric cars of the literary profession. Without regard to life or limb, they roll crashing into that margin of existence which is reserved for other human exactions. They lie in wait for one's hour of maddening pre-engagement. They lurk, watching for one's direst emergency. They select the confusing occasions of public amusement, and are well known to prefer a houseful of company. They delight to hit the eve of a journey. They meet the exhausted traveller at the door of his hotel. (286)

Not only did Phelps provide for her audience such insights into the emotional and psychological strains in a writer's daily life, but the story itself was structured around the heroine's repeated "nervous journey to the post-office" (287) as she awaits the response of publishers to her second novel. "Love's Daily Bread," just completed, was needed to save the family from poverty. The narrator tells readers: "The history of that first winter in the hired house at Cantelope Corner was the history of a manuscript" (288).

That history is, of course, a series of heartbreaking rejections by publishers, appropriately named "Bind and Blow," "Scowl and Critic," "Frisky and Flourish." The heroine's lowest moment comes when she loses a baby and her very survival becomes questionable. At that point Phelps's story recalls Mark Twain's "About Magnanimous-Incident Literature" (discussed earlier), in which books 'do not tell the whole story'; for she has her heroine tell her husband: "Oh, I've tried—to do my share—to help along. But it isn't easy doing. . . . so many things. Don't let Popsy take to writing" (291).

The family is saved, however, by a "prince of American publishers" (289), who sees the virtues of "Love's Daily Bread" when no other figure in the profession does. He is described in terms that one would think embarrassed the editors at *Harper's* when printed on the magazine's pages for January 1893: this paragon "will be remembered longer for his great, good heart, and for his exquisite courtesy to timid and troubled authors, than he will for the high quality of the success which gave him his unique position in the advancement of American literature" (289). The publisher's wisdom pertains to the human hearts of his authors but also to the larger reading public as well: he "was wisest of the wise in the mysterious laws that govern the great freshets of public taste and whim" (290). His saving power was perhaps best revealed in the story's one illustration. The mother/author, lying as if on her deathbed, hears her daughter: " 'Mummer,' said Popsy, severely, 'You've dwopped a good-luck letter' " (292), the publisher's check for "one thousand dollars" (292) included in his correspondence accepting the novel. According to such stories as Phelps's, the powerful, benevolent figure of publisher towers over the literary landscape in the 1890s, granting fortune to certain Americans. Both within works of literature and in editorial discussion of current events on neighboring pages of the magazines, the context of this social pattern framed the meaning of literature.

The recognition of context insisted on by the periodical format in the nineteenth century was also related to another important theme in American literature, the tension between isolation and community. In Mary Catherine Lee's 1893 short story, *An Island Plant: In Three Parts,* the importance of the social and physical environment to an individual's life was stressed; at the same time, the form of this work, its installment appearance in a periodical, made a similar point about the nature of literature in context. Indeed, the story's one direct allusion was to a central voice in the American tradition of literary communities. The narrator asked at one point, "who does live alone?" (599), and then allowed Oliver Wendell Holmes to answer: " 'This body in which we journey across the isthmus between the two oceans,' says Dr. Holmes, 'is not a private carriage, but an omnibus' " (599).

Lee's Hawthornesque tale took place in a settlement of houses "isolated upon the western end of the island" (597), Nantucket. The story's first part, published in the May 1893 *Atlantic* under the title of "The Roots," told the story of Phebe Nichols, who lived in the "[m]ost isolated, most lonely" (597) of the settlement's houses. Nearly driven mad by her solitary condition, she created fantasies of a lover "lost at sea" (599) and talked with "invisible communicants" (600). After a particularly dazzling sunset underscored "the desolation of her separated life" (602), Phebe accepted the proposal of James Newbegin, a "ruddy, middle-aged simpleton, white-eyed, comfortable, invertebrate . . . just the germ of a soul, a mere register of dim sensations" (604). His lack of ties to the larger human community was stressed by the fact that he navigated the island's sandy beaches in a unique "two-wheeled cart" equipped with sail, "luffing and keeping off, jibing and tacking and reefing" (603).

The second installment of Lee's story appeared in the June *Atlantic* and further stressed the theme of isolation by depicting the later terrible alienation of Phebe's three grown daughters, Anne, Mary, and a second Phebe. Despite the efforts of some good Quakers living on the island, each daughter tasted the possibility of joining the human community only once, when each encountered in turn the romantic Cap'n Dudley. But this wild character, for whom there was "too much room to caper in ashore" (753), left the island for a career at sea in the story's second chapter, "The Green Branches." Years later he returned to find that the three sisters were all mad, one wandering the island like her father, "one staring out of a window that looks toward the town," and a third "gazing into the fire" (764–65). Entitled "The Results of Drought and Winter," the third chapter emphasized the effects of the three sisters' isolation from society, the "wastes of womanhood" (767). Although Captain Dudley had possessed in his youth "an earnest wish to adore something" (757), and the sisters had wanted at the same time "to be *liked*,—more and more" (756), their separation had resulted in doom, "the dead body of tender passion, that had died not in hard struggles, but in long, slow, wasting sickness" (768).

As Mary Catherine Lee explored the theme of alienation in her fiction, the form of the *Atlantic*, in which *An Island Plant: in Three Parts* appeared, also argued for the importance of context and relationship, that is, for Holmes's theory of the "omnibus" carrying many passengers. Lee's story was surrounded by the familiar features of a thirty-five-year-old, popular literary magazine—other stories, parts of serial novels, articles, essays, and editorial commentary. Thus, it did not stand alone. Even much bleaker naturalistic works at this late point in the century, such as Stephen Crane's "The Open Boat," were framed by the familiar packaging of entertainment and information in an established literary periodical. Crane's story appeared in the June 1897 *Scribner's Magazine* (728–40), along with, among other items, the fourth installment of William Dean Howells's *The Story of a Play.*

The context of Catherine Lee's serial story, however, did reveal the changing climate of publishing in the 1890s: publication of long works in magazines was beginning to seem for many writers less conducive to creative effort; and issuing works first in inexpensive, single-volume editions was becoming more profitable. Whereas *An Island Plant* was divided into two installments for *The Atlantic*, the story had been structured in three parts. The magazine's installment division matched the story's shape to some degree, as the May number gave the mother's history and the June issue that of the daughters. And the gap in time between the mother's and the daughters' youths was stressed by the thirty-day pause between May and June. But the June issue had to encompass two temporal settings, the daughters' youth and their old age, whereas the May part had contained only one. Time's passing between the daughters' youth and their old age was not strengthened by any pause in publication between chapters 2 and 3. Each of the three chapters was about the same length, but the first magazine installment was only half the length of the second. Thus the structure organizing the narrative did not coincide exactly with that imposed by the periodical.

Any story's context, the magazine in which it appeared, added to its meaning for an original audience. This is true of serial fiction in periodicals from mid-century, when the publication format was accepted and used artistically by authors, and of works published in the 1880s and 1890s, when authors were straining against the limits imposed by installment issue. In separating stories from the magazines in which they first reached their nineteenth-century audiences, modern scholars and students have created special texts for study. Recovering fiction in its original context leads us back to the actual literary history of the last century.

AMERICA'S STORY

Just as themes like alienation and community were central to specific works of nineteenth-century American literature, the topic of national identity might be said to be involved in the overall history of serial fiction in periodicals from 1850 to 1900. Brian Lee discusses the "tensions and ironies created by conflicting social and political ideals" (6) in the latter half of the nineteenth century, concluding: "It is even possible to maintain that the American novel itself is a product of this period, and that the form did not really exist before the Civil War" (6). These years did see an effort by publishers to free themselves from a reliance on European fiction for the material in their literary periodicals. An attraction and resistance to the European model had been a feature of the American literary tradition from its beginnings, as Barbara Lewalski writes: "early American literature is as much a product of continuities as an indigenous creation" (24). And William L. Hedges reminds us that the "history of American literature is now commonly conceived as an evolution toward indigenousness" (190). In December 1868 *Lippincott's Magazine* linked an emerging national literature with the close of the Civil War: "The number of writers in this country is increasing, and those who watch the development of our literature must be struck with the fact that since the close of the great contest which has stirred the American mind to its profoundest depths, a decided improvement has taken place in the tone of the periodical press" (670).

Many American magazines publishing at mid-century realized that their native writers were not producing works comparable to the British masters of the time. The March 1854 *Putnam's* lamented: "We make it a point to read all the new American novels that come out, with the hope of by-and-by lighting upon one which deserves to be called American. But the coming novel has not yet appeared" (333). Circulation figures had made magazine editors well aware of the appeal of British writers, as Arthur John notes: "After the Civil War, [*Harper's*] monthly fell off in circulation so sharply that the House of Harper considered ending its publication. But the serialization of Charles Dickens's 'Our Mutual Friend' and Wilkie Collins's 'Armadale' restored its prewar leadership" (60). *Harper's* claimed in May 1866 that its audience demanded the kind of serial being written by English writers. Thus its pages featured fiction by Charles Reade and Mrs. Humphrey Ward "not because of the partiality of the editor for English authors, nor of any supposed preference of the reader for English stories, nor because they are 'stolen,' for they are liberally paid for, but simply because they are better adapted to the taste to which the magazine is addressed"

(803). *The Atlantic* at about the same time saw the publication of the definitively American *Miss Gilbert's Career* by J. G. Holland as unusual in January 1861: "And an additional satisfaction is caused by the fact, that the book, not only in origin, but in essence, is American from cover to cover" (126). *Lippincott's* claimed in its inaugural issue of January 1868, "American writers and American affairs will naturally claim the greater part of our space, but not to the exclusion of European topics" (114).

Some magazines resented the popularity foreign writers enjoyed in America. The July 1862 *Atlantic* expressed unhappiness at the demand for Victor Hugo's *Les Misérables*, the first book of which (*Fantine*) had just been published in English. The magazines claimed that the book's success was owing to "the most desperate of bookselling speculations" (124) rather than to literary merit. Other voices in the United States pointed out that the lack of a strong national literature derived from the country's own status as a developing culture. *Putnam's* said in October 1854: "America has no national novel, for the very good reason that there is no such thing as American society" (394). And, of course, these magazines were all subject to the forces of a free market and had to compete for prominent names to grace their table of contents. *Harper's*, for instance, added the phrase, "Written Exclusively for Harper's Magazine," after the title of Charles Reade's *Jack of All Trades: A Matter of Fact Romance* in 1857–58.

By the 1870s, however, a general agreement emerged that native periodicals and the serial novels important to their success should be distinctly American. This view coincided with a change in the authors dominating the literary scene, as Richard H. Brodhead explains: "With the deaths or retirements from authorship of the generation of Hawthorne, Melville, Emerson, and Poe in the 1850s and 1860s, then the emergence, just after the Civil War, of such new figures as Henry James, William Dean Howells, and Mark Twain, American literature undergoes one of the most thoroughgoing changes of the guard in its entire history" (467). The June 1857 *Putnam's Magazine* explained that it had come into being because no existing magazine was expressing a newly redefined American identity: "it was still felt that the intellectual independence and movement of the country had no organ; that there was a character, and talent, and literary requirement in the American mind, of which there was, as yet, no expression; and, from that conviction, in due season, sprang *Putnam's Monthly*—which did not necessarily clash with *Harper*, more than the *Weekly Tribune* with the *New York Ledger*" (294). *Putnam's* was one of the first to assert the strength of the American creative spirit, insisting on the first page in its inaugural issue of January 1853, "It is because we are confident that neither Greece nor Guinea can offer the American reader a richer variety of instruction and amusement in every kind, than the country whose pulses throb with his, and whose every interest is his own, that this Magazine presents itself to-day" (1).

By November 1875 *Scribner's Monthly* was also asserting the importance of American periodicals and American fiction: "We wish to call attention to the fact that we are endeavoring to make an American magazine. It seems as if American readers must be tired by this time of the ordinary English-society-novel. . . . There is nothing more interesting to an American than a good story, either of his own time or of the time which has hardly retired from his personal memory" (123). Three years later, in November 1878, the same magazine acknowledged that for "many years the American public depended upon the British novel" (146); now the magazine felt "that it could do no better for its own countrymen and for American literature than to discard utterly the British novel and get the best American novel it could, to take its place" (147). The "best" American novel was still suspect in some circles, however, as *Harper's* suggested in its April 1869 "Editor's Book Table": "While our table is covered with books of poetry, illustrated books, and books of travels, we look in vain for an American novel, or in truth for an American novelist. We have, indigenous to the soil, humorists, poets, moralists, historians, very readable magazine writers; but our novels, with one or two single exceptions, are poor copies of transatlantic productions" (423). And a March 1881 *Lippincott's* essay, "The Decline of Genius," complained: "The great writers of the century are nearly all gone, and there are no indications that a new race is coming on" (309).

Nevertheless, a change from European to American literary material was occurring in the book trade as well as in the periodical industry. In June 1878 *Harper's* announced that it would be bringing out a new series of books: "Harper's 'Library of American Fiction' will be a worthy companion of the familiar 'Library of Select Novels,' which has been the means of introducing to the general American public the more famous English and European novelists of the last thirty-five years" (146). By this time the conviction that America had a viable, if still young, literary tradition was more widely accepted, as a *Century* comment in June 1889 suggested: "The editors [of a new book on American literature] have given a liberal interpretation to the word literature; indeed, they have been forced to do so, for it is not much more than half a century that literature as a fine art has been practiced in this country with any success" (314). Sometimes editorial policy dictated a conspicuous selection of American works over foreign ones, as was perhaps the case in 1867 when the featured serial in *Harper's* was George F. Harrington's *The Virginians in Texas,* a work forgotten now but likely to have found enthusiastic readers in at least two states at the time.

That periodicals consciously promoted an American literature through editorial policy was, in fact, widely stated. *Harper's* editors said as early as January 1863 that they hoped to stimulate native literary production even when they were featuring the more established British authors: "Indeed, as one of the objects originally contemplated by us was to bring before the American reader, at the most reasonable rate, the good things that were scattered through foreign periodicals, and which were accessible only at the most unreasonable rates, so we may fairly say that our success, the success of an American magazine, itself stimulated American talent and business enterprise to enter the field as competitors. . . . now the foreign guests there [in our pages] are only of the most distinguished. . . . But generally the bulk of our contributors are American" (279). In a November 1890 article, "The Century's Twentieth Anniversary," *Century* claimed that its one enduring theme over the last two decades had been the American story: "If there is any one dominant sentiment which an unprejudiced reviewer would recognize as pervading these forty half-yearly volumes it is, we think, a sane and earnest Americanism" (148). In many ways, what Americans were attempting in the 1850s, 1860s, and 1870s, then, was the development of an audience, that is, a taste for American stories by American writers. This was a policy Charles Dudley Warner advocated in the June 1890 *Atlantic,* though his aim was to refine audience discrimination even further: "It is, perhaps, too much to say that all the American novel needs for its development is an audience, but it is safe to say that an audience would greatly assist it" (730).

Even late in the century, however, some voices expressed a need to continue drawing on the European tradition. In a December 1893 *Atlantic* article, "'Mere Literature,' " Woodrow Wilson argued: "If this free people to which we belong is to keep its fine spirit, its perfect temper amidst affairs, its high courage in the face of difficulties, its wise temperateness and wide-eyed hope, it must continue to drink deep and often from the old wells of English undefiled, quaff the keen tonic of its best ideals, keep its blood warm with all the great utterances of exalted purpose and pure principle of which its matchless literature is full" (828). *Century* also acknowledged in November 1895 that, in promoting native writers, it had not been ignoring the significant writers in Europe: "The literary history of America during the past twenty-five years involves to a very large extent the history of The Century Magazine. At the same time the magazine has numbered in the past and will in the future number among its contributors many of the best writers of the old world" (155). Because of rising national feeling, *Century* predicted a "revival of creative literature" for America in the twentieth century.

Others at the time felt so confident of the state of American letters that they were willing to offer space to other cultures. As the historian Francis Parkman noted in a preface to Mary Hartwell Catherwood's *The Romance of Dollard* (beginning its serial publication in the November 1888 *Century*), "The author is a pioneer in what may be called a new departure in American fiction," taking Canada as a subject (81). And, although its shape may have varied from expectations, such a thing as the American novel was generally agreed to have arrived in these decades. *Harper's* noted in its September 1881 "Editor's Easy

Chair," "It seems to be understood that the American novel, which has been so long anxiously expected, is gradually arriving, not, indeed, in the precise form which may have been anticipated, but in its essential substance" (626).

There was, of course, concern throughout the period that European and other nations understand American culture; and that meant native writers should accurately depict their land and people in their own periodicals. The April 1880 *Lippincott's* explained to Americans that they could be understood abroad through images created by others. In "Americans in English Fiction," the editors complained that European portraits of Americans did not accurately describe the nation because those novelists met only a few, unrepresentative Americans, the wealthy who traveled in Europe (512–14). The October 1878 *Harper's* noted that some readers had objected to the characterization of Americans in James's *Daisy Miller*: "But a party of intelligent American women, while they sew and embroider and crochet on a summer morning in the country, listening to 'Daisy Miller' read aloud, would probably unite in the declaration that it is a shame for an American to draw such a portrait of an American girl for the inspection of the English in an English magazine" (780). *Harper's* was recognizing not only an American sensitivity about its image abroad but also a resentment that native writers might choose to publish in foreign periodicals. The hope was that our writers would project a positive national character through our journals to other countries. *Harper's* had announced this potential a few years earlier in a March 1858 "Editor's Table": "Within the last fifteen years our literature—and especially that part of it more distinctly American—has begun to exert an influence over European mind" (554).

At a central place in this American effort to shape and exhibit a national character was the novel as a unique art form and the periodical as the place of its publication. In October 1854 *Putnam's* said of novels: "peculiarly are they the product of this nineteenth[-century] era when there is such a fecundity and such an overflowing of mental and psychal life" (396). Discussing the growth of a native novel industry, the March 1858 *Harper's* credited the generation of American writers after Irving and

Cooper and the new magazines with expanding the nation's influence in the world: "But it remained for our present generation of writers, living in an age of cheap printing, when the masses can be readily reached through those channels of intellectual communication which are every where open, to find general access to British readers. American genius at a shilling was a lucky idea" (554). The April 1886 *Lippincott's* also saw a great future for American literature: "When we come to formulate our demands of the Coming American Novelist, we will agree that he must be native-born. His ancestors may come from where they will, but we must give him a birthplace and have the raising of him" (440). This forward-looking essay even considered the possibility that the next century's man of letters might be of African ancestry. And in a further note of explanation the author concluded: "I have used the generic masculine pronoun [to represent the great novelist of the future] because it is convenient. . . . Why should not the coming novelist be a woman as well as an African?" (443).

The concern over the American character was directed inward as well as toward other countries in the last half of the nineteenth century. That is, regions of the United States wanted to prove their distinctive identity at the same time that they fit themselves into the country as a whole. Christopher P. Wilson explains that the Progressive Era at the end of the century "provided new means by which a writer could seek out previously unexplored areas of American life. It also enticed writers to voice democratic aspirations and gave several promising writers an audience they might otherwise have lacked" (xv). Thus, regionalism in literature was a part of a larger national desire to establish an identity; and serial fiction published in periodicals added to America's continuing story by defining elements of a larger union. The postwar South in particular faced the challenge of pronouncing its separateness while not denying the larger framework of the union that had defeated it. But such schizophrenic efforts found a medium in periodical publication, as the major literary monthlies gave ample space to regionalists like Mary Noallis Murphree, George Washington Cable, Sarah Orne Jewett, and Hamlin Garland. Werner Sollars also points out that periodicals not only featured regional writing but were "a rich resource for ethnic readings long before the more familiar book publications started" (579).

As one of the chief features of a modern urban industrial society, the new national magazine industry helped preserve regional and ethnic identity through fiction published in its pages at the same time that it asserted a national identity in the broad range of its subject matter and the great reach of its distribution. An acknowledgment of the nation's relationship to its regions appeared in *Harper's New Monthly Magazine*'s "Editor's Easy Chair" for December 1883: "With the vast increase of a heterogeneous population, and the extending area of the country, it may well be that no city or local group of men and women will ever again exert so mighty a dominance as that of New England and its capital [Boston]" (150). Christopher P. Wilson explains the same phenomenon from the perspective of the audiences for fiction now emerging across the country: "Measurable strides in literacy rates and education in the 1880s and 1890s undoubtedly expanded the available audience of mass industries of print; public high schools alone had tripled in number in the latter decade. Libraries also grew in numbers and were modernized in these years" (12).

Regionalism's endorsement of distinct local elements in the American character became linked to fundamental principles of democracy, the many making up the one. Eric J. Sundquist accounts for the connections between realism, regionalism, and democracy: "To the European insistence on precise description, authentic action and dialogue, and moral honesty, the American tradition [of realism] deriving from Walt Whitman, Nathaniel Hawthorne, Harriet Beecher Stowe and Herman Melville adds a democratic openness in subject matter and style that breaks down rigid hierarchies" (502). The November 1859 *Harper's* "Editor's Table" explained how the dramatic growth of inexpensive periodicals, featuring the best writing of the day, had been an essential feature of our developing country: "Without doubt literature is now the most democratic thing in existence—almost as much so as sunshine and air; and, moreover, the people are conscious of it, and appreciate the wonderful revolution [that has created 'readers by the million']" (838). G. P. Lathrop's August 1874 discussion of realism in *The Atlantic*, "The Novel and Its Future," also linked this literary mode to democratic principles: "The level of humanity is like that of the ocean; but each constituent particle rejoices in its own atomic being, and all have a chance to crest the highest waves, if wind and moon conspire favorably" (324).

This sentiment, that the wide distribution of literature was appropriate to our form of government, allowed at least one periodical to dismiss worries about "cheap literature" and any danger it might pose to society. The November 1859 *Harper's* asserted: "Our firm conviction in this matter, as in politics, is that the people may be trusted" (840). Later in the century, the April 1887 *Harper's* saw the spread of good literature around the globe as "one of the hopefulest signs of the world's progress" (826). Thus, as magazines prospered and serial novels found more and more vehicles to the public, nineteenth-century America established a mode of expression for its expanding, heterogeneous population. Richard H. Brodhead concludes of the "quality" literary journals and their related publishing interests: "The literary institutions under gentry control in the later nineteenth century succeeded in creating, it may be, the closest thing to a coherent national literary culture that America has ever had" (472–73). As the subjects for the fictions published serially in magazines increasingly involved American citizens in their distinct regions of the country, the nation's history as a whole grew longer and deeper. After a generation of significant native writers had found a distinctly New World voice in the first half of the 1800s, and after the divisions of the Civil War, America's continuing story resumed in literary periodicals, shaped and nurtured by installment issue.

FROM SERIALS TO SHORT STORIES

In the last decade of the nineteenth century, new ideas about the purposes and forms of literature took shape. The many women writing fiction, as well as some men writing about women, had inaugurated new possibilities of subject matter for the novel. Cecelia Tichi notes: "It is fair to say that from the 1880s the new woman in theory and fact changed the canon of American literature, affecting writers' lives and invigorating the national literature with new fictional design in character, form, and theme" (590). The June 1891 *Scribner's Magazine* made a similar observation in its "Point of View" section:

> If the married woman is to be the heroine of the coming novel [as others have written] it must turn on something besides love-making. It must be the story of her career; of her professional or political success; of her painful accession through toilsome decades to the front rank of the doctors; of the money she made and what she did with it. American women are very much alive in these days. There is no special difficulty about writing interesting books about them without using men at all except as puppets or lay figures. (792)

Many of the old guard, however, expressed resentment at such social changes influencing the form of fiction. One voice in "The Contributors' Club" of the July 1898 *Atlantic,* for instance, regretted the necessity of including the "new woman" in fiction: "Let the story-teller sweep the horizon with his literary glasses. Everywhere he will see the army of new women demanding recognition. Choice is invidious, but choose he must" (141). And still others complained that women writers were occupying too much space, not just in less prestigious weekly and daily newspapers, but also in the major periodicals. Tichi points out that "artful male writers were subtler [than those who openly criticized change], but equally subversive of the new woman" (593).

Other forces affected the kinds of fiction authors contemplated writing in the 1890s. The debate continued about whether realism or romance was the proper mode for fiction, and European examples of aestheticism and decadence challenged assumptions about the moral value of art. *Harper's* "Editor's Study" for April 1896, for example, reacted negatively to the increasingly bleak portraits presented by realistic and naturalistic writers: "It has come about that the novels and stories which are to fill our leisure hours and cheer us in this vale of tears have become what is called tragic. It is not easy to define what tragedy is, but the term is applied in modern fiction to scenes and characters that come to ruin from no particular fault of their own—not even when the characters break most of the ten commandments, but by an unappeasable fate that dogs and thwarts them" (643). Such readers desired the morally uplifting tales more characteristic of mid-century.

The emergence of newer, cheaper periodicals, whose profit came more from advertising than from subscriptions, challenged the literary supremacy of the "quality" magazines. *McClure's, Munsey's, The Saturday Evening Post*, and others provided new space and a variety of formats to a growing class of fiction writers. And entrepreneurs like S. S. McClure began to offer serials by new writers like Robert Louis Stevenson to newspapers across the country through expanding syndicates. Christopher P. Wilson explains, "a series of related developments—the passage of the Postal Act of 1879, technological advancements in printing, engraving, and papermaking, and the growth of national advertising itself—opened up [for magazines] new vistas of circulation and increased reliance on advertising as a source of revenue" (48).

Within the widespread debate about the role of art in society, America's effort to define itself evolved toward a proclamation of the short story as the great national genre. Like serial novels, short stories had developed along with the growing periodical trade of an expanding industrial nation (John 163; Sollors 588). Arguments about the primacy of the short story began with assertions about the nature of life in the New World, its energy and capacity for rapid change. *Century* noted in its June 1890 "Topics of the Time": "[The editor] may even permit himself to ask whether the literary artist of our day has not caught somewhat of the hurry, the immediateness, of the time; whether, indeed, the present age is not too present with us; whether there is the slow, determined, sure, artistic work which made the successful careers of the earlier generation of American poets, romanticists, and essayists" (313). Similarly, J. S. Tunison, in the November 1897 *Atlantic* ("The Coming Literary Revival"), termed "characteristic of modern life" an "uneasy feeling that the world will never see long novels again as good as those of Fielding and Thackeray. . . . There are short stories and little poems which will live forever; but, on the whole, these two classes in literary art lack seriousness, if considered as an end in themselves. They are characteristic of a tentative, a waiting age" (698).

While Tunison found the short story lacking "seriousness," others began to claim it as a form marking the country's maturity in the literary world. As it announced what was to come in its next volume, the October 1891 *Century* noted the preeminence of the American short story: coming next was "a great number of shorter stories of American life, most of them single-number stories, which cover a large part of the continent in scene, and which in depiction of character and social phenomena seem to us to be very remarkable, and to prove again the truth of most of those appreciative and enthusiastic things said by American and foreign critics of the American short story—or short-story, as Mr. Brander Matthews calls it" (950). That the editor felt it necessary to identify these works as "single-number" stories shows how the parts format was still the norm in these years; but more and more works were appearing as whole units. And that there was some debate about what to call the form underscores a revaluation of its status as a literary genre.

Other voices linked an American development of the short story genre to special qualities in the national temperament. The February 1887 "Editor's Study" in *Harper's* announced: "But we are not sure, after all, as we hinted in the beginning, that the Americans have not brought the short story nearer perfection in the all-round sense than almost any other people, and for reasons very simple and near at hand. It might be argued from the national hurry and impatience that it was a literary form peculiarly adapted to the American temperament" (484) This column concluded that the "success of American magazines," which still "must have" serial novels, also now requires short stories (484). In an article entitled "The Short Story," the February 1892 *Atlantic* stated the claim to a national excellence even more strongly: "American writers, less greedy than Lord Bacon, have taken the short story as their province. . . . [T]here is no sign that the art is anywhere so rich, so varied, or so fresh as it is with us. . . . It appears to have become in truth, the national mode of utterance in the things of the imagination and, taking its own wherever it finds it, the short story has become more and more variously expressive" (261).

The popularity of the new genre for authors and audiences in these years was also marked by the publication of short story series in the "quality" monthlies. In most cases this new subgenre involved a group of stories sharing a common setting and cast of characters, all appearing as a continuing feature in a single periodical. Each monthly story appeared under the same heading, the title of the series; but one month's text also stood alone as a complete short story. Such works included: Stephen Crane's *Whilomville Stories* in *Harper's* (August 1899–August 1900); Margaret Deland's *Old Chester Tales* in *Harper's* (April–December 1898); Sarah Orne Jewett's *Country of the Pointed Firs* in *The Atlantic* (January–September 1896); Grace King's *Balcony Stories* in *Century* (December 1892–October 1893); Rudyard Kipling's *Stalky and Co.: A Series of Stories about Schoolboy Life* in *McClure's* (December 1898–June 1899); and Brander Matthews's *Vignettes of Manhattan* in *Harper's* (December 1893–August 1894).

Like novels initially published serially, most of these collections later appeared in volume editions, as a letter from Herman Justi ("How to Utilize Old Magazines") in the March 1897 *Century* explained. Justi admitted that some material from periodicals could, after it had been read, simply be discarded: "Serial stories, or even short storiettes if they have any merit, are likely to appear in book form, and consequently they, too, can be consigned, like some of our dear rejected manuscript, 'to outer darkness' " (793). As authors worked increasingly in this new mode, audiences also became accustomed to receiving their reading in complete, separate packages. Reviewing the volume edition of Grace King's *Balcony Stories*, for instance, the April 1894 *Atlantic* felt that the preface linking the stories together could be passed over after an initial reading: "A baker's dozen of sketches, or tales, follow upon a prelude which seeks to account for the title of the book. . . . [T]he fiction of the balcony ceases to trouble writer or reader after it has once done its work of pitching the note of the book" (557). The prelude had suggested a unifying context for her stories—women talking on warm summer evenings in the South, as children listened from their beds—that lent King's work a sense of continuity and development characteristic of the serial novel. By this point in the century, however, readers felt it was less important to see each short work as part of a larger whole.

Lippincott's, in fact, began another new publishing practice in the late 1880s, the publishing of one entire novel in each issue of the magazine. One of the first of what might now be called "novellas" was Julian Hawthorne's *Sinfire: A Novel*, which took up pages 1 to 84 of the January 1887 number. The *Lippincott's* cover reprinted Julian Hawthorne's comment from the *New York World:* "By this plan the subscribers will get twelve novels a year instead of one or two, and will get them straight instead of mangled out of shape and recognition by the serial process, which has so long been the curse of fictitious literature." Novels released in this way were not to be republished in any other form; they were available "now or later" only through purchase of the magazine.

A June 1891 *Atlantic* article, "New England in the Short Story," linked such changing sensibilities as the development of the novella and the vogue for short stories to phases of regionalism in American literature: "There are two periods in the life of a country when the short story is peculiarly adapted to display the characteristics of the people: the first is when the country is virgin soil for the novelist; the second is when the soil, in agricultural phrase, is worn out" (845). According to this analysis, the American South and Southwest were "virgin" territories for writers; thus short stories depicting the traits of these generally unknown parts of the country abounded in the 1880s and 1890s. New England, on the other hand, had been "worn out" by novelists; so here too short stories dominated because full-length treatment of the region's character would have been unnecessary or redundant: "when a country has been appraised by the historian, the political economist, the sociologist, the philosopher, the novelist, there comes to be a certain common significance attached to it, so that as soon as it is named the mind responds with a tolerably definite concept of the character embodied in the country and people" (845). In this division of the country into old and new, the short story remained the dominant genre.

American affection for the short story even began to alter the model of the novel, as critics interpreted long, whole works as collections of individual, smaller texts. *Harper's* September 1887 "Editor's Study," for instance, suggested that long novels were really series of short stories: "A big book is necessarily a group of episodes more or less loosely connected by a thread of narrative, and there seems no reason why this thread must always be supplied. Each episode may be quite distinct, or it may be one of a connected group; the final effect will be from the truth of each episode, not from the size of the group" (640). We might even link this change in the theory of fiction to larger shifts in American thought. Brian Lee identifies the conflict between individual freedom and social conformity as perhaps the central theme in our literary history from the mid-nineteenth century to the present (12). In the serial, the dominant form before 1900, each part, though it is to be read alone, must take its place within the larger whole. A short story, rising in importance in the final decade of the last century, asserts more individual freedom than one installment, even though it too can have its place in a collection of related stories. And a novel published in a single volume, the form which will dominate modern literature, claims a virtual autonomy from any larger context.

Some novelists in the late nineteenth century were working within a concept of what *Harper's* called the "big book," a collection of separate "episodes more or less loosely connected by a thread of narrative." Unlike mid-century serials, installment novels by James and others in the 1880s and 1890s were sometimes made up of individual parts that resembled short stories. The single part of an earlier novel had generally depended heavily on knowledge of what had come before, and it looked insistently toward a continuation of its own story. In fact, the practice of printing "To Be Continued" at the end of each periodical installment in a serial novel increased near the close of the nineteenth century, in part because without the tag readers could not tell what works were completed short stories and which were ongoing serial stories. Earlier, the serial's continuation could be assumed by editor and audience.

The demand for short stories in periodicals could account in part for the fact that the first installments of many late nineteenth-century novels stood alone as short stories. For instance, Henry James's first three chapters of *The Princess Casamassima*, included in the September 1885 *Altantic*, formed a neat unit with distinct beginning, middle, and end. Chapter 1 of *The Princess Casamassima* described Mrs. Bowerbank's visit to Amanda Pynsent, a "little dressmaker" (289) living at Lomax Place in north London, and her revelation that a woman dying in prison wished to see her son, Hyacinth Robinson, who had been adopted by Miss Pynsent. Chapter 2 presented Mr. Vetch's talk with Miss Pynsent about the adopted child, which indirectly suggested their sad love story and the unsatisfactory class structure of English society. And the third chapter took readers to the prison for the crucial meeting of Florentine and Hyacinth. So powerful was this interview between the dying woman and her ten-year-old son that no detailed explanation was necessary to show that the boy's subsequent life would be shaped by the kiss in a dark, frightening prison: his mother's arms "closed about him, and the poor dishonoured head pressed itself against his little cheek. It was a terrible, tremendous embrace, to which Hyacinth submitted with instant patience" (311).

It was not necessary for subscribers to the September 1885 *Atlantic* to read beyond that text for an understanding of basic themes. Whether the boy would turn out to be totally unlike his parents or would live a life remarkably similar to theirs was in many ways irrelevant: his course would be determined by this seminal event, by the forces at work in this scene. Mrs. Bowerbank explained how this kiss was the culmination of an unstated history and thus summed up the past before this short story: she told Amanda that Florentine wanted the "kiss her lips have been famished for for years" (293). Mrs. Bowerbank also knew that the relationship of Hyacinth to the dying woman would shape the future, no matter what he was told at this time: "Oh, he'd be sure to know [if Miss Pynsent kept his origin secret from him], one of these days. We see a great deal of that— the way things come out" (293). And Miss Pynsent recognized that there was a certain "way things come out," which she would be unable to control: "She had had her picture of the future, painted in rather rosy hues, hung up before her now for a good many years; but it seemed to her that Mrs. Bowerbank's heavy hand had suddenly punched a hole in the canvas" (297).

The sense that the seeds of the future were contained in this moment was also suggested by Vetch, who was prepared to "watch [Hyacinth] with curiosity, to see what he grows into" (301). Vetch believed the boy's character would also affect that future and the people like Amanda who would make it up: "he will, in his imagination (and that will always persuade him), subject you to some extraordinary metamorphosis; he will dress you up" (302). And Mellicent Henning, whom Amanda called a "naughty little girl" (290), was introduced in this installment to suggest an alternative type for Hyacinth to associate with in the future. Like his mother, Mellicent had kissed Hyacinth on this most meaningful day of his life; and he would not accept Miss Pynsent's characterization of her: "Why is she bad? I don't think she is bad; I like her very much" (295).

As it was clear in the first installment that these characters would shape the protagonist's future, James's September 1885 text also insisted that the larger structure of society would be a factor in the outcome of events. Miss Pynsent's world was organized by simplistic concepts, which "she had read in a novel" (292). And her sewing suggested a tendency to fantasies common to her class: "she told fibs as freely as she invented trimmings" (292). Hyacinth had clearly learned from her: readers of *The Atlantic* first encountered him at "the little sweet-shop on the other side of the street [in Lomax Place], an establishment where periodical literature, as well as tough toffy and hard lollipops was dispensed, and where song-books and pictorial sheets were attractively exhibited in the small-paned, dirty window" (290). So Hyacinth would take his path in life guided by ideas packaged for him in cheap magazines: "He used to stand there for half an hour at a time, spelling out the first pages of the romances in the Family Herald and the London Journal, and admiring the obligatory illustration, in which the noble characters (they were always of the highest birth) were presented to the carnal eye" (290). In these three chapters, then, the matrix that would frame Hyacinth's entire life—a contrast of "noble characters" and "carnal eye"—was fully presented. The Sep-

120

tember part concluded with Miss Pynsent worried that Hyacinth would ask too many questions after leaving the prison: "To her surprise, however, he completely neglected them; he sat in silence, looking out of the window [of the cab], till they reëntered Lomax Place" (311).

As the central character's prospects were defined and restricted by the magazine industry he encountered in the sweet-shop, so Henry James, the author, had to endure the constraints built into the publication system of his day. By making this installment of *The Princess Casamassima* as complete and self-contained as a short story, however, James seemed to block out the framework of the periodical issue of his own novel. There was only one conspicuous concession to the shape of the fiction beyond this part, a link to future installments: the narrator admitted near the end, "What thoughts were begotten at that moment in [Hyacinth's] wondering little mind Miss Pynsent was destined to learn at another time" (311). But even this hint did not absolutely need extended dramatization, given Mrs. Bowerbank's and Vetch's predictions within the installment. That Amanda would learn the consequences of her action was the primary point, just as that Hyacinth would be affected by the deathbed scene remained James's essential thematic note, the conclusion to his short story in the September 1885 *Atlantic*.

Despite an intense interest in the short story form that was altering the shape of fiction, many writers were, of course, still at work on traditional, full-length novels in the 1880s and 1890s. J. S. Tunison insisted that the short story had limits in his November 1897 *Atlantic* piece, "The Coming Literary Revival." For him and others, the way toward the great literature of the future was "not to rest in the boasted excellence of some light form of literature, for example the American short story" (701). The long novel published serially in a periodical remained a major mode of expression for many established authors. The pervasive voice of William Dean Howells, for instance, ended the century with an installment novel, *Their Silver Wedding Journey*. It is tempting, in fact, to see this work in *Harper's* as closing out the tradition that has been the subject of this introduction: serial fiction in periodicals from 1850 to 1900. The twelve installments of *Their Silver Wedding Journey* ran neatly through the last twelve months of the century, January–December 1899. This late novel was also a sequel to Howells's early work, *Their Wedding Journey*, which appeared in parts from July to December 1871 in *The Atlantic*. Thus the early novel and the later novel, with many parts titles in between, suggested a serial development to Howells's entire career and to the novel genre, which is analagous to his many individual installment tales.

As is well known, other powerful voices in fiction began to prefer the single-volume edition to publication in periodicals after 1900, feeling that editorial constraints were less burdensome in that mode. However, the serial tradition did not end at 1900. James West reports: "During the first half of the twentieth century the American author could publish stories and serialize novels in an unprecedented number and variety of such [popular] magazines" (103). Furthermore, explains West, "Money from the magazines was extremely important to writers before 1940. Indeed, they often made a good deal more from serial rights than from book royalties" (107). Among the many twentieth-century serials appearing in American magazines were: Rudyard Kipling's *Kim* in *McClure's* (1900–1901); Pauline Hopkins's *Hagar's Daughter* in the *Colored American Magazine* (1901); H. G. Wells's *First Man in the Moon* in *Cosmopolitan* (1901); Booth Tarkington's *Two Vanrevels* in *McClure's* (1902); Frank Norris's *Pit* in *The Saturday Evening Post* (1902); Jack London's *Call of the Wild* in *The Saturday Evening Post* (1903); Edith Wharton's *The House of Mirth* in *Scribner's* (1905); Charlotte Perkins Gilman's *Herland* in *The Forerunner* (1915); Willa Cather's *Professor's House* in *Colliers* (1925); and Ernest Hemingway's *A Farewell to Arms* in *Scribner's* (1929). Thus, America's continuing story was told through novels in parts well into the modern age.

Works Cited in Introduction

Note: All citations to nineteenth-century periodicals (and works published serially in these magazines) are made in the text and include page numbers along with the month and year of publication.

Anesko, Michael. *"Friction with the Market"*: Henry James and the Profession of Authorship. New York: Oxford University Press, 1986.

Baker, Houston. "Figurations for a New American Literary History." *Blues, Ideology, and Afro-American Life: A Vernacular Theory*. Chicago: University of Chicago Press, 1984. Rpt. in *Reconstructing American Literary History*, ed. Sacvan Bercovitch, 147–71.

Ballou, Ellen. *The Building of the House*. Boston: Houghton Mifflin Company, 1970.

Baym, Nina. *Novels, Readers, and Reviewers: Responses to Fiction in Antebellum America*. Ithaca and London: Cornell University Press, 1984.

———— . "The Rise of the Woman Author." In *Columbia Literary History of the United States*, ed. Emory Elliot, 288–305.

Bercovitch, Sacvan. "Introduction." In *Reconstructing American Literary History*. ed. Sacvan Bercovitch. Cambridge, Mass.: Harvard University Press, 1986.

————, and Myra Jehlen. *Ideology and Classic American Literature*. Cambridge: Cambridge University Press, 1986.

Berthoff, Warner. "Culture and Consciousness." In *Columbia Literary History of the United States*, ed. Emory Elliot, 482–98.

Brodhead, Richard H. "Literature and Culture." In *Columbia Literary History of the United States*, ed. Emory Elliot, 467–81.

Callow, James T., and Robert J. Reilly. *A Guide to American Literature from Emily Dickinson to the Present*. New York: Barnes and Noble, 1977.

Charvat, William. *The Profession of Authorship in America, 1800–1870*. Columbus: Ohio State University Press, 1968.

Colby, Robert A. "Quill and Olive Branch: Walter Besant Corresponds with Brander Matthews." *Columbia Library Columns* 41 (November 1991): 13–22.

Columbia Literary History of the United States. Ed. Emory Elliot. New York: Columbia University Press, 1988.

Coultrap-McQuin, Susan. *Doing Literary Business: American Women Writers in the Nineteenth Century*. Chapel Hill: University of North Carolina Press, 1990.

Davidson, Cathy N.. "Introduction: Toward a History of Books and Readers." In *Reading in America: Literature and Social History*, ed. Cathy N. Davidson. Baltimore and London: Johns Hopkins University Press, 1989.

Douglas, Ann. *The Feminization of American Culture*. New York: Alfred A. Knopf, 1977.

Feltes, N. N. *Modes of Production of Victorian Novels*. Chicago: University of Chicago Press, 1986.

Gates, Henry Louis. "Foreword." *The Magazine Novels of Pauline Hopkins*. Intro. Hazel V. Carly. New York and Oxford: Oxford University Press, 1988.

Gilmore, Michael T. *American Romanticism and the Marketplace*. Chicago: University of Chicago Press, 1985.

Hamer, Mary. *Writing by Numbers: Trollope's Serial Fiction*. Cambridge: Cambridge University Press, 1987.

Hedges, William L. "Toward a National Liteature." In *Columbia Literary History of the United States*, ed. Emory Elliot, 187–202.

Hughes, Linda K., and Michael Lund. *The Victorian Serial.* Charlottesville: University Press of Virginia, 1991.

James, Henry. *The Letters of Henry James.* Vol. 1. Ed. Percy Lubbock. New York: Charles Scribner's Son, 1920. 2 Vols.

John, Arthur. *The Best Years of the Century.* Urbana: University of Illinois Press, 1981.

Johnson, Robert Underwood. *Remembered Yesterdays.* Boston: Little, Brown, and Company, 1923.

Kirby, David K. *American Fiction to 1900: A Guide to Information Sources.* Detroit, Mich.: Gale Research Company, 1975.

Kolodny, Annette. "The Integrity of Memory: Creating a New Literary History." *American Literature* 57 (May 1985): 291–307.

Lee, Brian. *American Fiction: 1865–1940.* London and New York: Longman, 1987.

Lewalski, Barbara Kiefer. "English Literature at the American Moment." In *Columbia Literary History of the United States,* ed. Emory Elliot, 24–32.

Ludwig, Richard M., and Clifford A. Nault, Jr., eds. *Annals of American Literature, 1602–1983.* New York: Oxford University Press, 1986.

Lund, Michael. *Reading Thackeray.* Detroit, Mich.: Wayne State University Press, 1988.

Lynn, Kenneth S. *William Dean Howells: An American Life.* New York: Harcourt, Brace, Jovanovich, 1970, 1971.

Martin, Wendy. "Emily Dickinson." In *Columbia Literary History of the United States,* ed. Emory Elliot, 609–26.

McClure, S. S. *My Autobiography.* New York: Frederick Ungar, 1963.

Milder, Robert. "Herman Melville." In *Columbia Literary History of the United States,* ed. Emory Elliot, 429–47.

Mott, Frank Luther. *A History of American Magazines.* Cambridge: Harvard University Press, 1930, 1938, 1957. 4 Vols.

The Norton Anthology of American Literature. Vol. 2. Ed. Nina Baym et al. New York: W. W. Norton, 1979. 2 Vols.

Parker, Hershel. *Flawed Texts and Verbal Icons: Literary Authority in American Fiction.* Evanston, Ill.: Northwestern University Press, 1984.

Pease, Donald. *Visionary Compacts: American Renaissance Writings in Cultural Context*. Madison: University of Wisconsin Press, 1987.

Porter, Carolyn. "Social Discourse and Nonfictional Prose." In *Columbia Literary History of the United States*, ed. Emory Elliot, 345–63.

Reeves, John K. *William Dean Howells. Their Wedding Journey*. Bloomington and London: Indiana University Press, 1968.

Reynolds, David. S. *Beneath the American Renaissance*. New York: Knopf, 1988.

Rogal, Samuel J. *A Chronological Outline of American Literature*. New York: Greenwood Press, 1987.

Seelye, John. "Charles Brockden Brown and Early American Fiction." In *Columbia Literary History of the United States*, ed. Emory Elliot, 168–86.

Sicherman, Barbara. "Sense and Sensibility: A Case Study of Women's Reading in Late-Victorian America." In *Reading in America: Literature and Social History*, ed. Cathy N. Davidson, 201–25.

Silverman, Kenneth. "From Cotton Mather to Benjamin Franklin." In *Columbia Literary History of the United States*, ed. Emory Elliot, 101–12.

Smith, Herbert F. *The Popular American Novel: 1865–1920*. Boston: Twayne-G. K. Hall, 1980.

Sollors, Werner. "Immigrants and Other Americans." In *Columbia Literary History of the United States*, ed. Emory Elliot, 568–84.

Spiller, Robert E., et al. *A Literary History of the United States*. 3rd. ed. New York: Macmillan, 1963.

Sundquist, Eric. J. "Realism and Regionalism." In *Columbia Literary History of the United States*, ed. Emory Elliot, 501–24.

Tichi, Cecelia. "Woman Writers and the New Woman." In *Columbia Literary History of the United States*, Emory Elliot, 589–606.

Tompkins, Jane. *Sensational Designs: The Cultural Work of American Fiction*. New York: Oxford University Press, 1985.

Vann, J. Don. *Victorian Novels in Serial*. New York: Modern Language Association, 1985.

126

West, James L. W., III. *American Authors and the Literary Market-place Since 1900*. Philadelphia: University of Pennsylvania Press, 1988.

Wilson, Christopher P. *The Labor of Words: Literary Professionalism in the Progressive Era*. Athens: University of Georgia Press, 1985.

Wood, James Playsted. *Magazines in the United States*. 3rd. ed. New York: Ronald Press, 1971.

Appendix A

"Magazine Novels"
from *The Galaxy*, "Driftwood" by Philip Quilibet
(January 1869: 130–32)

With their new year and new volumes, all the magazines are flinging out promises of fresh attractions for the twelvemonth to come. 'Tis the season of gifts and forthputtings, and those of the magazines are prospectuses. One observes how important a part the serial novel plays among these announcements of good things in store; though, for that matter, the serial novel has become a prime necessity to the popular magazine.

It was born with magazines—grew with their growth, and strengthened with their strength, from early days of "Blackwood" and "Fraser" to yesterday's issue of "St Paul's" and "Belgravia," warm from the press. The French serial novelists find their channel in the *feuilleton*, made illustrious by Balzac, the two Dumas, Sue, About, Alphonse Karr, and a hundred others, just as the magazine serial has been immortalized by Dickens, Reade, Thackeray, Bulwer, Lever, and a hundred other Englishmen.

But, in one sense, some last-century novels may be called serials, being published (like "Tristram Shandy,") one or two volumes at a time—for a novel in less than five volumes was then accounted as unorthodox as a tragedy in less than five acts. Nay, let us push *back*, while we are about it, and boldly declare that "serials" were old as that household of learned slaves purchased by a rich Roman as live editions of the old bards whose works they had memorized. They were wont to deliver their "continued stories," in occasional parts, to their master. Happier than we, he suited his instalments to his own patience and interest, nor suffered tortures, as we do, from an intensely piqued curiosity. And yet even this grand owner of living and breathing libraries could not always have his "serials" as he liked. "Disappointments sometimes occurred. Perhaps the deputy 'Pindar' was out of the way; or a sudden indisposition of 'Homer' interrupted Ulysses in the middle of an harangue, and left Hector stretching out his arms to the child." Could G. P. R. James himself leave us more helplessly dependent in a *dénouement*, with his "Turn we to other scenes?"

Now, in our modern days, when books are material instead of vital, and the Press is literally not "bond" but *free*—unpleasant interruption at the most interesting moment is the foundation-principle of the serial novel. It is a rough and unfeeling principle, at best, and wanting in human kindness, whichever way you look at it. Take your own case, gentle reader, and confess your foibles. Is it or is it not agreeable for you to leave your hero for a month in a bandit's cave with a Colt's pistol presented, capped and cocked, at his head? Do you find it pleasant or unpleasant to have him suspended over a chasm by a cord which snaps, and is "to be continued in our next?" Or a thousand miles high in a balloon, with the gas stealthily leaking? How did you fancy, in your very last romance, being cut off just as Matilda had stabbed the Count?

These are home questions, for every man to ask of himself; and who knows, after all, but that it is from such considerations that Thackeray (who was very kindly) and Miss Thackeray (his own daughter) usually give us the end of a serial novel with the beginning, and remove all doubts and fears by making the hero tell his own story, or else by assuring you in the first number that "he is alive and well at this moment?"

Now, one would say, of course, and with perfect truth, that the serial novel starts enormously handicapped in the race for popular favor. That readers *must* wait a month, whether they will or no, for every new instalment; that only enough is then given them to whet their appetite (like that of the hero of a famous English serial) for "more;" that a tale which could be

129

dispatched in a few winter evenings is made to stretch from January to January again; that the memory is taxed in a way that loose readers (who use book-marks) do not like—these and other obvious objections would seem to condemn the serial novel to unpopularity from the start. How, therefore, comes it to pass that, in reality, this strange and imperious literary device rules the reading world—as all the world knows that it does? How is it that many magazines live, move, and have their being through serial novels? That one of Charles Reade's *floats* the "Argosy," and one of Miss Braddon's builds "Belgravia?" How is it that the magazine publishers vie with each other to get the best serial novelists, and to them surrender most valuable space? And, finally, how is it that, when they have been successful or unsuccessful, they tell you a single serial represents a gain or a loss to them of 10,000, 20,000, 30,000 subscribers?

The answer lies in the serial novel itself, as viewed in the best works of its great masters. Their genius has made it possible to construct a story, obviating for the reading world the disadvantages just set forth, by being interesting in every detached part, and yet complete and connected as a whole. The serial novel must be various, and must shift its scenes as quickly as real life shifts them; it must be founded on nature and yet be filled with the "romance of real life;" it must be probable, so far as consists with the experience that "truth is stranger than fiction;" it must be vivid and dramatic, with apt and natural dialogue and eloquent situations; it must delineate character with the touch of a master, and deal with society as it exists, though the choice of circumstance and of *dramatis pesonae* be left to the writer; and, while it is entrancing in each number, it must march progressively, and without perceptible breaks, to the end.

In a word, therefore, the successful serial novel defies the disadvantages of its interrupted publication; or, to speak more truly, it somehow turns these very disadvantages to account. It makes capital of the very curiosity which we dislike to have aroused without being satisfied, by adroit manipulation and artistic skill.

Yet, thirty years ago, the "Edinburgh Review," in discoursing of a famous novelist, said:

The difficulties to which Mr. Dickens is exposed in his present periodical mode of writing are, in some respects, greater than if he allowed himself a wider field, and gave his whole work to the public at once. But he would be subjected to a severer criticism if his fiction could be read continually—if his power of maintaining a sustained interest could be tested—if his work could be viewed as a connected whole, and its object, plan, consistency, and arrangement brought to the notice of the reader at once. This ordeal cannot be passed triumphantly without the aid of other qualities than necessarily belong to the most brilliant sketcher of detached scenes.

The real truth is, however, as we now know from larger experience, that the serial novel includes the other; and that whoever succeeds in the magazine equally suceeds in the book. But the reverse is not true. The serial demands as much force and originality as the other, as much invention, as much analytic power, as picturesque a style; and, beyond all that, it demands a special literary ingenuity and artistic skill. Not every great novelist can write a magazine novel. "Romola," one of George Eliot's greatest books (and how great that must be let the readers of "Adam Bede" say), was a dead failure in "Cornhill" as a serial. Dr. Holmes's "Guardian Angel" was not constructed like a true serial, and suffers infinite depreciation with those who read it in that way. In a continuous volume, some dull or distracting chapters may be launched without hazard; but not so in the serial, where the merciless public demands that each instalment shall in some sort justify itself, and none escape by vicarious surplusage.

One batch of dry leaves, twenty pages of digression, may ruin all, with this inexorable judge. Ordinary constructive ability will not suffice for a serial, for it must display in every number a man master of his materials, and the polished workmanship of an artist. A 'prentice hand is quickly seen to be out of place here. Dr. Russell, illustrious and crowned with laurels won in other fields, lately undertook a serial in "Tinsley's Magazine." The "Adventures of Dr. Brady" started off very finely; but presently it flopped down with an Icarus-tumble. The Edinburgh Reviewer's dictum regarding "the power of maintaining a sustained interest" must be reversed; for a novelist's sustaining power cannot be more severely tried than when he leaps a chasm of a month with his reader on his back, at the end of every two or three chapters.

Charles Dickens may be regarded as the projector and inventor of the modern serial novel, as it exists in our language today. He established it by sheer genius, and by sheer genius gave it an immeasurable lease of life. The chances were all against it, and predictions must have been abundant that it would fail. "My friends," says Dickens, dryly, "told me it was a low, cheap form of publication, by which I should ruin all my rising hopes; and how right my friends turned out to be, everybody now knows." When from the "Sketches by Boz," begun in the "Morning Chronicle," and ended in magazines, he launched "Pickwick" upon the world in monthly instalments, it marked a new epoch in the publisher's trade, as well as in literature. The loose construction of these "Papers," which did not pretend to plan or plot, favored the form of publication—or, perhaps, was the result of it. But, when, after 30,000 copies of Pickwick had been sold, he tried in the same method a connected, progressive novel, and made it a success, the new serial method was assured. To show the progress of the serial novel, let the sketchiness of immortal "Pickwick" be compared with some modern magazine story, complete in each part, and yet overlaid with plot and sub-plot, coming from the master-hand of Wilkie Collins or Charles Reade. But Dickens followed the instinct of his selfconscious and confident genius at the start, improving always in art, until his monthly green covers became as heartsome by the fireside, and as welcome to the eyes, as the sight of green fields in spring.

Then Thackeray, after his semi-serial experience in "Fraser," followed in the wake of his brother craftsman, and strewed abroad the monthly yellow covers of "Vanity Fair"—and a very worthy sort of "yellow-covered" literature it was, too.

In due time, monthly magazines rose to great popularity, and multiplied. The serial novel then established its home in them, and the best writers resorted to these vehicles, or rather were besought to help them on. Dickens, in "Household Words;" Thackeray with "Lovel, the Widower," and with "Philip" in "Cornhill;" Bulwer with "My Novel," in "Blackwood;" Lever

132

(and no novelist, by the way, is more underrated in the critical world than the author of "Charles O'Malley," and "Sir Brooke Fossbrooke") with "Maurice Tiernay," in the "Dublin University"—in a word, the famous novel-writers all lent their pens to the magazines. And soon amid the illustrious galaxy of English novelists suddenly appeared the star of Charles Reade, and shot rapidly up the heavens, where to-day it is in the zenith of favor.

In the English magazine the serial plays a far more important *rôle* than in the American. Two serials are common enough in ours, as also in our popular weekly papers; but in England the monthly magazines *mean* novelists. They are adventured by publishers mainly on the strength of the names and fames of popular novelists; so that Charles Reade, for example, said with perfect truth of his "Griffith Gaunt," that it "floated the 'Argosy.' " Continued stories are their main features, and the rest is expressively termed "padding." "Cornhill," "Temple Bar," "London Society," "The Argosy," "Belgravia," "Tinsley's," "Good Words," "Gentleman's Magazine," (which has surrendered to its fate and, after a century, comes out in modern style and runs a serial), "St. Paul's" "St. James,"—what do these and others mean, if not Reade, Trollope, Wilkie Collins, Miss Braddon, Mrs. Edwards, Mrs. Wood, George Eliot, Miss Mulock, Sala, Yates, Miss Thackeray, and other popular novelists of the day? One or two such names, secured to any periodical, ensure its success.

So it turns out that serial-novel writing has become a regular branch of the literary calling, and even a distinct profession in itself—as much as law, or medicine, or divinity. Hundreds of writers are engaged in this calling, and turn out their novel per annum as regularly and methodically as a builder builds a house, haply planning all at first, but developing it day by day, instead of bringing it before the public at one stroke. Literature too, like law, has grown to wear more of a business or commercial aspect than in days gone-by.

As for the exigency of daily, weekly, or monthly publication, that is accepted by the feuilletonist or magazinist as a custom of his trade, and, as I said, is commonly turned to advantage. For instance, the serial novelist habitually watches the reception given to his characters—the applause or hisses that greet his

Appendix B

Teaching in Installments

In most high school, college, and university literature courses, teachers and students proceed by reading whole works in a chronological sequence. The historical pattern of the literary tradition is often underscored in a class syllabus by the dates of volume publication included for each title. In such a course a work is read and discussed individually and yields a meaning, a set of assumptions about the universe, which impressed itself on its original audience at the time of publication and on its audience's memory thereafter. Knowledge of these great works of literature and their lessons about the human condition are a significant part of what we usually term "culture," values shared by citizens in a particular tradition. Put another way, the content of a traditional course in literature, to be mastered by students, is a major expression of culture.

For about the last dozen years I have been organizing most of my courses in literature along a different line. I schedule the reading of works in installments, re-creating as much as possible the way in which they were first read, because so many titles, especially in the nineteenth and twentieth centuries, were first published serially. Over the course of a fourteen-week academic semester, I alternate the reading of parts of perhaps eight to ten different works originally published serially from the beginning of a historical period to its end.

At the end of this section is the syllabus for my fall 1991 undergraduate course, "Introduction to American Literature," designed for the general education program at Longwood College. I will be referring to the experience of students in this class to flesh out what teaching literature in installments, rather than in whole units, accomplishes.

I should note that I serialized several titles in this course that were not originally published in installments, Vikram Seth's *The Golden Gate* and Eric Kraft's *Herb 'n' Lorna*. This reformatting is particularly fortuitous in Eric Kraft's case because his work consciously follows the serial tradition of the nineteenth century. His brilliant *Personal History, Adventures, Experiences, and Observations of Peter Leroy* (1982–) tells the story of a David Copperfield-like protagonist whose maternal grandparents' history is recounted in *Herb 'n' Lorna*. And more installments in the ongoing series are scheduled for release. For this course I also taught several works in a traditional fashion, in one sustained reading: Longfellow's *Courtship of Miles Standish* and Eudora Welty's *Delta Wedding*.

The first impetus for this manner of reading was simply convenience: I could get more students to read long works when they were broken into parts than when I assigned them to be read as whole units. In a survey conducted near the end of the semester, most of the forty-seven students in my two sections found this approach easier than they had expected. Among the responses to this method were these comments:

"To be frank, at first I thought it was going to be very difficult to assimilate so much material, but to my surprise it wasn't. The reading was given to us in limited quantity, which made it much easier to grasp and understand the subject." ". . . it gave me a goal piece by piece, and being a procrastinator I need goals and deadlines in order to perform well. It also had an anticipatory effect when I returned to each novel." "I have read more this semester than I thought I could because I didn't think I would have the time. However, the assignments were not unreasonable and I never fell behind." "I've read more this semester than I have in my *entire* life!" "I thought you were crazy when the syllabus said to buy eight novels. But I seem to be reading them all, except for *Golden Gate*." ". . . it really hasn't seemed like we were reading eight long books. It was more like reading three short stories a week."

Because this course is taken by non-majors, I was especially gratified that many students read far more than they antici- pated: "I cannot believe I actually will have read all of these books. I am amazed at myself, considering I do not like to read." "I was surprised, and dare I say proud of myself. When I look back and see how much I read it dazzles me. I never would have thought that each assignment added up to be so much."

In my survey I also asked if students felt confused by reading a number of thematically related stories all at the same time. Most had no major difficulty remembering characters and plot. Nor did they confuse our many storylines:

"It was very difficult at the beginning of each novel because the stories and/or characters hadn't taken any concrete form in my mind yet. As I read more of each, the stories not only got more interesting, but they became clearer and it became easier to dis- tinguish among them." "I thought it would be hard to keep all of the characters straight, and at first it was. The more we did it, though, the easier it got." "I am not much of a reader and when I first began reading all of the books I thought I'd get all of the books mixed up. It has been easier than I thought because you cleared up all of the confusion when you went over the assign- ments in class." "If I had been assigned to read the book all at once, to be truthful it would have been half read and flipped through."

More than two-thirds of the class even felt that reading in in- stallments made them better readers by the end of the semester.

"Towards the close of the semester I found myself reading faster and faster as well as analyzing the text." "I became more aware of details that I normally would have completely overlooked if we hadn't discussed the works as we went along." "I learned what to look for—which details were important and which were not." "I feel that discussing each part helped me to understand the works more. If I would have just had to read the whole book and then discuss it, I probably wouldn't have gotten that much out of it." "By reading in segments and then discussing plot and

> character, I learned to be more particular in how I read things, and I learned what to look for, to relate books back to our topic."

While there were those who complained of the restrictions (they were not allowed to read ahead), many more were happy to have limited assignments that created a continuing story.

In both kinds of courses—those organized by whole texts and those featuring serial structure—students accumulate much of the same knowledge. The individual works and their meanings represent a tradition that has both reflected and shaped social change in America over the last two centuries. For the fall 1991 course, I chose works having to do with courtship, marriage, and divorce in American society. Students traced throughout the semester such themes as the relationship of religion to matrimony, the changing influence of gender on behavior, the impact of mobility associated with urban, industrialized life. Their study, or course, involved not merely the accumulation and consumption of the facts of history, but the imaginative responses of great men and women to their times. Authors put into aesthetic shape lasting visions of history, which subsequently have guided individuals and cultures.

I did not ignore such traditional meanings of individual works or the collective tradition for this course in American literature; but reading works like Harriet Beecher Stowe's *The Minister's Wooing* (1858–59), William Dean Howells's *A Modern Instance* (1881–82), Pauline Hopkins's *Hagar's Daughter* (1901–2) and Edith Wharton's *Age of Innocence* (1920) in installments over an entire semester focused some of our attention in other directions. As diagrams 1 and 2, illustrating whole work versus installment syllabi, suggest, I have especially recognized three major components of literary works: beginnings (on which I concentrate in the first several weeks at the start of the term); middles (which dominate class time, taking up eight to ten weeks of meetings); and endings (which become the focus in the final two weeks of the course). Not only do students know (I hope) what each work says about the world and what the whole tradition says, but they also know something about what reading literature means, what reading literature says about the world.

138

1 WHOLE WORK SYLLABUS

August 26	September 2	October 2			November 1	December 6
Henry Wadsworth Longfellow *The Courtship of Miles Standish* (1858)	Harriet Beecher Stowe *The Minister's Wooing* (1859)	William Dean Howells *A Modern Instance* (1881)	Pauline Hopkins *Hagar's Daughter* (1902)	Edith Wharton *Age of Innocence* (1920)	Eudora Welty *Delta Wedding* (1946) — Vikram Seth *The Golden Gate* (1987)	Eric Kraft *Herb 'n' Lorna* (1988)

---

2. INSTALLMENT SYLLABUS

August 26	September 2	October 2	November 1	December 6

Eric Kraft, *Herb 'n' Lorna* (————————————————————————— 1989)

Harriet Beecher Stowe, *The Minister's Wooing* (Dec. 1858 ——————— Dec. 1859)

William Dean Howells, *A Modern Instance* (Dec. 1881 ——————————— Oct. 1881)

Henry Wadsworth Longfellow, *The Courtship of Miles Standish* (1858)

Vikram Seth, *The Golden Gate* (———————————————————— 1987)

Edith Wharton, *Age of Innocence* (July 1920 ——————— October 1920)

Pauline Hopkins, *Hagar's Daughter* (March 1901 ——————— March 1902)

Eudora Welty, *Delta Wedding* (1946)

Traditional literary criticism deals extensively with beginnings and ends, since these elements of form tend to underscore or even determine the basic shape of each work. The
aesthetic principle of a text is a logical subject for any structur-
alist or post-structuralist approach. My concentration on beginnings and endings at particular moments of the course,
however, put added emphasis (and perhaps new light) on the
value of these aspects of a work of literature. When we begin
three or more works in the same month (as my students did at
the beginning of the semester), we are or should be made aware
of what a good thing it is to have new projects and possibilities
dominating our lives. Story after story opened up for us in the
first weeks of the semester, and we could see the value of inau-
guration. Similarly, at the end of this course in American literature there was an extra sense of resolution, of process
completed underscored by our bringing to a close many stories
essentially all at once. The belief that tasks can be undertaken,
sustained, and concluded, then, is a key feature of literary experience given special visibility in the way Longwood students
read in the fall 1991 semester.

However, even more important is what such an installment
reading schedule reveals about the middle of a work of literature, because it is there that less frequently explored values of
literary experience are apparent. The middle is not ordinarily
the primary subject of a literary criticism interested in unity or
harmony; and it can even be seen as bulky, bothersome material
that gets between the linked beginning and end in an organic
work of art. Yet there is meaning in middles; and that meaning
becomes evident in the less conventional approach of reading
serially. Far more than half of the students' time in this American literature course was devoted to being in the middles of
long works without specific knowledge of how things were going to work out. Yet my students and I were hardly without
things to say throughout all that time.

While there are certainly key principles or themes endorsed
by each work in this course, there appears also to be a tendency
in many works—particularly long works like most of those in
this syllabus—not to endorse a specific position or set of guidelines but instead to seek an attitude or an approach capable of

providing direction in a number of (if not all) situations. The Countess Olenska in Edith Wharton's portrayal of New York's high society in the 1870s, for instance, knows far better than Newland Archer how to negogiate her way among tricky obstacles; yet Newland embodies absolute knowledge of the fixed New York social code. No matter where we catch Mary Scudder (*The Minister's Wooing*) or Lorna Huber (*Herb 'n' Lorna*) in their journeys through life, each demonstrates a quality of mind and heart that enables her to make wise choices for the future. An important meaning of these (and many other) works, then, is that quality of heart and mind that charts an intelligent path forward at any moment in time. What I would like to do here is to identify more precisely what this quality is and link it to the installment structure of so much nineteenth-century publication and reading.

Can we slice the pie of the American literary tradition in a different way from a whole-work-by-whole-work approach? Can we identify not only overall themes derived from complete texts but also, seeing the middles of works together, can we discover what is revealed in the movement from part to part? What, for example, do many works share in their middles that might also be portrayed by their protagonists? Are there consistent features visible in the formal structure of installments that are analogous to what key characters of the novels represent? I will propose here five key virtues or values of reading, things students can learn as they move from part to part. I propose these five qualities as additional, not alternative, meanings for these texts, efforts to get at what is of value in reading (not only what is of value after reading).

1) *Foresight* (or anticipating). Some central characters of these American literary works have an ability to look into the future, to predict what might or could happen. While for some this foresight could bring trouble, it is still clear that it is better to anticipate than to go blindly into the future. Marcia Gaylord Hubbard learned this lesson all too slowly in Howells's tale, to her own sorrow. Similarly, we readers are encouraged in the middles of novels to look ahead, to make predictions. This feature of all literature is often ignored when discussion of a work takes place after it is read, when the characters' futures have

been decided. At ends of works readers, students, and teachers tend to forget their speculation while reading, particularly their wrong or mistaken anticipations. Foresight is, of course, much intensified in the serial form, with its built-in pauses of publication where expectation is heightened by private and public anticipation. And, obviously, I have built into this syllabus pauses—space between classes and the spaces of classes devoted to other works. Even when a class's suspicions about what will happen are wrong, reaction to what actually does happen is intensified through long involvement with the question. Such suspicions of possibilities would (and often do in some classes) fill up journals.

In the survey I asked my students whether they enjoyed being kept in suspense and if they had become better at speculating about "what happens next" in literature:

> "I enjoy speculating about what might happen because it draws my interest into the book." "I feel like I'm a detective looking for clues to solve the mystery." "A lot of things that were hinted at in the stories, I missed while reading, but when they were brought up in class, I understood them better." "It was fun [guessing] what was going to happen next. I do think I got better at it over the semester (or if not better, more interested)." "I think having to stop at certain points creates suspense for us, giving us something to look forward to when we *do* read the novel again." "Also it made me speculate as to what might happen, forcing me to think about what has happened, thus understanding more." "I have enjoyed it because it has kept me intrigued in each book—you always have something to look forward to in this way." ". . . each new novel and each new situation within 'seasoned' me better before I tackled the next."

One of the most positive accomplishments of the class was the development of reasoned doubt in some students' minds, an awareness that their expectations about literature and life had been naive: "Honestly, I can't say that I got better at speculating but now I make more *realistic* forecasts of the characters I'm reading about." "I dislike speculating because sometimes the actual events were a disappointment compared to what I had hoped would happen."

2) *Memory* (or remembering). Many characters we admire in fiction are sensitive to the past, to the lessons and applications of yesterday. Hagar in Pauline Hopkins's magazine novel *Hagar's Daughter* knows the price still to be paid for slavery twenty years after the Civil War; but that lesson must be learned by Cuthbert Sumner, as well as by Hopkins's turn-of-the-century readers. Installment readers also must remember what has happened in earlier numbers in order to react fully to what is going on in any present number. Memory is clearly operative in each middle installment, as readers add to or alter their understanding of character and event in light of new developments. Our mastery of the text already read is tested in the assimilation of new material. While memory is often called upon in the traditional approach using whole texts, students are not always required to remember early material in reading the new. In a serial approach, the testing of memory increases through the length of any academic term as considerable time separates a first encounter with a work from the last.

Two-thirds of my students found no difficulty in remembering characters and events in the different works, though those who had trouble expressed it strongly.

> "Once the characters are mentioned, the story comes right along with it." "It can be hard sometimes when you first pick the book up again but then it comes back." ". . . for the most part, I have slipped smoothly back into each novel." ". . . everything has built on what we already know."

Again, sometimes failures produced positive results: "I have had a little bit of trouble because I didn't start out taking notes. The notes help to keep the names straight with the stories." "The idea of using a character sheet for each book is a good way in remembering." "I suggest a kind of plot time line of events, brief, but it may help the next class."

3) *Sympathy* (or identifying with others). If there is a fundamental flaw in many nineteenth-century literary characters, it is often an inability to understand how others feel. Newland Archer remains remarkably unable to see the complexity of knowledge and understanding possessed by his wife May throughout

their thirty years of marriage. In each part of a work's middle readers move into a fictional world, sharing the joys and sorrows of the major characters at those moments (regardless of where those characters will end up). This ability to see the relationship of one character (even ourselves) to another (in one work or another) involves seeing differences or contrasts as well as similarities. The discovering of relationships—similarities and contrasts—is a key virtue of literature generally; however, the permeation of the fiction into the reader's world is a particularly strong feature of the serial novel, where interest must be sustained over weeks, months, and even years. Since this kind of sympathy must also accomodate changes in the characters with new installments, it may be even deeper than identification with characters in works read all at once.

While it is hard to measure such subjective experience, students in my American literature course generally felt that the longer time of involvement with fictional worlds intensified their relationships to characters:

> "I think I'll *remember* the stories longer because we spent more time reading each work. I've thought about some of the different characters we've read and people they resemble that I personally know today." "Marcia Hubbard is not a woman I want to become." "If you read straight through a book, it's over. Reading them like this gave the illusion of days, weeks, months, etc." "This kind of reading gives us the opportunity to grow with the characters." "An example that comes to mind is Lorna [from Kraft's *Herb 'n' Lorna*.] I found myself having more time to 'put myself in her shoes' and try to experience in my mind what she was experiencing." " . . . this semester each character and book has stayed out in the open. For example, Herb and Lorna really seem like grandparents, at least for me, because I feel like I have really been let into their lives, and [have been] watching them for several months."

If class discussion is also a measure of involvement, I should add that students reading in installments are almost always more open and interested than students assigned to read whole works on their own: "the reading does not bog you down and the atmosphere is very relaxed and open. The class gives you an opportunity to express yourself and to hear others." "It is interesting to hear what my peers think in comparison to my views upon reading a selection."

4) *Balance* (or establishing priorities). Deciding what is important to an individual or to society is certainly a regular theme of much literature, but when you know the end of the processes you receive confirmation of certain values. Exactly how Ben Halleck should respond to the plight of Marcia Hubbard in her unhappy marriage (*A Modern Instance*) is easiest to understand when all the facts are in, at the end of that novel; but how characters and readers arrive at that evaluation is the substance of the middle pages of the work. To move wisely from the July to the August 1881 installment of Howells's novel, one must discover key matters and weigh their relative importance while reading, with confirmation delayed for a time. Dismissing the trivial and focusing on the essential is a virtue, in fact, that Bartley Hubbard never does achieve and which the reader struggles to attain.

Students did feel better able to judge individual works, though they most often equated high quality with those books they most wanted to read: "I have begun to see parallels between my relationships and some of the characters' relationships and it helped me make some decisions." "I think reading them all at once gave the characters greater contrast to each other. Wimpy Marcia [Hubbard] stands apart from insane Hagar, flashy Madame Olenksa, or wild Aurelia [Walker]." Many found that lively class discussion challenged them to decide which works were relevant to their own lives: "I think in some ways I got better at anticipating but in other ways, we had so many different possibilites generated in class that it was difficult to decide which was right."

5) *Patience* (or waiting). Certainly, patience—the ability to wait for material to come together, to make sense—is a virtue in any class; but the long work read serially rewards those who know (or learn) that simply sticking with something pays off in any learning process. A model for patience is Harriet Beecher Stowe's Mary Scudder (*The Minister's Wooing*), in part because, as a woman, no other course of action is available to her; she must wait for the men (and the right man) to come to her. How

long she waits would best be understood by the readers of the *Atlantic Monthly* who took thirteen months in 1858–59 for their patience to be rewarded. Perhaps only after one has exercised this quality of patience does one truly appreciate its rewards.

A large number of my students claimed they had not learned to be more patient in reading or to appreciate in new ways the rewards of long-term effort. But these comments suggest that the semester-long effort had been profitable.

> "Reading in installments does not cure my impatience; it strengthens my anticipation. I never did turn to the back to see how the book would end because this action would also terminate my anticipation and kill the suspense." "I like waiting to see what's going to happen because it gives me a chance to decide what I think is going to happen." "I think that waiting to read the next passage to one of the books you like is difficult, but enjoyable." "I turned to the back of *Age of Innocence* and was sorry I did. I didn't do so until the last reading but it still ruined it."

Of course, some answers revealed that students can be very patient with certain titles: "On some books I wanted to look at the end like *Hagar's Daughter*. Then other books like *Minister's Wooing* I didn't care at all."

I have one more quality of reading I am tempted to throw in as a sixth virtue or meaning in this course: *humor*. Academic discussions of humor often end up rather dry, and after students have read an entire work, attempts in class to re-create the laughter we might have experienced while reading have always been difficult. I do know that my students and I laughed during our semester together; and that laughter must have been a key part of our literary experience, somehow present in the meaning of these novels. Furthermore, I believe that our appreciation of humor increased through our sharing of early instances of comedy in group discussions. But exactly what humor is, or how we develop an appreciation of it, is difficult to determine.

The five primary qualities of mind, then—foresight, memory, sympathy, balance, and patience—are displayed and developed, I submit, by serial literature. I believe that some of the attitudes encouraged by this form are built into American literary history, since so many of our works were issued and read in various serial modes. What students should have learned in this course was not simply a number of facts and principles about the evolution of modern society (though, again, I trust they have learned that, too). If the course was truly successful, all of them now possess greater ability than when they began the course—more foresight, sympathy, memory, balance, and patience. They are, I hope, better prepared for the next moment in history (theirs and the world's) because in reading they have sharpened these qualities.

The real test of this course—and of all teaching—does not come in the classroom, but after it. A memorable *New Yorker* cartoon once showed a family watching television in their living room, with characteristically blank faces. An announcer was stating rather matter-of-factly the words printed as the caption for the cartoon: "We now return you to your own lives, which are already in progress." Our own and students' lives are more important than any fiction (television or novel), but the time spent in reading or viewing can—and I hope, does—improve students' lives "already in progress."

SAMPLE SYLLABUS

English 203   American Literature   Fall 1991

August 26: Eric Kraft's *Herb 'n' Lorna* (NAL/Dutton) [7–54: 1989]

28: Harriet Beecher Stowe's *Minister's Wooing* (Stowe-Day) [1–40: Dec. 1858]

30: William Dean Howells's *A Modern Instance* (Penguin) [3–48: Dec. 1881]

September 2: *Herb 'n' Lorna* (55–113)

4: Henry Wadsworth Longfellow's *Courtship of Miles Standish* (New American Library) [195–241: 1858]

6: Longfellow, cont.

9: *Minister's Wooing* (41–116: Jan.–Feb. 1859)

11: *A Modern Instance* (49–118: Jan.–Feb. 1882)

13: Vikram Seth's *Golden Gate* (Random House) [3–52: 1987]

16: Edith Wharton's *Age of Innocence* (Macmillan) [1–90: July 1920]

18: *Herb 'n' Lorna* (114–64)

20: *Minister's Wooing* (117–212: March–May 1859)

23: Exam

25: Discussion of Exam

27: *A Modern Instance* (119–66: March–April 1882)

30: Pauline Hopkins's *Hagar's Daughter* (Oxford University Press) [3–54: March–April 1901]

October 2: *The Golden Gate* (53–122)

4: *Age of Innocence* (91–175: August 1920)

7: *Herb 'n' Lorna* (165–220)

9: In-Class Essay

11: *Minister's Wooing* (213–85: June–July 1859)

14: *Hagar's Daughter* (55–100: May–July 1901)

16: *A Modern Instance* (167–243: May–June 1882)

18: *Age of Innocence* (177–284: Sept. 1920)

*** Fall Break ***

23: *Hagar's Daughter* (100–147: Aug.–Sept. 1901)

25: *Herb 'n' Lorna* (221–62); *The Golden Gate* (123–72)

28: *Hagar's Daughter* (148–90: Nov.–Dec. 1901)

30: *Minister's Wooing* (286–374: Aug.–Sept. 1859)

November 1: *A Modern Instance* (244–333: July–Aug. 1882)

4: *Hagar's Daughter* (190–234: Jan.–Feb. 1902)

6: *Age of Innocence* (285–362: Oct. 1920)

8: *Herb 'n' Lorna* (263–89); *The Golden Gate* (173–233)

11: *Hagar's Daughter* (235–84: March 1902)

13: *Minister's Wooing* (375–490: Oct.–Nov. 1859)

15: Exam

18: Eudora Welty, *Delta Wedding* (Harcourt, Brace, Jovanovich) [3–117: 1946]

20: Welty, cont. (118–247)

22: Reading Day; Out-of-Class Essay Due

25: *A Modern Instance* (334–453: Sept.–Oct. 1882)

*** Thanksgiving ***

December 2: *Minister's Wooing* (490–578: Dec. 1859)

4: *The Golden Gate* (234–307)

6: *Herb 'n' Lorna* (290–310)

WORKS OF SERIAL FICTION

Aldrich, Thomas Bailey

Prudence Palfrey
The Atlantic Monthly, Vol. 33
Jan. 1874:   I–IV (1–13)
Feb. 1874:   V–VI (144–57)
March 1874:   VII–VIII (257–68)
April 1874:   IX–XII (385–402)
May 1874:   XIII–XVI (513–527)
June 1874:   XVII–XVIII
                (672–683)

□

The Queen of Sheba
The Atlantic Monthly, Vol. 40
July 1877:   I–III (1–10)
Aug. 1877:   IV–V (174–87)
Sept. 1877:   VI–VII (257–68)
Oct. 1877:   VIII–IX (385–400)
Nov. 1877:   X–XI (513–24)

□

The Stillwater Tragedy
The Atlantic Monthly, Vols. 45–46
April 1880:   I–V (433–48)
May 1880:   VI–IX (577–93)
June 1880:   X–XIII (721–40)
July 1880:   XIV–XVII (1–16)
Aug. 1880:   XVIII–XXII
                (145–62)
Sept. 1880:   XXIII–XXVIII
                (289–309)

□   □   □   □   □

Aldrich, Thomas Bailey, and M. O. W. Oliphant

The Second Son
The Atlantic Monthly, Vols. 59–61
Jan. 1887:   I–IV (1–21)
Feb. 1887:   V–VIII (145–66)
March 1887:   IX–XII (324–42)
April 1887:   XIII–XVI (449–68)
May 1887:   XVII–XIX (682–93)
                " '. . . that can
                never have any-
                thing to do with
                you.' "
June 1887:   XIX, cont.–XXI
                (804–15)
                "Lily had gone on
                towards the
                lodge . . ."
July 1887:   XXII–XXIV (44–56)
Aug. 1887:   XXV–XVII (173–86)
Sept. 1887:   XXVIII–XXXI
                (300–18)
Oct. 1887:   XXXII–XXXV
                (487–506)
Nov. 1887:   XXXVI–XXXIX
                (655–73)
Dec. 1887:   XL–XLII (734–47)
Jan. 1888:   XLIII–XLV (57–71)
Feb. 1888:   XLVI–XLVIII
                (165–77)

□   □   □   □   □

Allen, James Lane

Sister Dolorosa
The Century Magazine, Vol. 41;
n.s. 19
Dec. 1890:   I–III (265–74)

Allen, James Lane (continued)

Jan. 1891:   IV–V (432–43)
Feb. 1891:   VI–XII (580–92)

□   □   □   □   □

Anderson, Hans Christian

Lucky Peer
Scribner's Monthly (later *Century*), Vol. 1

Jan. 1871:   I–II (270–76)
Feb. 1871:   III–V (391–98)
March 1871:   VI–X (505–16)
April 1871:   XI–XVII (625–39)

□   □   □   □   □

Ballestier, Wolcott, and Rudyard Kipling

Benefits Forgot
The Century Magazine, Vols. 45–46; n.s. 23–24

Dec. 1892:   I–II (192–206)
Jan. 1893:   III (407–13)
Feb. 1893:   IV–V (525–38)
March 1893:   VI–VIII (766–79)
April 1893:   IX–XII (937–49)
May 1893:   XIII–XV (51–64)
June 1893:   XVI–XIX (285–303)
July 1893:   XX–XXIV (446–61)
Aug. 1893:   XXV–XXVII (611–23)
Sept. 1893:   XXVIII–XXXI (697–708)
Oct. 1893:   XXXII–XXXV (939–51)

□   □   □   □   □

Bonner, Sherwood [Catherine McDowell]

The Valcours
Lippincott's Magazine, Vol. 28

Sept. 1881:   I–IV (243–58)
Oct. 1881:   V–VIII (345–61)
Nov. 1881:   IX–XIII (444–62)
Dec. 1881:   XIV–XVI (555–70)

□   □   □   □   □

Boyesen, Hjalmar Hjorth

A Norseman's Pilgrimage
The Galaxy, Vols. 18–19

Dec. 1874:   I–III (779–93)
Jan. 1875:   IV–VI (55–74)
Feb. 1875:   VII–IX (232–44)
March 1875:   X–XI (378–90)
April 1875:   XII–XIII (483–97)
May 1875:   XIV–XV (659–69)

□

Falconberg
Scribner's Monthly (later *Century*), Vols. 16–17

Aug. 1878:   Prelude-II (496–507)
Sept. 1878:   III–V (728–41)
Oct. 1878:   VI–VII (824–36)
Nov. 1878:   VIII–X (20–32)
Dec. 1878:   XI–XII (248–60)
Jan. 1879:   XIII–XIV (363–72)
               ". . . into a tin pail which hung on her arm."
Feb. 1879:   XIV, cont.–XVI (537–47)
               "As she saw the young girl, . . ."

March 1879:   XVII–XIX (672–82)
April 1879:   XX–XXII (816–28)

□

Queen Titania
Scribner's Monthly (later *Century*),
Vol. 22
Aug. 1881:   I–VII (593–607)
Sept. 1881:   VIII–XII (761–69)
Oct. 1881:   XIII–XVII (841–50)

□

A Problematic Character
The Century Magazine, Vol. 28;
n.s. 6
Aug. 1884:   I–V (608–19)
Sept. 1884:   VI–XI (745–60)
Oct. 1884:   XII–XIV (893–902)

□

A Perilous Incognito
Scriber's Magazine, Vol. 2
July 1887:   Part I, I–III
              (120–28)
Aug. 1887:   Part II, IV–V
              (222–28)

□ □ □ □ □

Burnett, Frances Hodgson

That Lass O' Lowrie's
Scribner's Monthly (later *Century*),
Vols. 12–14
Aug. 1876:   I–II (544–52)
Sept. 1876:   III–V (624–33)
              ". . . without any
              higher fruition."

Oct. 1876:   V, cont.–VIII
              (827–35)
              " 'I have seen Joan
              Lowrie,' said
              Anice; . . .''
Nov. 1876:   IX–XIII (32–40)
Dec. 1876:   XIV–XVI (260–66)
Jan. 1877:   XVII–XX (305–12)
Feb. 1877:   XXI–XXIV (512–20)
March 1877:   XXV–XXVII
              (707–14)
April 1877:   XXVIII–XXXIV
              (832–46)
May 1877:   XXXV–XLIII
              (18–28)

□

Haworth's
Scribner's Monthly (later *Century*),
Vols. 17–18
Nov. 1878:   I–VII (113–27)
Dec. 1878:   VIII–XI (193–204)
Jan. 1879:   XII–XVII (385–400)
Feb. 1879:   XVIII–XXII
              (512–25)
March 1879:   XXIII–XXVII
              (652–64)
April 1879:   XXVIII–XXXII
              (784–95)
May 1879:   XXXIII–XXXVII
              (79–93)
June 1879:   XXXVIII–XL
              (183–91)
July 1879:   XLI–XLIV (367–74)
Aug. 1879:   XLV–XLVIII
              (527–35)
Sept. 1879:   XLIX–LI (683–91)
Oct. 1879:   LII–LIV (874–82)

□

May 1880:	XXX–XXXVI (24–34)
June 1880:	XXXVII–XL (194–204)
July 1880:	XLI–XLV (380–91)
Aug. 1880:	XLVI–XLIX (527–35)
Sept. 1880:	L–LIV (696–704)
Oct. 1880:	LV–LXI (812–24)

□

Madame Delphine
Scribner's Monthly (later *Century*), Vol. 22

May 1881:	I–VI (22–31)
June 1881:	VII–XI (191–99)
July 1881:	XII–XV (436–43)

□

Dr. Sevier
The Century Magazine, Vols. 27–28; n.s. 5–6

Nov. 1883:	I–VII (54–68)
Dec. 1883:	VIII–XIV (237–51)
Jan. 1884:	XV–XVII (422–30)
Feb. 1884:	XVIII–XXII (529–42)
March 1884:	XXIII–XXVI (753–65) ". . . why Mary Richling's window shone all night long."
April 1884:	XXVI[?]–XXX (873–86) (chapters apparently misnumbered) "Round goes the wheel forever . . ."

May 1884:	XXXI–XXXVI (70–81)
June 1884:	XXXVII–XLII (257–70)
July 1884:	XLIII–XLVII (418–26)
Aug. 1884:	XLVIII–LII (596–608)
Sept. 1884:	LIII–LV (698–711)
Oct. 1884:	LVI–LX (820–32)

□

Carancro
The Century Magazine, Vol. 33; n.s. 11

Jan. 1887:	Part I, Chpts. I–V (355–65)
Feb. 1887:	Part II, Chpts. VI–X (544–57)

□

Au Large
The Century Magazine, Vol. 35; n.s. 13

Nov. 1887:	I–IV (88–99)
Dec. 1887:	V–VIII (213–26)
Jan. 1888:	IX–XIII (344–56)
Feb. 1888:	XIV–XVII (548–55)
March 1888:	XVIII–XXII (732–40)

□

Strange True Tales of Louisiana
The Century Magazine, Vols. 37–38; n.s. 15–16

Nov. 1888:	Introduction and "The Young Aunt with the the White Hair" (110–16)

157

Carey, Alice

Jan. 1867:	Part I (239–50)		June 1881:	X–XIII (551–64)
	". . . there ever		July 1881:	XIV–XVIII (31–46)
	was between the		Aug. 1881:	XIX–XXIV (135–56)
	two women."			

Feb. 1867:   Part II (312–18)
"As before stated,
Matilda was for a
time . . ."

□

The Rose Rollins
The Atlantic Monthly, Vol. 20
Oct. 1867:   Part I (420–30)
". . . she drooped
her eyelids mod-
estly and
resumed."
Nov. 1867:   Part II (545–57)
" 'It was a Sunday
evening that was
coming on . . .' "

□   □   □   □   □

Catherwood, Mary Hartwell

Lilith
Lippincott's Magazine, Vol. 27
Jan. 1881:   I–V (28–41)
Feb. 1881:   VI–VIII (130–43)
March 1881:   IX–XIII (238–51)

□

Craque-O'-Doom
Lippincott's Magazine, Vols. 27–28
April 1881:   I–V (350–66)
May 1881:   VI–IX (443–52)

□

Stephen Guthrie
Lippincott's Magazine, Vol. 29
Jan. 1882:   I–V (21–38)
Feb. 1882:   VI–VIII (122–38)
March 1882:   IX–XV (230–54)
April 1882:   XVI–XXI (329–46)
May 1882:   XXII–XXIII
(436–49)
June 1882:   XXIV–XXVI
(540–54)

□

The Romance of Dollard
The Century Magazine, Vol. 37;
n.s. 15
Nov. 1888:   Preface–V (81–95)
Dec. 1888:   VI–XI (261–275)
Jan. 1889:   XII–XVI (345–57)
Feb. 1889:   XVII–XX (528–40)

□

The Lady of Fort St. John
The Atlantic Monthly, Vol. 68
July 1891:   Prelude–III (1–14)
Aug. 1891:   IV–VIII (145–58)
Sept. 1891:   IX–XII (389–401)
Oct. 1891:   XIII–XV (492–506)
Nov. 1891:   XVI–XVIII (577–96)

□

Old Kaskaskia: In Four Parts
The Atlantic Monthly, Vol. 71

Catherwood, Mary Hartwell (continued)

Jan. 1893: Part First "The Bonfire of St. John" (1–14)

Feb. 1893: Part Second "A Field Day" (145–58)

March 1893: Part Third "The Rising" (289–303)

April 1893: Part Fourth "The Flood" (433–43)

□

The White Islander
The Century Magazine, Vol. 46; n.s. 24

June 1893: Part I (222–30)
July 1893: Part II (335–44)
Aug. 1893: Part III (533–42)
Sept. 1893: Part IV (729–36)

□

The Spirit of an Illinois Town: in Three Parts
The Atlantic Monthly, Vol. 78

Aug. 1896: Part One (168–74)
Sept. 1896: Part Two (338–47)
Oct. 1896: Part Three (480–91)

□

The Days of Jeanne D'Arc
The Century Magazine, Vols. 53–54; n.s. 31–32

April 1897: I–II (883–97)
May 1897: III–IV (118–27)
June 1897: V–VI (231–45)
July 1897: VII–VIII (406–19)

Aug. 1897: IX–XI (603–15)
Sept. 1897: XII–XIII (684–96)
Oct. 1897: XIV–XVI (910–24)

□ □ □ □ □

Chesebro', Caroline

Hearts of Oak
Knickerbocker Magazine, Vol. 38

Oct. 1851: I–VI (397–411)
Nov. 1851: VII–X (515–25)

□

Bernice Atherton
Graham's Magazine, Vols. 44–45

April 1854: I–III (375–84)
May 1854: IV–VI (472–79)
June 1854: VII–IX (585–95)
July 1854: X–XIV (43–54)
Aug. 1854: XV–XVII (145–55)
Sept. 1854: XVIII–XX (241–50)
Oct. 1854: XXI–XXIV (335–46)
Nov. 1854: XXV–XXX (425–30)

□

The Birth of Fleance Krüger
Knickerbocker Magazine, Vol. 46

Nov. 1855: Part One (457–71)
Dec. 1855: Part Two (573–86)

□

The Pure Pearl of Diver's Bay
The Atlantic Monthly, Vol. 1

April 1858: I–III (686–96)
". . . the ears of those that heard her."

May 1858:   IV–IX (821–34)
"Did she talk of
flesh and
blood . . ."

□

*Her Grace, the Drummer's
Daughter*
The Atlantic Monthly, Vol. 2
Oct. 1858:   [Part I] (532–50)
"The three were
surely one now."
Nov. 1858:   [Part II] (656–72)
"The girl whose
suggestion had
brought
about . . ."

□

Victor and Jacqueline
The Atlantic Monthly, Vol. 5
Aug. 1860:   I–VI (168–85)
Sept. 1860:   VII–XI (271–87)

□

*For Better, For Worse: In Three
Parts*
Harper's New Monthly Magazine,
Vol. 26
March 1863:   I–III (501–11)
". . . to suit their
own sense of
fitness."
April 1863:   IV–VI (647–57)
"Nothing but
prosperity . . ."
". . . and she had
leaned upon it."

May 1863:   VII–IX (747–58)
"The study was
no place for . . ."

□

The Foe in the Household
The Atlantic Monthly, Vols. 23–24
March 1869:   I–III (323–37)
April 1869:   IV–VII (462–76)
May 1869:   VIII–XI (568–80)
June 1869:   XII–XV (686–99)
July 1869:   XVI–XVIII (26–39)
Aug. 1869:   XIX–XX (168–76)
Sept. 1869:   XXI–XXIII (282–94)
Oct. 1869:   XXIV–XXVI
(420–30)
Nov. 1869:   XXVII–XXIX
(534–42)
Dec. 1869:   XXX–XXXII
(722–30)

□

Lavinia: Her Progress
Putnam's Magazine, Vol. 4, n.s.
July 1869:   Part I, I–III (53–62)
Aug. 1869:   Part II, IV–VII
(179–90)
Sept. 1869:   Part III, VIII–XI
(326–35)
Oct. 1869:   Part IV, XII–XVI
(411–23)

□

From Generation to Generation
The Atlantic Monthly, Vols. 27–28
June 1871:   Part I (691–703)
". . . 'I never saw
one.' "

Chesebro', Caroline (continued)

July 1871:   Part II (9–20)
"Pauline Bynner
was a girl of great
good sense . . ."

□

*Probationer Leonhard; or, Three
Nights in the Happy Valley
Lippincott's Magazine*, Vol. 11
Jan. 1873:   I–III (45–54)
Feb. 1873:   IV–IX (161–76)
March 1873:   X–XV (331–44)

□   □   □   □   □

Child, Lydia Maria

*Loo Loo
The Atlantic Monthly*, Vols. 1–2
May 1858:   Scenes I–III
(801–12)
". . . was always
the wisest and
best."
June 1858:   Scenes IV–V
(32–42)
"They had lived
thus nearly a
year . . ."

□   □   □   □   □

Chopin, Kate

*Athenaise: A Story of a Tempera-
ment: In Two Parts
The Atlantic Monthly*, Vol. 78

Aug. 1896:   Part One, I–V
(232–41)
". . . abroad touch-
ing his personal
safetly."
Sept. 1896:   Part Two, VI–XI
(404–13)
"Athenaise
reached her desti-
nation . . ."

□   □   □   □   □

Collins, Wilkie

*Armadale
Harper's New Monthly Magazine,*
Vols. 30–33
Dec. 1864:   Book the First, I–
III (79–97)
Jan. 1865:   Book the Second, I
(213–29)
Feb. 1865:   II–III (336–52)
March 1865:   IV–V (490–504)
April 1865:   Book the Third,
I–II (647–63)
May 1865:   III–IV (760–73)
June 1865:   V–VII (76–91)
July 1865:   VIII–IX (196–208)
Aug. 1865:   X–XII (344–57)
Sept. 1865:   XIII; Book the
Fourth, I–II
(481–95)
Oct. 1865:   III–IV (625–38)
Nov. 1865:   V–VII (768–83)
Dec. 1865:   VIII–IX (67–81)
Jan. 1866:   X (188–202)
Feb. 1866:   XI–XIII (327–42)
March 1866:   XIV (446–60)
April 1866:   XV (601–13)
May 1866:   Book the Fifth,
I–III (738–56)
" '. . . why are you
not at lunch.' "

| June 1866: | III, cont.; Book the Last, I (75–92) " 'If I had been less anxious . . .' " |
| July 1866: | II; Epilogue, I–II (186–209) |

□

The New Magdalen
Harper's New Monthly Magazine,
Vols. 45–47

Oct. 1872:	First Scene: Preamble, I–V (754–68)
Nov. 1872:	Second Scene: Preamble, VI–VIII (901–13)
Dec. 1872:	IX–XI (117–26)
Jan. 1873:	XII–XV (283–96)
Feb. 1873:	XVI–XIX (439–51)
March 1873:	XX–XXI (597–607)
April 1873:	XXII–XXIII (753–63)
May 1873:	XXIV–XXVII (914–26) ". . . Horace as she went on."
June 1873:	XXVII, cont.–XXIX; Epilogue, I–IV (104–21) "What was it possible for a friendless . . ."

□   □   □   □   □

Cooper, James Fenimore

Old Ironsides [a piece of "naval biography" posthumously published from manuscript]

Putnam's Magazine, Vol. 1

| May 1853: | [Part I] (473–87) ". . . she was now so soon to undergo." |
| June 1853: | [Part II] (592–607) "Rumors of an approaching war . . ." |

□   □   □   □   □

Crane, Stephen

Whilomville Stories
Harper's New Monthly Magazine,
Vols. 99–101

Aug. 1899:	"I. The Angel Child" (358–64)
Sept. 1899:	"II. Lynx-Hunting" (552–57)
Oct. 1899:	"III. The Lover and the Telltale" (759–63)
Nov. 1899:	"IV. 'Showing Off' " (855–60)
Dec. 1899:	"V. Making an Orator" (25–28)
Jan. 1900:	"VI. Shame" (320–24)
Feb. 1900:	"VII. The Carriage Lamps" (366–72)
March 1900:	"VIII. The Knife" (591–98)
April 1900:	"IX. The Stove" (798–804)
May 1900:	"X. The Trial, Execution, and Burial of Homer Phelps" (963–68)
June 1900:	"XI. The Fight" (56–63)

Crane, Stephen (continued)

July 1900:   "XII. The City Ur-
            chin and the
            Chaste Villagers"
            (216–21)
Aug. 1900: "XIII. A Little Pil-
            grim" (401–04)

□ □ □ □ □

Daudet, Alphonse [trans. Henry James]

Pact Tarascon—The Last Adventures of the Illustrious Tartarin
Harper's New Monthly Magazine,
Vol. 81
June 1890:   Preface, Intro.;
            Book First, I–III
            (3–25)
July 1890:   IV–VI (166–85)
Aug. 1890:   Book Second, I–II
            (327–40)
Sept. 1890: III–V (521–37)
Oct. 1890:   Book Third, I–III
            (683–99)
Nov. 1890:   IV–VI (937–55)

□ □ □ □ □

Davis, Rebecca Blaine Harding

A Story of To-Day
The Atlantic Monthly, Vols. 8–9
Oct. 1861:   Part I (471–86)
            "Do you think
            their work is
            lost?"

Nov. 1861:   Part II (582–97)
            "Margaret stood
            looking
            down . . ."
            ". . . if we only
            had chosen."
Dec. 1861:   Part III (707–18)
            "Now that I have
            come to the love
            part . . ."
            ". . . then followed
            the phaeton down
            the hill."
Jan. 1862:   Part IV (40–51)
            "An hour after,
            the evening
            came . . ."
            ". . . with one
            backward look
            went in."
Feb. 1862:   Part V (202–13)
            "There was a dull
            smell of
            camphor . . ."
            ". . . to make one
            day for Lois
            happier."
March 1862: Part VI (282–98)
            "It was later than
            Holmes
            thought . . ."
            ". . . the face of
            my father in the
            New Year."

□

David Gaunt
The Atlantic Monthly, Vol. 10
Sept. 1862: Part I (257–71)
            ". . . And so he
            left her."

Oct. 1862: Part II (403–21)
"It was late . . ."

□

Paul Blecker
The Altantic Monthly, Vols. 11–12
May 1863: Part I (580–98)
". . . what things
are needed for a
tired girl's soul."
June 1863: Part II (677–91)
"You do not like
this Lizzy
Gurney? . . ."
". . . and then for
an exchange."
July 1863: Part III (52–69)
" 'Skin cool,
damp. Pha!' . . ."

□

George Bedillion's Knight
The Altantic Monthly, Vol. 19
Feb. 1867: Part I, I–II (155–67)
". . . Sim had
turned hastily
away."
March 1867: Part II, III–IV
(289–300)
"Back in his shop-
window . . ."

□

Dallas Galbraith: An American
Novel
Lippincott's Magazine, Vols. 1–2
Jan. 1868: I–III (5–27)

Feb. 1868: IV–VI (121–43)
March 1868: VII–X (233–53)
April 1868: XI–XIV (345–69)
May 1868: XV–XVII (457–76)
June 1868: XVIII–XXII
(569–95)
July 1868: XXIII–XXVI (9–34)
Aug. 1868: XXVII–XXIX
(121–46)
Sept. 1868: XXX–XXXIII
(233–54)
". . . Dallas Gal-
braith, hunted
down, stood at
bay."
Oct. 1868: XXXIII, cont.–
XXXVIII (345–73)
"There was a little
toll-gate . . ."

□

Natasqua
Scribner's Monthly (later *Century*),
Vol. 3
Nov. 1870: I–III (58–69)
Dec. 1870: IV–VI (159–69)
Jan. 1871: VII–IX (283–90)

□

Berrytown
Lippincott's Magazine, Vols. 11–12
April 1873: I–V (400–411)
May 1873: VI–VII (579–87)
June 1873: VIII–X (697–707)
July 1873: XI–XV (35–48)

□

Davis, Rebecca Blaine Harding
(continued)

Earthen Pitchers
Scribner's Monthly (later *Century*),
Vol. 7

Nov. 1873:	I–II (73–81)
Dec. 1873:	III–VI (199–207)
Jan. 1874:	VII–IX (274–81)
Feb. 1874:	X–XII (490–94)
March 1874:	XIII–XIV (595–600)
April 1874:	XV–XVII (714–21)

□

A Law Unto Herself
Lippincott's Magazine Vol. 20

July 1877:	I–II (39–49)
Aug. 1877:	III–V (167–82)
Sept. 1877:	VI–IX (292–308)
Oct. 1877:	X–XIII (464–78)
Nov. 1877:	XIV–XVIII (614–28)
Dec. 1877:	XIX–XXII (719–31)

□

By-Paths in the Mountains
Harper's New Monthly Magazine,
Vol. 61

July 1880:	I (166–85) "... said the doctor, meekly."
Aug. 1880:	II (353–69) "Early in June of the following year . . ." " '. . . that bridge, I reckon.' "
Sept. 1880:	III (532–47) "Our adventurers with difficulty . . ."

□

Here and There in the South
Harper's New Monthly Magazine,
Vol. 75

July 1887:	I (235–46)
Aug. 1887:	II (431–43)
Sept. 1887:	III (593–605)
Oct. 1887:	IV (747–60)
Nov. 1887:	V (914–25)

□   □   □   □   □

Davis, Richard Harding

The Princess Aline
Harper's New Monthly Magazine,
Vol. 90

Jan. 1895:	Part I (240–51) " '. . . the same roof shelters us both!' "
Feb. 1895:	Part II (456–70) " 'The course of true love certainly . . .' " ". . . no detaining fingers on Nolan's arm."
March 1895:	Part III (595–606) " 'You are coming now, Miss Morris . . .' "

□

Soldiers of Fortune
Scribner's Magazine, Vol. 21

Jan. 1897:	I–II (29–47)
Feb. 1897:	III–IV (161–77)
March 1897:	V–VIII (333–50)

April 1897:   IX–XI (449–64)
May 1897:   XII–XIII (607–25)
June 1897:   XIV–XV (693–707)

□   □   □   □   □

De Forest, John W.

Doctor Hawley: In Two Parts
Harper's New Monthly Magazine,
Vol. 26
Feb. 1863:   Part I (312–22)
               ". . . to observe
               once more, that
               such is life?"
March 1863:   Part II (468–77)
               "Lucky was it for
               Doctor
               Hawley . . ."

□

Parole D'Honneur: In Two Parts
Harper's New Monthly Magazine,
Vol. 37
Aug. 1868:   Part I (372–78)
               ". . . but it
               crushed the Cap-
               tain, and he
               went."
Sept. 1868:   Part II (483–90)
               "Many a blow fails
               of half . . ."

□

The Man and Brother
The Atlantic Monthly, Vol. 22
Sept. 1868:   Part I (337–48)
               ". . . no more of
               Jim and Bill
               Stigall."

Oct. 1868:   Part II (414–25)
               "Dialogues similar
               in nature . . ."

□

The Lauson Tragedy
The Atlantic Monthly, Vol. 25
April 1870:   I (444–55)
               ". . . had an hour
               since been
               consumed."
May 1870:   II (565–75)
               "The search for
               the missing Aunt
               Mercy . . ."

□

Overland
The Galaxy, Vols. 10–11
Aug. 1870:   I–V (149–75)
Sept. 1870:   VI–X (293–320)
Oct. 1870:   XI–XIII (483–97)
Nov. 1870:   XIV–XVII (638–56)
Dec. 1870:   XVIII–XXI
               (785–802)
Jan 1871:   XXII–XXIV (53–65)
Feb. 1871:   XXV–XXVII
               (205–18)
March 1871:   XXVIII–XXX
               (387–400)
April 1871:   XXXI–XXXIII
               (535–47)
May 1871:   XXXIV–XXXVI
               (662–75)
June 1871:   XXXVII–XXXIX
               (801–16)
July 1871:   XL–XLII (41–56)

□

167

De Forest, John W. (continued)

Kate Beaumont
The Atlantic Monthly, Vols. 27–28
Jan. 1871:   I–IV (70–92)
Feb. 1871:   V–VII (184–201)
March 1871:   VIII–XI (298–321)
April 1871:   XII–XIV (446–62)
May 1871:   XV–XVII (573–89)
June 1871:   XVIII–XX (726–43)
July 1871:   XXI–XXIII (45–63)
Aug. 1871:   XXIV–XXVI
              (189–206)
Sept. 1871:   XXVII–XXIX
              (289–306)
Oct. 1871:   XXX–XXXII
              (483–99)
Nov. 1871:   XXXIII–XXXV
              (546–63)
Dec. 1871:   XXXVI–XXXIX
              (660–77)

□

The Wetherel Affair
The Galaxy, Vols. 14–17
Dec. 1872:   I–IV (727–40)
Jan. 1873:   V–VIII (15–29)
Feb. 1873:   IX–XII (149–63)
March 1873:   XIII–XVI (293–307)
April 1873:   XVII–XX (437–51)
May 1873:   XXI–XXIV
              (590–604)
June 1873:   XXV–XXVIII
              (735–50)
July 1873:   XXIX–XXXII
              (16–32)
Aug. 1873:   XXXIII–XXXVI
              (157–73)
Sept. 1873:   XXXVII–XLI
              (305–23)
Oct. 1873:   XLII–XLV (456–71)

Nov. 1873:   XLVI–XLIX
              (615–30)
Dec. 1873:   L–LII (735–46)
Jan. 1874:   LIII–LVI (15–30)

□   □   □   □   □

Deland, Margaret

Sidney
The Atlantic Monthly, Vols. 65–66
Jan. 1890:   I–III (1–18)
Feb. 1890:   IV–VI (159–78)
March 1890:   VII–IX (343–60)
April 1890:   X–XIII (497–516)
May 1890:   XIV–XVI (648–65)
June 1890:   XVII–XIX (749–65)
July 1890:   XX–XXII (45–62)
Aug. 1890:   XXIII–XXV
              (145–60)
Sept. 1890:   XXVI–XXVIII
              (355–70)
Oct. 1890:   XXIX–XXXI
              (433–46)

□

The Story of a Child
The Atlantic Monthly, Vol. 70
Sept. 1892:   I–IV (288–306)
Oct. 1892:   V–X (446–63)
Nov. 1892:   XI–XV (577–97)

□

Philip and His Wife
The Atlantic Monthly, Vols. 73–74
Jan. 1894:   I–III (1–20)
Feb. 1894:   IV–VII (145–62)
March 1894:   VIII–X (289–306)
April 1894:   XI–XIII (433–46)

May 1894: XIV–XVI (577–92)
June 1894: XVII–XIX (721–38)
July 1894: XX–XXII (1–14)
Aug. 1894: XXIII–XXV (145–58)
Sept. 1894: XXVI–XIX (289–308)
Oct. 1894: XXX–XXXIV (433–51)

□

Old Chester Tales
Harper's New Monthly Magazine,
Vols. 96–98
April 1898: "The Promises of Dorothea," I–VIII (664–79)
May 1898: "Good for the Soul," I–V (880–95)
June 1898: "Miss Maria," I–VI (25–42)
July 1898: "The Thief," I–V (260–75)
Aug. 1898: "The Child's Mother," I–V (406–22)
Sept. 1898: "Justice and the Judge," I–VI (522–39)
Oct. 1898: "Where the Laborers are Few," I–V (780–96)
Nov. 1898: "Sally," I–VI (863–79)
Dec. 1898: "The Unexpectedness of Mr. Horace Shields," I–VII (142–60)

□ □ □ □ □

Dickens, Charles

Bleak House
Harper's New Monthly Magazine,
Vols. 4–7
April 1852: I–IV (649–68)
May 1852: V–VII (809–28)
June 1852: VIII–X (87–106)
July 1852: XI–XIII (229–48)
Aug. 1852: XIV–XVI (358–78)
Sept. 1852: XVII–XIX (505–24)
Oct. 1852: XX–XXII (638–57)
Nov. 1852: XXIII–XXV (791–810)
Dec. 1852: XXVI–XXIX (93–112)
Jan. 1853: XXX–XXXII (222–41)
Feb. 1853: XXXIII–XXXV (381–400)
March 1853: XXXVI–XXXVIII (523–41)
April 1853: XXXIX–XLII (670–89)
May 1853: XLIII–XLVI (812–30)
June 1853: XLVII–XLIX (93–112)
July 1853: L–LIII (245–63)
Aug. 1853: LIV–LVI (389–408)
Sept. 1853: LVII–LIX (525–44)
Oct. 1853: LX–LXVII (659–86)

□

Little Dorrit
Harper's New Monthly Magazine,
Vols. 12–15
Jan. 1856: I–IV (234–58)
Feb. 1856: V–VIII (383–402)
March 1856: IX–XI (526–46)
April 1856: XII–XIV (669–89)

169

□

□

□ □ □ □ □

du Maurier, George

□

Trilby
Harper's New Monthly Magazine,
Vols. 88–89

Jan. 1894:	Part First (168–89)
Feb. 1894:	Part Second (329–50)
March 1894:	Part Third (567–87)
April 1894:	Part Fourth (721–41)
May 1894:	Part Fifth (825–47)
June 1894:	Part Sixth (67–87)
July 1894:	Part Seventh (261–84)
Aug. 1894:	Part Eighth (351–74)

□

The Martian
Harper's New Monthly Magazine,
Vols. 93–95

Oct. 1896:	Part I (659–78)
Nov. 1896:	Part II (869–88)
Dec. 1896:	Part III (39–59)
Jan. 1897:	Part IV (186–206)
Feb. 1897:	Part V (420–41)
March 1897:	Part VI (589–607)
April 1897:	Part VII (691–709)
May 1897:	Part VIII (839–60)
June 1897:	Part IX (129–46)
July 1897:	Part X (182–99)

□ □ □ □ □

Eggleston, Edward

Roxy
Scribner's Monthly (later *Century*),
Vols. 15–16

Nov. 1877:	I–III (32–44)
Dec. 1877:	IV–VII (192–202)

Jan. 1878:	VIII–XI (320–33)
Feb. 1878:	XII–XVIII (496–508)
March 1878:	XIX–XXIV (648–61)
April 1878:	XXV–XXIX (768–80)
May 1878:	XXX–XXXIV (16–27)
June 1878:	XXXV–XXXIX (224–36)
July 1878:	XL–XLIV (328–42)
Aug. 1878:	XLV–XLVIII (568–77)
Sept. 1878:	XLIX–LII (624–39)
Oct. 1878:	LIII–LIX (792–807)

□

The Graysons: A Story of Illinois
The Century Magazine, Vols. 35–36; n.s. 13–14

Nov. 1887:	I–III (40–47)
Dec. 1887:	IV–VII (298–308)
Jan. 1888:	VIII–IX (368–78)
Feb. 1888:	X–XII (562–74)
March 1888:	XIII–XV (681–92)
April 1888:	XVI–XIX (834–45)
May 1888:	XX–XXIII (78–90)
June 1888:	XXIV–XXVI (265–75)
July 1888:	XXVII–XXX (341–52)
Aug. 1888:	XXXI–XXXIII (528–35)

□

The Faith Doctor
The Century Magazine, Vols. 41–42; n.s. 19–20

Feb. 1891:	I–V (540–57)

Eggleston, Edward (continued)

March 1891:	VI–VII (661–72)
April 1891:	VIII–XI (932–44)
May 1891:	XII–XVI (45–58)
June 1891:	XVII–XXII (246–59)
July 1891:	XXIII–XXVI (396–408)
Aug. 1891:	XXVII–XXXI (609–22)
Sept. 1891:	XXXII–XXXVI (708–19)
Oct. 1891:	XXXVII–XLI (939–49)

□ □ □ □ □

Eliot, George

Romola
Harper's New Monthly Magazine,
Vols. 25–27

Aug. 1862:	Proem–V (380–404)
Sept. 1862:	VI–VIII (545–60)
Oct. 1862:	IX–XII (669–85)
Nov. 1862:	XIII–XIV (772–81)
Dec. 1862:	XV–XX (50–71)
Jan. 1863:	XXI–XXVI (206–21)
Feb. 1863:	XXVII–XXXII (322–42)
March 1863:	XXXIII–XXXVII (478–94)
April 1863:	XXXVIII–XLI (621–36)
May 1863:	XLII–XLVI (758–75)
June 1863:	XLVII–LI (77–90)
July 1863:	LII–LVI (220–33)
Aug. 1863:	LVII–LXI (361–74)
Sept. 1863:	LXII–LXVII (496–514)

Oct. 1863:	LXVIII–LXXII, Epilogue (647–61)

□

Daniel Deronda
Harper's New Monthly Magazine,
Vols. 52–53

Feb. 1876:	Book I, I–X (425–59)
March 1876:	Book II, XI–XIV (594–610)
April 1876:	Book II, XV–XVIII (753–68)
May 1876:	Book III, XIX–XXVII (899–927)
June 1876:	Book IV, XXVIII–XXXIV (109–41)
July 1876:	Book V, XXXV–XL (266–302)
Aug. 1876:	Book VI, XLI–XLIX (425–61)
Sept. 1876:	Book VII, L–LVII (592–621)
Oct. 1876:	Book VIII, LVIII–LXX (745–82)

□ □ □ □ □

Foote, Mary Hallock

In Exile: A Story in Two Parts
The Atlantic Monthly, Vol. 48

Aug. 1881:	Part I (184–92) ". . . and somewhat defiant existence."
Sept. 1881:	Part II (322–30) "The autumn rains set in early . . ."

□

The Led-Horse Claim: A Romance of the Silver Mines
The Century Magazine, Vol. 25; n.s. 3

Nov. 1882:	I–IV (101–14)
Dec. 1882:	V–VII (209–22)
Jan. 1883:	VIII–X (367–79)
Feb. 1883:	XI–XIII (582–93)
March 1883:	XIV–XVII (688–97)

☐

John Bodewin's Testimony
The Century Magazine, Vol. 31; n.s. 9

Nov. 1885:	I–V (60–73) "... had already proved a pitfall to her discretion."
Dec. 1885:	V, cont.–IX (229–43) " 'Isn't she charming' Mrs. Craig said . . ."
Jan. 1886:	X–XIV (377–88)
Feb. 1886:	XV–XIX (559–72)
March 1886:	XX–XXII (665–76)
April 1886:	XXIII–XXVI (829–38)

☐

The Last Assembly Ball: A Pseudo-Romance of the Far West
The Century Magazine, Vols. 37–38; n.s. 15–16

March 1889:	Introductory–V (773–89) "... the voice of the 'enemy' had

the quality which carries."

April 1889:	Part II, I–IV (879–90) "It was two months or more . . ." ". . . to complete Milly's triumph, and his own."
May 1889:	Part III, The Catastrophe, I–III (105–12)
June 1889:	Part III, concluded; IV (180–88)

☐

The Chosen Valley
The Century Magazine, Vol. 44; n.s. 22

May 1892:	I–III (106–18)
June 1892:	IV–VI (206–18)
July 1892:	VII–XI (400–13)
Aug. 1892:	XII–XIV (525–35)
Sept. 1892:	XV–XVII (702–12)
Oct. 1892:	XVIII–XXI (823–33)

☐

Coeur D'Alene
The Century Magazine, Vols. 47–48; n.s. 25–26

Feb. 1894:	I–III (502–14)
March 1894:	IV–VI (722–31)
April 1894:	VII–X (895–908)
May 1894:	XI–XIV (102–15)

☐

173

Foote, Mary Hallock (continued)

The Trumpeter: In Two Parts
The Atlantic Monthly, Vol. 74
Nov. 1894: Part One (577–97)
"... a long way
toward feeling that
one is that man."
Dec. 1894: Part Two (721–29)
"It was at
Laramie, between
the mountains,
and ..."

□

The Hanshaw Bride
The Century Magazine, Vol. 52;
n.s. 30
May 1896: [Part I] (90–104)
"... she had
made her wishes
plain."
June 1896: [Part II] (228–41)
"Camp at the
Thousand Springs.
A little grass ..."

□ □ □ □ □

Frederic, Harold

Seth's Brother's Wife
Scribner's Magazine, Vols. 1–2
Jan. 1887: I–V (22–36)
Feb. 1887: VI–IX (184–98)
March 1887: X–XII (308–22)
April 1887: XIII–XVII (479–99)
May 1887: XVIII–XX (615–27)
June 1887: XXI–XXIII (731–44)

July 1887: XXIV–XXV
(97–105)
Aug. 1887: XXVI–XXVIII
(185–96)
Sept. 1887: XXIX–XXX
(283–91)
Oct. 1887: XXXI–XXXII
(404–11)
Nov. 1887: XXXIII–XXXV
(532–40)

□

In the Valley
Scribner's Magazine, Vols. 6–8
Sept. 1889: I–III (284–97)
Oct. 1889: IV–VII (436–50)
Nov. 1889: VIII–XI (573–88)
Dec. 1889: XII–XIV (663–76)
Jan. 1890: XV–XVII (73–86)
Feb. 1890: XVIII–XX (221–34)
March 1890: XXI–XXIV (318–35)
April 1890: XXV–XXVIII
(497–513)
May 1890: XXIX–XXXI
(587–602)
June 1890: XXXII–XXXIV
(757–70)
July 1890: XXXV–XXXVII
(81–94)

□

The Copperhead
Scribner's Magazine, Vol. 14
July 1893: I–II (112–20)
Aug. 1893: III–V (194–204)
Sept. 1893: VI–VIII (343–53)
Oct. 1893: IX–XI (514–24)
Nov. 1893: XII–XIV (622–32)

□ □ □ □ □

Fuller, Henry B.

The Chatelaine of La Trinite
The Century Magazine, Vol. 44,
n.s. 22
June 1892:   I–II (232–44)
July 1892:   III–IV (427–40)
Aug. 1892:   V–VI (549–60)
Sept. 1892:   VII–VIII (732–42)
Oct. 1892:   IX–X (929–39)

☐   ☐   ☐   ☐   ☐

Garland, Hamlin

Ol' Pap's Flaxen
The Century Magazine, Vols. 43–
44; n.s. 21–22
March 1892:   [Part I] (743–51)
               ". . .steadily on,
               founding a great
               state."
April 1892:   II (912–23)
               "One morning,
               eight years
               later, . . ."
               ". . . apparently
               dropping off to
               sleep."
May 1892:   [Part III] (39–47)
               "It was in
               June, . . ."

☐   ☐   ☐   ☐   ☐

Grant, Robert

An Average Man
The Century Magazine, Vols. 27–
28; n.s. 5–6
Dec. 1883:   I–III (288–304)

Jan. 1884:   IV–V (375–87)
Feb. 1884:   VI (606–14)
March 1884:   VII–VIII (706–19)
April 1884:   IX–X (850–58)
May 1884:   XI–XII (91–102)
June 1884:   XIII–XIV (177–90)

☐

The Reflections of a Married Man
Scribner's Magazine, Vol. 11
March 1892:   I–III (354–77)
April 1892:   IV–VI (425–38)
May 1892:   VII–VIII (556–65)
June 1892:   IX–X (722–31)

☐

The Opinions of a Philosopher
Scribner's Magazine, Vols. 13–14
June 1893:   I–II (777–90)
July 1893:   III–V (38–55)
Aug. 1893:   VI–VIII (226–45)
Sept. 1893:   IX–X (357–69)

☐

Search-light Letters
Scribner's Magazine, Vols. 25–26
Jan. 1899:   "To a Young Man
               or Woman in
               Search of the
               Ideal," I–IV
               (96–111)
March 1899:   "To a Modern
               Woman with So-
               cial Ambition,"
               I–IV (361–78)
July 1899:   "To a Young Man
               Wishing to be an
               American," I–IV
               (104–16)

Grant, Robert (continued)

Sept. 1899: "To a Political Optimist," I–III (364–79)

□ □ □ □ □

Hale, Edward Everett

What Will Become of Them?
The Atlantic Monthly, Vol. 14
Aug. 1864: Part I (170–84)
"... landlord's temper were equally pitiless."
Sept. 1864: Part II (320–32)
"Gentleman Bill, full of confidence . . ."

□

Philip Nolan's Friends; or "Show Your Passports!"
Scribner's Monthly (later *Century*), Vols. 11–13
Jan. 1876: I–IV (400–416)
Feb. 1876: V–VII (504–19)
March 1876: VIII–IX (648–60)
April 1876: X–XI (790–96)
May 1876: XII–XIV (16–28)
June 1876: XV–XVI (176–87)
". . . At an earlier hour the three Fathers had started on theirs." [No Chapter XVII]
July 1876: XVIII–XX (400–412)
"It is time to go back to the fortunes of poor Will Harrod, . . ."

Aug. 1876: XXI–XXIV (499–511)
Sept. 1876: XXV–XXVIII (708–20)
Oct. 1876: XXIX–XXXII (877–88)
Nov. 1876: XXXIII–XXXVII (41–59)
Dec. 1876: XXXVIII–XXXIX (248–60)

□

A New England Boyhood
The Atlantic Monthly, Vol. 70
Aug. 1892: I–II (148–60)
Sept. 1892: III (338–46)
Oct. 1892: IV (495–505)
Nov. 1892: V (608–17)
Dec. 1892: VI–VII (765–76)
March 1893: "My College Days" (355–63)
April 1893: "My College Days-II" (458–67)

□ □ □ □ □

Hardy, Thomas

Return of the Native
Harper's New Monthly Magazine, Vols. 56–58
Feb. 1878: Book First, I–IV (415–30)
March 1878: V–VII (573–86)
April 1878: VIII–XI (735–49)
May 1878: Book Second, I–V (895–909)
June 1878: VI–VIII (92–104)
July 1878: Book Third, I–IV (272–86)

Aug. 1878:   V–VIII (435–48)
Sept. 1878:   Book Fourth, I–IV (586–99)
Oct. 1878:   V–VIII (754–65)
Nov. 1878:   Book Fifth, I–IV (911–22)
Dec. 1878:   V–VIII (83–95)
Jan. 1879:   IX; Book Sixth, I–IV (285–300)

□

A Laodicean
Harper's New Monthly Magazine,
Vols. 62–64
Jan. 1881:   Book the First, I–IV (289–303) " '. . . the religion of reasonable persons.' "
Feb. 1881:   IV, cont.–VIII (449–66) "They walked on, and came . . ."
March 1881:   IX–XIII (609–24)
April 1881:   XIV–XVI; Book the Second, I–II (769–85)
May 1881:   III–VII (929–43) ". . . Dare rose and followed her."
June 1881:   VII, cont.–VIII; Book the Third, I–III (129–43) " 'Oh, it is you, Miss . . .' "
July 1881:   IV–VII (289–303)
Aug. 1881:   VIII–XI (449–63)
Sept. 1881:   Book the Fourth, I–V (609–23)
Oct. 1881:   Book the Fifth, I–V (769–83)

Nov. 1881:   VI–X (929–44)
Dec. 1881:   XI–XIV (129–41)
Jan. 1882:   Book the Sixth, I–V (289–306)

□

Two on a Tower
The Atlantic Monthly, Vols. 49–50
May 1882:   I–IV (577–95)
June 1882:   V–IX (722–40)
July 1882:   X–XV (1–19)
Aug. 1882:   XVI–XXI (146–64)
Sept. 1882:   XXII–XXVII (289–308)
Oct. 1882:   XXVIII–XXXII (433–50)

□

Wessex Folk
Harper's New Monthly Magazine,
Vols. 82–83
March 1891:   [Part I] (587–99)
April 1891:   "The Superstitious Man's Story" "Andrew Satchel's Experience as a Musician" (698–705)
May 1891:   "Absent-Mindedness in a Parish Choir" "The Winters and the Palmleys" (890–97)
June 1891:   "Incident with Life of Mr. George Crookhill" "Netty Sargent's Copyhold" (121–27)

□

Hardy, Thomas (continued)

Hearts Insurgent (later *Jude the Obscure*)
Harper's New Monthly Magazine, Vols. 90–91

Dec. 1894:	The Simpletons I–VI (65–81)
Jan. 1895:	VII–XI (188–202)
Feb. 1895:	XII–XVI (349–64)
March 1895:	XVII–XXI (567–82)
April 1895:	XXII–XXV (722–36)
May 1895:	XXVI–XXIX (940–57)
June 1895:	XXX–XXXII (117–29)
July 1895:	XXXIII–XXXVI (251–67)
Aug. 1895:	XXXVII–XL (411–26)
Sept. 1895:	XLI–XLIV (585–602)
Oct. 1895:	XLV–XLVIII (753–67) ". . . everybody right for going home.' "
Nov. 1895:	XLVIII, cont.–LI (894–903) "When Arabella, Jude, and Donn had disappeared . . ."

□   □   □   □   □

Harris, Joel Chandler

A Rainy Day with Uncle Remus
Scribner's Monthly (later *Century*), Vol. 22

June 1881:	I–V (241–48)

July 1881:	VI–X (443–53)
Aug. 1881:	XI–XV (608–16)

□

At Teague Poteet's: A Sketch of the Hog Mountain Range
The Century Magazine, Vol. 26; n.s. 4

May 1883:	Part I (137–50) ". . . from a revenue point of view.'
June 1883:	Part II (185–94) "Woodward was aroused during the night . . ."

□

Nights With Uncle Remus
The Century Magazine, Vol. 26; n.s. 4

July 1883:	I–VI (340–49)
Aug. 1883:	VII–XI (611–23)
Sept. 1883:	XII–XVI (772–81)

□

Azalia
The Century Magazine, Vol. 34; n.s. 12

Aug. 1887:	I–III (540–52)
Sept. 1887:	IV–V (712–22)
Oct. 1887:	VI–VIII (881–87)

□

The Old Bascom Place
The Century Magazine, Vol. 38; n.s. 16

Aug. 1889:	I–III (607–15)
Sept. 1889:	IV–VI (768–78)
Oct. 1889:	VII–X (909–14)

□

The Sea Island Hurricanes
Scribner's Magazine, Vol. 15
Feb. 1894: "The
           Devastation," I–
           VIII (229–47)
March 1894: "The Relief," I–VII
           (267–84)

□

The Chronicles of Aunt Minervy Ann
Scribner's Magazine, Vols. 25–26
Feb. 1899: "How She Ran
           Away from Home
           and Then Ran
           Back Again"
           (175–87)
May 1899: "How She Went
           into Business"
           (544–54)
June 1899: "Major Perdue's
           Bargain" (694–704)
July 1899: "An Evening with
           the Ku-Klux"
           (34–46)
Sept. 1899: "When Jess Went
           A-Fiddlin' "
           (310–19)
Oct. 1899: "How She and
           Major Perdue
           Frailed out the
           Gossett Boys";
           "How She Joined
           the Georgia Legis-
           lature" (433–45)

□ □ □ □ □

Harrison, Constance Cary

Anglomaniacs
The Century Magazine, Vol. 40;
n.s. 18
June 1890: I–II (269–82)
July 1890: III–IV (435–46)
Aug. 1890: V–VI (575–86)
Sept. 1890: VII–VIII (677–86)

□

Sweet Bells Out of Tune
The Century Magazine, Vols. 45–
46; n.s. 23–24
Nov. 1892: I–III (13–28)
Dec. 1892: IV–V (215–22)
Jan. 1893: VI–VII (457–66)
Feb. 1893: VIII–IX (499–506)
March 1893: X–XI (741–52)
April 1893: XII–XIII (858–66)
May 1893: XIV–XV (23–31)

□

A Bachelor Maid
The Century Magazine, Vols. 48–
49; n.s. 26–27
July 1894: I–II (427–38)
Aug. 1894: III–IV (559–72)
Sept. 1894: V–VI (710–22)
Oct. 1894: VII–IX (876–88)
Nov. 1894: X–XII (73–86)

□

An Errant Wooing
The Century Magazine, Vols. 49–
50; n.s. 27–28

Harrison, Constance Cary (continued)

Dec. 1894:   I–III (262–75)
Jan. 1895:   IV–VI (370–85)
Feb. 1895:   VII–VIII (517–27)
March 1895:   IX–X (674–86)
April 1895:   XI–XII (894–904)
May 1895:   XIII–XIV (133–43)

□

Good Americans
The Century Magazine, Vol. 55;
n.s. 33
Nov. 1897:   I–II (57–69)
Dec. 1897:   III–IV (186–97)
Jan. 1898:   V–VI (330–38)
Feb. 1898:   VII–VIII (498–508)
March 1898:   IX–X (659–71)
April 1898:   XI–XII (912–24)

□   □   □   □   □

Harte, Bret

An Episode of Fiddletown
Scribner's Monthly (later *Century*),
Vol. 6
Aug. 1873:   I (433–39)
               ". . . untenanted
               except by motes
               and sunbeams."
Sept. 1873:   II (576–82)
               "When it was
               fairly known that
               Mrs.
               Tretherick . . ."
               ". . . snored
               peacefully."

Oct. 1873:   III (696–703)
               "A week before
               Christmas day,
               1870 . . ."

□

Gabriel Conroy
Scribner's Monthly (later*Century*),
Vols. 11–12.
Nov. 1875:   I–VII (16–31)
Dec. 1875:   VIII–XII (240–56)
Jan. 1876:   XIII–XVII (367–84)
Feb. 1876:   XVIII–XXII
               (552–69)
March 1876:   XXIII–XXVII
               (670–90)
April 1876:   XXVIII–XXXII
               (840–62)
May 1876:   XXXIII–XXXVII
               (29–46)
June 1876:   XXXVIII–XLIII
               (188–211)
July 1876:   XLIV–XLVIII
               (312–32)
Aug. 1876:   XLIX–LVI (512–29)

□

The Heir of the McHulishes
The Century Magazine, Vol. 46;
n.s. 24
Sept. 1893:   Part I, i–ii (763–71)
               ". . . was that of
               Malcolm
               McHulish."
Oct. 1893:   Part II (921–26)
               "A journey to
               Kelpie Island . . ."

□   □   □   □   □

Hawthorne, Nathaniel

The Dolliver Romance
The Atlantic Monthly, Vols. 14–15

July 1864:	"A Scene from The Dolliver Romance" (101–09) ". . . just now wandering over them."
Jan. 1865:	"Another Scene from The Dolliver Romance" (1–7) "We may now suppose Grandsir Dolliver . . ."

□

Septimus Felton; or, The Elixir of Life
The Atlantic Monthly, Vols. 29–30

Jan. 1872:	[Part I] (5–14) ". . . murmured Rose pityingly to herself."
Feb. 1872:	II (129–38) "Septimus went into his house . . ." ". . . even if a successful one."
March 1872:	III (257–66) "Septimus, the next day, . . ." ". . . be welcome to his own."
April 1872:	IV (475–84) "A faint smile seemed to pass . . ."
	". . . for the sake of saving his life."
May 1872:	V (566–76) " 'It tastes as if it might have great potency . . .'" ". . . breathing upon it, had its effect."
June 1872:	VI (645–55) "It is not in our power, . . ." ". . . can make any more of it."
July 1872:	VII (1–16) "Septimus, meanwhile, had betaken himself . . ." ". . . I must away into another obscurity."
Aug. 1872:	VIII (129–144) "With almost a regret, . . ."

□

An Ancestral Footstep Outlines of an English Romance
The Atlantic Monthly, Vols. 50–51

Dec. 1882:	I (823–39) ". . . the secret compartment. 'There is nothing else.' "
Jan. 1883:	II (47–63) "May 5th, Wednesday. The father . . ." ". . . a humorous work, or nothing."

Hawthorne, Nathaniel (continued)

Feb. 1883:   III (180–95)
               "May 12th,
               Wednesday. Mid-
               dleton found . . ."

□   □   □   □   □

Hearn, Lafcadio

Youma
Harper's New Monthly Magazine,
Vol. 80
Jan. 1890:   I–VIII (218–35)
               ". . . before she
               could answer a
               word."
Feb. 1890:   IX–XIV (408–25)
               "A strange coast is
               that on
               which . . ."

□   □   □   □   □

Higginson, Thomas Wentworth

Malbone An Oldport Romance
The Atlantic Monthly, Vol. 23
Jan. 1869:   Prelude–III (1–12)
Feb. 1869:   IV–VI (137–47)
March 1869:   VII–X (265–78)
April 1869:   XI–XIV (393–405)
May 1869:   XV–XVIII (521–31)
June 1869:   XIX–XXIII (649–62)

□

Cheerful Yesterdays
The Atlantic Monthly, Vols. 78–79

Nov. 1896:   I (586–96)
Dec. 1896:   II (758–68)
Jan. 1897:   III (53–63)
Feb. 1897:   IV (241–51)
March 1897:   V (344–55)
April 1897:   VI (483–92)
May 1897:   VII (665–78)
June 1897:   VIII (780–91)

□   □   □   □   □

Holland, J. G.

Arthur Bonnicastle
Scribner's Monthly (later *Century*),
Vols. 5–6
Nov. 1872:   I (32–43)
Dec. 1872:   II (168–80)
Jan. 1873:   III (320–33)
Feb. 1873:   IV (480–93)
March 1873:   V–VII (544–58)
April 1873:   VIII–IX (688–700)
May 1873:   X–XII (32–47)
June 1873:   XIII–XV (208–24)
July 1873:   XVI–XVIII (304–19)
Aug. 1873:   XIX–XX (445–61)
Sept. 1873:   XXI–XXII (540–54)
Oct. 1873:   XXIII–XXIV
               (704–11)

□

The Story of Sevenoaks
Scribner's Monthly (later *Century*),
Vols. 9–11
Jan. 1875:   I–II (312–20)
Feb. 1875:   III–V (467–83)
March 1875:   VI–VIII (568–85)
April 1875:   IX–X (696–710)
May 1875:   XI–XII (21–37)
June 1875:   XIII–XV (151–68)

July 1875:	XVI–XVIII (328–44)
Aug. 1875:	XIX–XXI (432–46)
Sept. 1875:	XXII–XXIII (592–607)
Oct. 1875:	XXIV–XV (736–52)
Nov. 1875:	XXVI–XVII (80–90)
Dec. 1875:	XXVIII–XXIX (159–71)

□

Nicholas Minturn
Scribner's Monthly (later *Century*),
Vols. 13–14

Dec. 1876:	I–II (224–38)
Jan. 1877:	III–IV (384–99)
Feb. 1877:	V–VII (464–79)
March 1877:	VIII–X (592–608)
April 1877:	XI–XII (784–99)
May 1877:	XIII–XV (48–65)
June 1877:	XVI–XVIII (208–24)
July 1877:	XIX–XXI (288–302)
Aug. 1877:	XXII–XXIV (528–42)
Sept. 1877:	XXV–XXVII (608–22)
Oct. 1877:	XXVIII–XXX (744–60)

□ □ □ □ □

Holmes, Oliver Wendell

The Autocrat at the Breakfast Table
The Atlantic Monthly, Vols. 1–2

Nov. 1857:	(48–57)
Dec. 1857:	(175–84)
Jan. 1858:	(312–20)
Feb. 1858:	(457–69)

March 1858:	(614–25)
April 1858:	(734–44)
May 1858:	(871–83)
June 1858:	(102–11)
July 1858:	(234–45)
Aug. 1858:	(360–70)
Sept. 1858:	(496–506)
Oct. 1858:	(619–33)

□

The Professor at the Breakfast Table
The Atlantic Monthly, Vols. 3–4

Jan. 1859:	(85–96)
Feb. 1859:	(232–41)
March 1859:	(350–61)
April 1859:	(492–503)
May 1859:	(609–20)
June 1859:	(760–70)
July 1859:	(119–28)
Aug. 1859:	(232–43)
Sept. 1859:	(369–79)
Oct. 1859:	(500–11)
Nov. 1859:	(622–34)
Dec. 1859:	(751–66)

□

The Professor's Story
The Atlantic Monthly, Vols. 5–7

Jan. 1860:	"Preliminary Correspondence"–II (88–99)
Feb. 1860:	III–IV (222–35)
March 1860:	V–VI (347–57)
April 1860:	VII (470–86)
May 1860:	VIII–X (602–14)
June 1860:	XI–XII (735–46)
July 1860:	XIII–XIV (95–105)
Aug. 1860:	XV–XVI (215–27)

Our Hundred Days in Europe
The Atlantic Monthly, Vols. 59–60

March 1887:	I (343–56)
April 1887:	II (533–45)
May 1887:	III (638–49)
June 1887:	IV (832–42)
July 1887:	V (116–26)
Aug. 1887:	VI (213–25)
Sept. 1887:	VII (289–99)
Oct. 1887:	VIII (462–74)

□

Over the Teacups
The Atlantic Monthly, Vols. 61, 65–66

March 1888:	"Over the Teacups" (323–28)
Jan. 1890:	II (111–21)
Feb. 1890:	III (232–43)
March 1890:	IV (402–12)
April 1890:	V (549–60)
May 1890:	VI (691–703)
June 1890:	VII (829–41)
July 1890:	VIII (92–105)
Aug. 1890:	IX (236–48)
Sept. 1890:	X (387–400)
Oct. 1890:	XI (535–47)
Nov. 1890:	XII (660–71)

□ □ □ □ □

Hope, Anthony

"The Wheel of Love"—A Comedy in Narrative
Scribner's Magazine, Vol. 18

Aug. 1895:	I–VI (149–66) ". . . Certitude could no farther go."

Sept. 1895:	VII–XIII, Postscript (374–93) " 'It's a curious thing,' observed Roger Deane . . ."

□

Phroso: A Tale of Brave Deeds and Perilous Ventures
McClure's Magazine, Vols. 6–7

April 1896:	I–III (449–64)
May 1896:	IV–VI (544–60)
June 1896:	VII–X (46–64) ". . . on the occasion of our arrival."
July 1896:	X, cont.–XI (182–91) "The old men with the picture . . ."
Aug 1896:	XII–XV (245–67)
Sept. 1896:	XVI–XIX (332–53)
Oct. 1896:	XX–XXIII (441–60)

□

Rupert of Hentzau
McClure's Magazine, Vols. 10–11

Dec. 1897:	I–III (129–43)
Jan. 1898:	IV–V (235–45)
Feb. 1898:	VI–VIII (322–38)
March 1898:	IX–XII (455–75)
April 1898:	XIII–XIV (547–56)
May 1898:	XV–XVII (57–72)
June 1898:	XVIII–XIX (143–54) ". . . have ridden here to tell the king."

185

Hope, Anthony (continued)

July 1898:   XIX, cont.–XXI
              (271–80)
              "Sapt finished his
              lesson . . ."

□

The King's Mirror
Munsey's Magazine, Vols. 20–21
Jan. 1899:   I–IV (568–83)
              " '. . . in its prison
              of tradition?' "
Feb. 1899:   IV, cont.–VI
              (690–703)
              "A boy that would
              not have
              worshipped . . ."
              ". . . cruel forcing
              of a girl's
              inclination."
March 1899:   VI, cont.–IX
              (843–56)
              "Victoria received
              my advances . . ."
              ". . . but the king's
              infatuation."
April 1899:   IX, cont.–XI
              (20–31)
              "We were sitting
              by the fire . . ."
              ". . . her love had
              laid to rest."
May 1899:   XI, cont.–XIV
              (179–92)
              " 'What is it?' the
              countess
              cried . . ."
              ". . . was inter-
              ested and
              amused."

June 1899:   XIV, cont.–XVII
              (369–83)
              " 'Briande is al-
              ways
              deploring . . .' "
              " '. . . are you
              ready?' "
July 1899:   XVII, cont.–XIX
              (550–60)
              "We signified our
              assent . . ."
              ". . . and there
              ended the matter."
Aug. 1899:   XIX, cont.–XXI
              (710–20)
              "A low laugh
              escaped . . ."
              ". . . very happy
              together."
Sept. 1899:   XXI, cont.–XXIII
              (905–17)
              "I saw that Wetter
              rallied me . . ."
Oct. 1899:   XXIV–XXV (61–72)
Nov. 1899:   XXVI–XXVIII
              (268–80)

□   □   □   □   □

Howells, William Dean

A Day's Pleasure
The Atlantic Monthly, Vol. 26
July 1870:   I—The Morning
              (107–14)
              ". . . as never to
              have noticed her
              arrival."
Aug. 1870:   II—The Afternoon
              (223–30)
              "It is noticeable

how many peo-
ple . . ."
" '. . . Well, bring
on the lost
child.' "
Sept. 1870:   III—The Evening
(341–46)
" 'Well, where is
the lost
child? . . .' "

□

Their Wedding Journey
The Atlantic Monthly, Vol. 28
July 1871:   I (29–40)
Aug. 1871:   II–III (162–76)
Sept. 1871:   IV–V (345–57)
Oct. 1871:   VI (442–59)
Nov. 1871:   VII–VIII (605–23)
Dec. 1871:   IX–X (721–40)

□

A Chance Acquaintance
The Atlantic Monthly, Vol. 31
Jan. 1873:   I (17–28)
Feb. 1873:   II–III (181–96)
March 1873:   IV–VI (339–56)
April 1873:   VII–IX (431–48)
May 1873:   X–XII (563–78)
June 1873:   XIII–XIV (693–704)

□

A Foregone Conclusion
The Altantic Monthly, Vol. 34
July 1874:   I–II (1–15)
Aug. 1874:   III–VI (145–60)
Sept. 1874:   VII–IX (345–60)

Oct. 1874:   X–XII (475–87)
Nov. 1874:   XIII–XV (534–50)
Dec. 1874:   XVI–XVII (641–58)

□

Private Theatricals
The Atlantic Monthly, Vols. 36–37
Nov. 1875:   I–II (513–22)
Dec. 1875:   III–IV (674–87)
Jan. 1876:   V–VII (1–20)
Feb. 1876:   VIII (182–95)
March 1876:   IX–X (329–44)
April 1876:   XI–XII (437–49)
May 1876:   XIII–XV (559–74)

□

Out of the Question: Comedy
The Atlantic Monthly, Vol. 39
Feb. 1877:   I–II (195–208)
March 1877:   III–IV (317–29)
April 1877:   V–VI (447–61)

□

A Counterfeit Presentment: Comedy
The Atlantic Monthly, Vol. 40
Aug. 1877:   Part First, I–VIII
(148–61)
Sept. 1877:   Part Second, I–V
(296–305)
Oct. 1877:   Part Third, I–V
(448–60)

□

The Lady of the Aroostook
The Atlantic Monthly, Vols. 42–43
Nov. 1878:   I–VI (597–618)

Howells, William Dean (continued)

Dec. 1878:	VII–X (727–46)
Jan. 1879:	XI–XIV (25–41)
Feb. 1879:	XV–XXI (193–216)
March 1879:	XXII–XXVII (338–67)

□

The Undiscovered Country
The Atlantic Monthly, Vols. 45–46

Jan. 1880:	I–II (66–84)
Feb. 1880:	III–VII (216–40)
March 1880:	VIII–XI (336–54)
April 1880:	XII–XIV (499–523)
May 1880:	XV–XVII (641–60)
June 1880:	XVIII–XXII (780–805)
July 1880:	XXIII–XXVIII (83–111)

□

A Fearful Responsibility
Scribner's Monthly (later *Century*), Vol. 22

June 1881:	I–VI (276–93)
July 1881:	VII–XIII (390–414)

□

Dr. Breen's Practice
The Atlantic Monthly, Vol. 48

Aug. 1881:	I–III (143–64)
Sept. 1881:	IV–VI (289–309)
Oct. 1881:	VII–VIII (433–52)
Nov. 1881:	IX–X (577–93)
Dec. 1881:	XI–XII (721–34)

□

A Modern Instance
The Century Magazine, Vols. 23–24; n.s. 1–2

Dec. 1881:	I–IV (241–58)
Jan. 1882:	V–VII (367–75)
Feb. 1882:	VIII–X (577–91)
March 1882:	XI–XII (753–60)
April 1882:	XIII–XV (921–31)
May 1882:	XVI–XVIII (114–27)
June 1882:	XIX–XXII (257–72)
July 1882:	XXIII–XXVI (409–25)
Aug. 1882:	XXVII–XXX (569–86)
Sept. 1882:	XXXI–XXXV (740–63)
Oct. 1882:	XXXVI–XLI (897–919)

□

A Woman's Reason
The Century Magazine, Vols. 25–26; n.s. 3–4

Feb. 1883:	I–II (513–28)
March 1883:	III–V (753–68)
April 1883:	VI–VII (887–98)
May 1883:	VIII–IX (115–27)
June 1883:	X–XI (233–48)
July 1883:	XII–XIV (433–49)
Aug. 1883:	XV–XVII (592–611)
Sept. 1883:	XVIII–XIX (659–71)
Oct. 1883:	XX–XXI (907–21)

□

The Rise of Silas Lapham
The Century Magazine, Vols. 29–30; n.s. 7–8

Nov. 1884:	I–II (13–26)
Dec. 1884:	III–V (242–54)

Jan. 1885:   VI–VIII (370–84)
Feb. 1885:   IX–X (581–92)
March 1885:   XI–XII (661–76)
April 1885:   XIII–XIV (858–72)
May 1885:   XV–XVIII (15–27)
June 1885:   XIX–XXI (241–55)
July 1885:   XXII–XXV (353–73)
Aug. 1885:   XXVI–XXVII
                (513–26)

□

Indian Summer
Harper's New Monthly Magazine,
Vols. 71–72
July 1885:   I–IV (261–77)
Aug. 1885:   V–VII (433–51)
Sept. 1885:   VIII–X (616–34)
Oct. 1885:   XI–XIII (780–97)
Nov. 1885:   XIV–XVI (854–72)
Dec. 1885:   XVII–XVIII
                (apparently mis-
                numbered) (25–34)
Jan. 1886:   XX (283–93)
Feb. 1886:   XXI–XXIV (448–60)

□

The Minister's Charge; or The Ap-
prenticeship of Lemuel Barker
The Century Magazine, Vols. 31–
33; n.s. 9–11
Feb. 1886:   I–IV (500–15)
March 1886:   V–VII (718–29)
April 1886:   VIII–X (860–72)
May 1886:   XI–XIII (21–36)
June 1886:   XIV–XVI (249–59)
July 1886:   XVII–XIX (350–60)
Aug. 1886:   XX–XXI (511–21)
Sept. 1886:   XXII–XXIII
                (734–44)

Oct. 1886:   XXIV–XXVII
                (880–92)
Nov. 1886:   XXVIII–XXXI
                (38–46)
Dec. 1886:   XXXII–XXXVI
                (183–92)

□

April Hopes
Harper's New Monthly Magazine,
Vols. 74–75
Feb. 1887:   I–VII (381–96)
March 1887:   VIII–XIII (589–606)
April 1887:   XIV–XVIII
                (788–801)
May 1887:   XIX–XXIII (934–51)
June 1887:   XXIV–XXVII
                (99–112)
July 1887:   XXVIII–XXXII
                (246–58)
Aug. 1887:   XXXIII–XXXVI
                (344–52)
Sept. 1887:   XXXVII–XLII
                (605–20)
Oct. 1887:   XLIII–XLVIII
                (713–29)
Nov. 1887:   XLIX–LII (925–43)

□

Annie Kilburn
Harper's New Monthly Magazine,
Vol. 77
June 1888:   I–V (128–44)
July 1888:   VI–IX (270–85)
Aug. 1888:   X–XII (407–22)
Sept. 1888:   XIII–XVIII
                (569–84)
Oct. 1888:   XIX–XXIV
                (700–718)
Nov. 1888:   XXV–XXX (869–88)

□

189

Howells, William Dean (continued)

The Shadow of a Dream
Harper's New Monthly Magazine,
Vol. 80

March 1890:	Part First, I–VIII (510–29)
April 1890:	Part Second, I–VIII (766–82)
May 1890:	Part Third, I–IX (865–81)

□

An Imperative Duty
Harper's New Monthly Magazine,
Vol. 83

July 1891:	I–V (191–204)
Aug. 1891:	VI–VII (416–28)
Sept. 1891:	VIII–X (517–27)
Oct. 1891:	XI–XIII (765–76)

□

The World of Chance
Harper's New Monthly Magazine,
Vols. 84–85

March 1892:	I–VII (604–18)
April 1892:	VIII–XII (669–81)
May 1892:	XIII–XVI (856–68)
June 1892:	XVII–XX (36–46)
July 1892:	XXI–XXIV (229–39)
Aug. 1892:	XXV–XXVIII (400–410)
Sept. 1892:	XXIX–XXXIV (544–60)
Oct. 1892:	XXXV–XXXIX (740–54)
Nov. 1892:	XL–XLVI (927–42)

□

A Circle in the Water
Scribner's Magazine, Vol. 17

March 1895:	I–IV (293–303) ". . . than she expected me to do so."
April 1895:	V–VIII (428–40) "The Haskeths lived in a house . . ."

□

An Open-Eyed Conspiracy: An Idyl of Saratoga
The Century Magazine, Vol. 52;
n.s. 30

July 1896:	I–IV (345–57)
Aug. 1896:	V–IX (607–20)
Sept. 1896:	X–XIV (659–71)
Oct. 1896:	XV–XVIII (836–46)

□

The Story of a Play
Scribner's Magazine, Vols. 21–22

March 1897:	I–III (290–305)
April 1897:	IV–VII (477–92)
May 1897:	VIII–X (641–51)
June 1897:	XI–XIII (764–75)
July 1897:	XIV–XX (99–120)
Aug. 1897:	XXI–XXV (245–54)

□

Their Silver Wedding Journey
Harper's New Monthly Magazine,
Vols. 98–100

Jan. 1899:	Part I, I–VIII (193–210)
Feb. 1899:	Part II, IX–XIV (392–408)

March 1899: Part III, XV–XXI (546–60)

April 1899: Part IV, XXII–XX-VII (787–802)

May 1899: Part V, XXVIII–XXXII (923–38)

June 1899: Part VI, XXXIII–XXXVIII (109–24)

July 1899: Part VII, XXXIX–XLV (269–86)

Aug. 1899: Part VIII, XLVI–L (374–92)

Sept. 1899: Part IX, LI–LVI (570–88)

Oct. 1899: Part X, LVII–LXII (763–81)

Nov. 1899: Part XI, LXIII–LXX (926–49)

Dec. 1899: Part XII, LXXI–LXXV (85–106)

□ □ □ □ □

James, Henry

Poor Richard
The Atlantic Monthly, Vols. 19–20

June 1867: Part I (694–706)
". . . of this little act of justice."

July 1867: Part II (32–42)
"Richard got through the following week . . ."
". . . looked grave and pronounced him very ill."

Aug. 1867: Part III (166–78)
"In country districts, where life is quiet . . ."

□

Gabrielle De Bergerac
The Atlantic Monthly, Vol. 24

July 1869: Part I (55–71)
". . . 'I will wait for you.' "

Aug. 1869: Part II (231–41)
"I remember distinctly the incidents . . ."
". . . and Loquelin in the rich avowal of her tears."

Sept. 1869: Part III (352–61)
"A week after this memorable visit . . ."

□

Travelling Companions
The Atlantic Monthly, Vol. 26

Nov. 1870: I (600–614)
". . . treasures we may help each other to find."

Dec. 1870: II (684–97)
"At the end of my three days' probation, . . ."

□

A Passionate Pilgrim, in Two Parts
The Atlantic Monthly, Vol. 27

March 1871: Part First (352–71)
". . . *Keep the American.*"

April 1871: Part Second (478–99)
" 'Keep the American!' Miss Searle, . . ."

□

191

James, Henry (continued)

Watch and Ward
The Atlantic Monthly, Vol. 28
Aug. 1871:   Part First, I–II
                    (232–46)
Sept. 1871:   Part Second, III–IV
                    (320–39)
Oct. 1871:   Part Third, V–VI
                    (415–31)
Nov. 1871:   Part Fourth, VII–
                    VIII (577–96)
Dec. 1871:   Part Fifth, IX–XI
                    (689–710)

□

Guest's Confession, in Two Parts
The Atlantic Monthly, Vol. 30
Oct. 1872:   Part First, I–III
                    (385–403)
                    ". . .'But— I'm
                    madly in love!' "
Nov. 1872:   Part Second, IV–VI
                    (566–83)
                    "My situation, as I
                    defined it to Craw-
                    ford . . ."

□

Madame de Mauves: In Two Parts
The Galaxy, Vol. 17
Jan. 1874:   Part First: I–IV
                    (216–33)
Feb. 1874:   Part Second: V–
                    VIII (354–74)

□

Adina
Scribner's Monthly (later *Century*),
Vol. 8

May 1874:   Part I (33–43)
                    ". . . a sort of talis-
                    man against trou-
                    ble,—Angelo
                    Beati."
June 1874:   Part II (181–91)
                    "Sam Scrope
                    looked extremely
                    annoyed . . ."

□

Eugene Pickering: In Two Parts
The Atlantic Monthly, Vol. 34
Oct. 1874:   Part I (397–410)
                    ". . . some
                    supreme incarna-
                    tion of levity."
Nov. 1874:   Part II (513–26)
                    "Madame Blumen-
                    thal seemed, for
                    the time, . . ."

□

Roderick Hudson
The Atlantic Monthly, Vols. 35–36
Jan. 1875:   I, "Rowland"
                    (1–15)
Feb. 1875:   II, "Roderick"
                    (145–60)
March 1875:   III, "Rome"
                    (297–313)
April 1875:   IV, "Experience"
                    (422–36)
May 1875:   V, "Christina"
                    (515–31)
June 1875:   VI, "Frascati"
                    (644–58)
July 1875:   VII, "Saint Cecil-
                    ia's" (58–70)

Aug. 1875:   VIII, "Provoca-
tion" (129–40)

Sept. 1875:   IX, "Mary Garland" (269–81)

Oct. 1875:   X, "The Cavaliere"
(385–406)

Nov. 1875:   XI, "Mrs. Hudson" (553–70)

Dec. 1875:   XII, "Switzerland"
(641–65)

□

The American
The Atlantic Monthly, Vols. 37–39

June 1876:   I–III (651–73)
July 1876:   IV–V (15–31)
Aug. 1876:   VI–VII (155–70)
Sept. 1876:   VIII–X (310–29)
Oct. 1876:   XI–XII (461–74)
Nov. 1876:   XIII–XIV (535–50)
Dec. 1876:   XV–XVI (641–57)
Jan. 1877:   XVII–XVIII (1–18)
Feb. 1877:   XIX–XX (161–75)
March 1877:   XXI–XXII (295–11)
April 1877:   XXIII–XXIV
(412–25)
May 1877:   XXV–XXVI
(530–44)

□

The Europeans
The Atlantic Monthly, Vol. 42

July 1878:   I–III (53–72)
Aug. 1878:   IV–VI (155–77)
Sept. 1878:   VII–IX (262–83)
Oct. 1878:   X–XII (404–28)

□

Confidence
Scribner's Monthly (later *Century*),
Vols. 18–19

Aug. 1879:   I–II (507–19)
Sept. 1879:   III–IV (668–82)
Oct. 1879:   V–VI (849–64)
Nov. 1879:   VII–VIII (65–80)
Dec. 1879:   IX–X (209–25)
Jan. 1880:   XI–XII (393–411)

□

Washington Square
Harper's New Monthly Magazine,
Vols. 61–62

July 1880:   I–VI (287–301)
Aug. 1880:   VII–XII (413–26)
Sept. 1880:   XIII–XVIII
(593–607)
Oct. 1880:   XIX–XXIV (753–66)
Nov. 1880:   XXV–XXIX
(907–18)
Dec. 1880:   XXX–XXXV
(129–44)

□

The Portrait of a Lady
The Atlantic Monthly, Vols. 45–47

Nov. 1880:   I–V (585–611)
Dec. 1880:   VI–X (740–66)
Jan. 1881:   XI–XIV (1–27)
Feb. 1881:   XV–XVIII
(176–205)
March 1881:   XIX–XX (335–59)
April 1881:   XXI–XXIV (449–77)
May 1881:   XXV–XXVIII
(623–47)
June 1881:   XXIX–XXXIV
(800–826)
July 1881:   XXXV–XXXVIII
(59–85)

James, Henry (continued)

Aug. 1881:	XXXIX–XLII (213–40)
Sept. 1881:	XLIII–XLVI (338–65)
Oct. 1881:	XLVII–XLIX (479–99)
Nov. 1881:	L–LII (620–40)
Dec. 1881:	LIII–LV (751–70)

□

Daisy Miller: A Comedy
The Altantic Monthly, Vol. 51

April 1883:	Act I (433–56)
May 1883:	Act II (577–97)
June 1883:	Act III (721–40)

□

The Impressions of a Cousin
The Century Magazine, Vol. 27; n.s. 5

Nov. 1883:	[Part I] (116–29) ". . . she is coming to Eunice, at Cornerville."
Dec. 1883:	[Part II] (257–75) "June 8—Late this afternoon . . ."

□

Lady Barberina
The Century Magazine, Vol. 28; n.s. 6

May 1884:	I–II (18–31)
June 1884:	III–IV (222–34)
July 1884:	V–VI (336–50)

□

A New England Winter
The Century Magazine, Vol. 28; n.s. 6

Aug. 1884:	I–V (573–87) ". . . of a little month she enjoyed this felicity."
Sept. 1884:	VI–VII (733–43) "Mrs. Mesh sat on one side . . ."

□

The Bostonians
The Century Magazine, Vols. 29–31; n.s. 7–9

Feb. 1885:	I–V (530–43)
March 1885:	VI–X (686–700) ". . . as if they really had 'struck' something."
April 1885:	X, cont.–XIV (893–908) "Even to Verena, as we know . . ."
May 1885:	XV–XVI (58–66)
June 1885:	XVII–XVIII (256–64)
July 1885:	XIX–XXI (423–37)
Aug. 1885:	XXII–XXIV (553–68)
Sept. 1885:	XXV–XXVIII (692–708)
Oct. 1885:	XXIX–XXXIII (861–81)
Nov. 1885:	XXXIV–XXXVI (85–98) ". . . 'I want you to come out with me, away from here.' "

Dec. 1885: XXXVI, cont.–
XXXVIII (205–14)
" 'You always
want me to come
out! . . ."
". . . the most
charming woman
in America."

Jan. 1886: XXXVIII, cont.–XL
(337–51)
"It is to be feared,
indeed . . ."

Feb. 1886: XLI–XLII (591–600)

□

The Princess s Casamassima
The Atlantic Monthly, Vols. 56–58
Sept. 1885: Book First, I–III
(289–311)
Oct. 1885: IV–VII (433–59)
Nov. 1885: VIII–XI (577–602)
Dec. 1885: XII–XIII (721–38)
Jan. 1886: Book Second,
XIV–XVI (66–90)
Feb. 1886: XVII–XXI (145–78)
March 1886: Book Third, XXII–
XXIV (326–51)
April 1886: XXV–XXVIII
(485–507)
May 1886: XXIX–XXXII
(645–68)
June 1886: XXXIII–XXXVI
(789–813)
July 1886: Book Fourth, XXX-
VII–XXXVIII
(58–76)
Aug. 1886: XXXIX–XL
(209–28)
Sept. 1886: XLI–XLII; Book
Fifth, XLIII–XLIV
(349–75)". . . the

letter that Schinkel
had given him."
Oct. 1886: XLIV [cont.?]–XLVI
(432–49)
" 'And Madame
Grandoni, then?'
asked Hyancinth,
reluctant . . .' "

□

The Aspern Papers: In Three Parts
The Atlantic Monthly, Vol. 61
March 1888: I–IV (296–315)
". . . and express
everything."
April 1888: V–VII (461–82)
"I was seldom at
home . . ."
". . . to-night in
the garden."
May 1888: VIII–IX (577–94)
"As it turned out,
the provision . . ."

□

The Liar
The Century Magazine, Vol. 36;
n.s. 14
May 1888: Part I, I–II (123–35)
". . . almost con-
soled, he would
be magnanimous."
June 1888: Part II, II, cont.–III
(213–23)
"Lyon finished his
picture . . ."

□

Dec. 1891: Part Second
(721–35)
"Lady Maresfield
had given her
son . . ."

□

The Old Things
The Atlantic Monthly, Vols. 77–78
April 1896: I–IV (433–50)
May 1896: V–VI (631–40)
June 1896: VII–IX (721–37)
July 1896: X–XIII (58–74)
Aug. 1896: XIV–XVI (201–18)
Sept. 1896: XVII–XIX (376–90)
Oct. 1896: XX–XXII (518–30)

□ □ □ □ □

Jewett, Sarah Orne

A Landless Farmer
The Altantic Monthly, Vol. 51
May 1883: Part I (627–37)
". . . when they
were in their
places."
June 1883: Part II (759–69)
"Serena's not very
tender heart . . ."

□

A Marsh Island
The Atlantic Monthly, Vol. 55
Jan. 1885: I–III (39–51)
Feb. 1885: IV–VII (145–60)
March 1885: VIII–X (347–60)
April 1885: XI–XIV (452–66)

May 1885: XV–XVIII (654–67)
June 1885: XIX–XXIII (773–90)

□

The Country of the Pointed Firs
The Atlantic Monthly, Vols. 77–78
Jan. 1896: I–VII (1–18)
Feb. 1896: VIII–XI (302–12)
July 1896: XII–XV (75–88)
Sept. 1896: XVI–XX (352–66)

□ □ □ □ □

Kennedy, John Pendleton

A Legend of Maryland
The Atlantic Monthly, Vol. 6
July 1860: I–VI (29–44)
". . . against the
Baltimore family."
Aug. 1860: VII–X, plus Post-
script (141–52)
"Let me now once
more shift the
scene."

□ □ □ □ □

King, Grace

Balcony Stories
The Century Magazine, Vols. 45–
46; n.s. 23–24
Dec. 1892: "The Balcony"
"The Drama of
Three" (279–82)
Jan. 1893: "La Grande De-
moisell" (323–27)

King, Grace (continued)

Feb. 1893:	"Mimi's Marriage" "The Miracle Chapel" (493–99)
June 1893:	"The Story of a Day" (230–35)
July 1893:	"Anne Marie and Jeanne Marie" "A Crippled Hope" (372–79)
Aug. 1893:	"One of Us" "The Little Con- vent Girl" (544–51)
Sept. 1893:	"Grandmother's Grandmother" "The Old Ladies Resoration" (722–27)
Oct. 1893:	"A Delicate Affair" "Pupasse" (884–94)

□　□　□　□　□

Kipling, Rudyard, and Wolcott **Balestier**

The Naulahka
The Century Magazine, Vols. 43–44; n.s. 21–22

Nov. 1891:	I–III (35–45)
Dec. 1891:	IV–VI (186–97)
Jan. 1892:	VII–IX (343–52) " '. . . why do men go to war?' "
Feb. 1892:	IX, cont.–XI (608–18) "Kate saw little of Tarvin . . ."

March 1892:	XII–XIII (666–78)
April 1892:	XIV–XVII (890–904)
May 1892:	XVIII–XIX (135–42)
June 1892:	XX (290–95)
July 1892:	XXI (375–83)

□　□　□　□　□

Kipling, Rudyard, and Wolcott **Ballestier**

Benefits Forgot
The Century Magazine, Vols. 45–46; n.s. 23–24

Dec. 1892:	I–II (192–206)
Jan. 1893:	III (407–13)
Feb. 1893:	IV–V (525–38)
March 1893:	VI–VIII (766–79)
April 1893:	IX–XII (937–49)
May 1893:	XIII–XV (51–64)
June 1893:	XVI–XIX (285–303)
July 1893:	XX–XXIV (446–61)
Aug. 1893:	XXV–XXVII (611–23)
Sept. 1893:	XXVIII–XXXI (697–708)
Oct. 1893:	XXXII–XXXV (939–51)

□　□　□　□　□

Kipling, Rudyard

Captains Courageous: A Story of the Grand Banks
McClure's Magazine, Vols. 8–10

Nov. 1896:	I–II (17–31)
Dec. 1896:	III (165–75)
Jan. 1897:	IV–V (222–35)

Feb. 1897:   VI–VIII (341–55)
". . . speaking gruffly to one another."

March 1897:   VIII, cont.–IX (424–31)
"The 'We're Here' was racing . . ."
". . . Harvey was waiting for them."

April 1897:   IX, cont.–X (521–29)
"After violent emotion . . ."
". . . I gained some. I'll tell you."

May 1897:   X, concluded (611–18)
"Cheyne pulled his beard . . ."

□

Stalky and Co.
McClure's Magazine, Vols. 12–13.

Dec. 1898:   [I.] "Stalky" (99–110)

Jan. 1899:   "II. An Unsavory Interlude" (210–23)

Feb. 1899:   "III. The Impressionists" (311–23)

March 1899:   "IV. The Moral Reformers" (427–38)

April 1899:   "V. A Little Prep" (564–76)

May 1899:   "VI. The Flag of Their Country" (3–15)

June 1899:   "VII. The Last Term" (112–24)

□ □ □ □ □

Lever, Charles

Lettice Arnold
Harper's New Monthly Magazine,
Vol. 1

June 1850:   I–IV (13–35)
July 1850:   V–VI (168–78)
Aug. 1850:   VII–X (353–383)

□ □ □ □ □

Lytton, Edward Bulwer

My Novel; or, Varieties in English Life
Harper's New Monthly Magazine,
Vols. 1–6

Oct. 1850:   Book One, I–IX (659–72)
Nov. 1850:   X–XIII (761–77)
Dec. 1850:   Book Two, I–VI (85–97)
Jan. 1851:   VII–XII (251–63)
Feb. 1851:   Book Three, I–XII (382–96)
March 1851:   XIII–XXIX (524–43)
April 1851:   Book Four, I–XII (682–98)
May 1851:   XIII–XXV (825–40)
June 1851:   Book Five, I–VI (111–21)
July 1851:   VII–XIX (256–72)
Aug. 1851:   Book Six, I–XII (394–411)
Sept. 1851:   XIII–XXV (541–56)
Oct. 1851:   Book Seven, I–XV (665–79)

Lytton, Edward Bulwer (continued)

Nov. 1851:	XVI–XX (816–32)
Dec. 1851:	Book Eight, I–VI (103–18)
Jan. 1852:	VII–XIV (239–52)
Feb. 1852:	Book Nine, I–VIII (371–84)
March 1852:	IX–XVII (525–40) ". . . their propria- tory smile he re- sumed gravely."
April 1852:	XVII, cont.-Book Ten, I–IX (673–88) " 'Your flatterers will tell you . . ."
May 1852:	X–XIX (793–808) ". . . Scotch women generally are."
June 1852:	XIX, cont.–XXV, Book Eleven I–X (36–60) " 'Brother, said Dick!' What do women . . ." ". . . details in their joint designs."
July 1852:	X, cont.–XII (180–85) "Randal walked home slowly . . ."
Aug. 1852:	XIII–XVI (378–92) ". . . —to fly from shame!"
Sept. 1852:	XVI, cont.–XX (494–504) "But, when the seas rolled . . ."
Oct. 1852:	Book Twelve, I– VIII (669–86)
Nov. 1852:	IX–XV (813–32)

	". . . of the rent and tortured soul."
Dec. 1852:	XV, cont.–XXIII (56–75) " 'Fool!' said the unhappy man . . ."
Jan. 1853:	XXIV–XXVII (241–52)
Feb. 1853:	XXVIII–XXXV (349–77)

☐ ☐ ☐ ☐ ☐

Matthews, Brander

Vignettes of Manhattan
Harper's New Monthly Magazine,
Vols. 88–89

Dec. 1893:	I, "A Thanksgiv- ing Dinner" (28–34)
Jan. 1894:	II, "A Midsummer Midnight" (221–30)
Feb. 1894:	III, "In the Little Church Down the Street" (463–66)
March 1894:	IV, "At a Private View" (491–98)
April 1894:	[V], "Spring in a Side Street" (678–83)
June 1894:	[VI], "In Search of Local Color" (33–40)
July 1894:	[VII], "Before the Break of Day" (222–27)

Aug. 1894: [VIII], "A Vista in Central Park" (457–62)

□

The Royal Marine: An Idyl of Narragansett Pier
Harper's New Monthly Magazine,
Vol. 89
Sept. 1894: Part I, I–III (577–92) ". . . was not able to sleep at all."
Oct. 1894: Part II, IV–VI (680–94) "The next morning, at a quarter before eleven, . . ."

□ □ □ □ □

Melville, Herman

Bartleby, the Scrivener: A Story of Wall Street
Putnam's Magazine, Vol. 2
Nov. 1853: [Part I] (546–57) ". . . He was more a man of preferences than assumptions."
Dec. 1853: [Part II] (609–15) "After breakfast, I walked down town, . . ."

□

The Enchantadas, or Enchanted Isles,
by Salvador R. Tarnmoor
Putnam's Magazine, Vol. 3
March 1854: Sketches First-Fourth (311–19)
April 1854: Sketches Fifth-Ninth (345–55)
May 1854: Sketches Tenth-Eleventh (460–66)

□

Israel Potter; or Fifty Years of Exile
Putnam's Magazine, Vols. 4–5
July 1854: I–III (66–75)
Aug. 1854: IV–VII (135–46)
Sept. 1854: VIII–XII (277–90)
Oct. 1854: XIII (371–78)
Nov. 1854: XIV–XVI (481–91)
Dec. 1854: XVII–XIX (592–601) ". . . should rage in unnatural fight."
Jan. 1855: XIX, cont.–XX (63–71) "Ere long, a horrible explosion . . ."
Feb. 1855: XXI–XXIII (176–82)
March 1855: XXIV–XXVII (288–93)

□

Benito Cereno
Putnam's Magazine, Vol. 6
Oct. 1855: [Part I] (353–67) ". . . trip lengthened by the continual recession of the goal."
Nov. 1855: [Part II] (459–73) "The advancing speck was observed . . ."

Melville, Herman (continued)

". . . in neighborly
style long
anchored
together."

Dec. 1855: [Part III] (633–44)
"Before returning
to his own vessel,
Captain
Delano . . ."

□ □ □ □ □

Meredith, George

The Amazing Marriage
Scribner's Magazine, Vols. 17–18
Jan. 1895: I–IV (33–48)
Feb. 1895: V–VIII (229–46)
March 1895: IX–XII (365–82)
April 1895: XIII–XVI (461–78)
May 1895: XVII–XX (640–56)
June 1895: XXI–XXIV (774–88)
July 1895: XXV–XXVIII
(110–28)
Aug. 1895: XXIX–XXXI
(248–61)
Sept. 1895: XXXII–XXXVI
(328–47)
Oct. 1895: XXXVII–XXXIX
(444–58)
Nov. 1895: XL–XLIV (629–50)
Dec. 1895: XLV–XLVI (681–92)

□ □ □ □ □

Murfree, Mary Noailles [Charles Egbert Craddock]

Drifting Down Lost Creek
The Atlantic Monthly, Vol. 53

March 1884: I (362–75)
" . . and she arose
and followed it."
April 1884: II (441–54)
"Following the
voice of the
Lord . . ."

□

The Prophet of the Great Smokey
Mountains
The Atlantic Monthly, Vols. 55–56
Jan. 1885: I (1–12)
Feb. 1885: II–III (186–200)
March 1885: IV–V (289–302)
April 1885: VI–VIII (433–43)
May 1885: IX–X (601–16)
June 1885: XI–XII (744–57)
July 1885: XIII–XIV (31–44)
Aug. 1885: XV (244–56)

□

In the Clouds
The Atlantic Monthly, Vols. 57–58
Jan. 1886: I–II (1–19)
Feb. 1886: III–IV (200–220)
March 1886: V–VII (389–408)
April 1886: VIII–X (517–40)
May 1886: XI–XIII (669–90)
June 1886: XIV–XVI (816–34)
July 1886: XVII–XVIII
(113–31)
Aug. 1886: XIX–XXI (243–62)
Sept. 1886: XXII–XXIII
(386–403)
Oct. 1886: XXIV–XXV
(519–38)
Nov. 1886: XXVI–XXVII
(666–84)

Dec. 1886:   XXVIII–XXX (829–51)

□

The Despot of Broomsedge Cove
The Atlantic Monthly, Vols. 61–63
Jan. 1888:   I–II (95–111)
Feb. 1888:   III–IV (194–212)
March 1888:   V–VI (366–86)
April 1888:   VII–VIII (532–56)
May 1888:   IX–X (661–80)
June 1888:   XI–XII (813–34)
July 1888:   XIII–XIV (68–89)
Aug. 1888:   XV–XVI (230–50)
Sept. 1888:   XVII–XIX (398–419)
Oct. 1888:   XX–XXI (536–59)
Nov. 1888:   XXII–XXIV (674–99)
Dec. 1888:   XXV–XXVII (808–34)

□

In the "Stranger People's" Country
Harper's New Monthly Magazine,
Vols. 82–83
Jan. 1891:   I–III (202–28)
Feb. 1891:   IV–VI (359–84)
March 1891:   VII–IX (526–50)
April 1891:   X–XII (725–42)
May 1891:   XIII–XIV (834–48)
June 1891:   XV–XVI (63–84)

□

His Vanished Star
The Atlantic Monthly, Vols. 72–73
July 1893:   I–II (1–18)

Aug. 1893:   III–IV (145–59)
Sept. 1893:   V–VI (289–306)
Oct. 1893:   VII–IX (505–20)
Nov. 1893:   X–XI (655–71)
Dec. 1893:   XII–XIII (789–805)
Jan. 1894:   XIV–XV (99–115)
Feb. 1894:   XVI–XVII (223–39)
March 1894:   XVIII–XIX (384–404)

□

The Casting Vote
The Century Magazine, Vol. 47;
n.s. 25
Nov. 1893:   Part I (47–56)
          ". . . 'I'll let ye
          know 'lection
          day."
Dec. 1893:   Part II (271–83)
          "It was a hot day
          in the little valley
          town . . ."

□

The Mystery of Witch-face
Mountain
The Atlantic Monthly, Vol. 76
Sept. 1895:   I–III (331–50)
Oct. 1895:   IV–VI (525–44)
Nov. 1895:   VII–X (651–68)

□

The Juggler
The Atlantic Monthly, Vols. 78–80
Nov. 1896:   I (597–609)
Dec. 1896:   II–III (804–22)
Jan. 1897:   IV (73–85)

203

Murfree, Mary Noailles (continued)

Feb. 1897:	V (188–98)
March 1897:	VI (386–99)
April 1897:	VII–VIII (508–527)
May 1897:	IX (651–64)
June 1897:	X (825–37)
July 1897:	XI–XII (106–20)
Aug. 1897:	XIII–XIV (241–63)

□ □ □ □ □

Oliphant, Margaret

Norah: The Story of a Wild Irish Girl
Scribner's Monthly (later *Century*), Vol. 2

May 1871:	I–III (49–61) "... to call forth the mention of one name."
June 1871:	III, cont.–V (149–62) "'Well, find the men, me dear child ...'"

□

The Two Mrs. Scudamores
Scribner's Monthly (later *Century*), Vol. 3

Nov. 1871:	I–III (85–94)
Dec. 1871:	IV–VII (198–208) "'I am sure you know.'"
Jan. 1872:	VII, continued–VIII (297–303) "'I don't know, indeed,' she said ...'"

□

At His Gates
Scribner's Monthly (later *Century*), Vols. 3–5

Jan. 1872:	I–III (355–68)
Feb. 1872:	IV–VI (441–55)
March 1872:	VII–IX (585–98)
April 1872:	X–XI (713–22)
May 1872:	XII–XIII (34–43)
June 1872:	XIV–XVII (169–87)
July 1872:	XVIII–XXI (313–34)
Aug. 1872:	XXII–XXV (426–55)
Sept. 1872:	XXVI–XXXI (584–612)
Oct. 1872:	XXXII–XXXVII (706–37)
Nov. 1872:	XXXVIII–XLI (44–63)
Dec. 1872:	XLII–XLV (201–21)

□

A Country Gentleman
The Atlantic Monthly, Vols. 55–57

Jan. 1885:	I–III (88–103)
Feb. 1885:	IV–VII (228–48)
March 1885:	VIII–X (372–86)
April 1885:	XI–XIII (507–22)
May 1885:	XIV–XVI (577–92)
June 1885:	XVII–XX (803–20)
July 1885:	XXI–XXIII (55–69)
Aug. 1885:	XXIV–XXVI (177–92)
Sept. 1885:	XXVII–XXIX (324–39)
Oct. 1885:	XXX–XXXIII (484–504)
Nov. 1885:	XXXIV–XXXVII (609–26)
Dec. 1885:	XXXVIII–XLII (769–91)
Jan. 1886:	XLIII–XLVII (99–120)

Feb. 1886: XLVIII–LII (230–53)

□ □ □ □ □

Page, Thomas Nelson

Little Darby
Scribner's Magazine, Vol. 16
Sept. 1894: I (285–95)
". . . and Mrs. Stanley never asked after her or came."
Oct. 1894: II (457–71)
"The company in which Little Darby and . . ."

□

Red Rock
Scribner's Magazine, Vols. 23–24
Jan. 1898: I–III (34–52)
Feb. 1898: IV–VIII (161–78)
March 1898: IX–XI (292–310)
April 1898: XII–XVI (481–96)
May 1898: XVII–XXI (613–32)
June 1898: XXII–XXVII (689–709)
July 1898: XXVIII–XXIX (113–22)
Aug. 1898: XXX–XXXI (237–51)
Sept. 1898: XXXII–XXXVI (350–70)
Oct. 1898: XXXVII–XL (470–88)
Nov. 1898: XLI–XLVII (578–96)

□ □ □ □ □

Phelps, Elizabeth Stuart

Friends: A Duet
The Atlantic Monthly, Vols. 47–48
Jan. 1881: I–III (86–96)
Feb. 1881: IV–V (145–55)
March 1881: VI–VIII (305–17)
April 1881: IX–X (490–507)
May 1881: XI–XIII (666–78)
June 1881: XIV–XV (836–44)
July 1881: XVI (98–106)

□

Doctor Zay
The Atlantic Monthly, Vols. 49–50
April 1882: I–II (518–30)
May 1882: III–V (630–50)
June 1882: VI–VII (764–79)
July 1882: VIII–IX (28–41)
Aug. 1882: X–XI (206–13)
Sept. 1882: XII–XIII (325–39)

□

Chapters from a Life
McClure's Magazine, Vols. 6–7
Dec. 1895: I (49–58)
Jan. 1896: [II] (191–98)
Feb. 1896: [III] (293–300)
March 1896: [IV] (361–68)
April 1896: [V] (490–95)
May 1896: [VI] (513–18)
June 1896: VII (3–11)
July 1896: VIII (114–21)
Aug. 1896: IX (234–44)
Sept. 1896: [X] (353–62)
Oct. 1896: [XI] (461–68)

□

Phelps, Elizabeth Stuart (continued)

A Singular Life
The Atlantic Monthly, Vols. 75–76
Jan. 1896:   I–III (1–16)
Feb. 1896:   IV–VI (145–64)
March 1896:   VII–VIII (353–69)
April 1896:   IX–XI (433–45)
May 1896:   XII–XIII (641–53)
June 1896:   XIV–XVII (721–36)
July 1896:   XVIII–XIX (77–90)
Aug. 1896:   XX–XXII (145–61)
Sept. 1896:   XXIII–XXVI
                (380–97)
Oct. 1896:   XXVII–XXX
                (433–48)

□   □   □   □   □

Reade, Charles

*Jack of All Trades: A Matter of Fact
Romance*
Harper's New Monthly Magazine,
Vol. 16
Dec. 1857:   I–II (109–14)
Jan. 1858:   III–V (189–97)
Feb. 1858:   VI–VIII (376–81)
March 1858:   IX–XI (481–92)

□

Griffith Gaunt; or, Jealousy
The Atlantic Monthly, Vol. 16
Dec. 1865:   I–IV (641–56)
                ". . . eyes full and
                searching on Grif-
                fith Gaunt."
Jan. 1866:   IV, cont.–V
                (100–18)
                "He uttered a little
                shout . . ."

Feb. 1866:   VI–VIII (221–37)
March 1866:   IX–XIV (365–82)
April 1866:   XV–XVII (507–22)
May 1866:   XVIII–XXV
                (596–621)
June 1866:   XXVI–XXVII
                (751–68)
July 1866:   XXVIII–XXXI
                (94–113)
Aug. 1866:   XXXII–XXXVIII
                (204–24)
Sept. 1866:   XXXIX–XL
                (323–37)
Oct. 1866:   XLI (492–505)
Nov. 1866:   XLII–XLV (606–25)

□

Put Yourself in His Place
The Galaxy, Vols. 8–11
March 1869:   I–III (309–27)
April 1869:   IV–V (469–85)
May 1869:   VI–VII (633–55)
June 1869:   VIII–IX (777–800)
July 1869:   X (5–21)
Aug. 1869:   XI (149–67)
Sept. 1869:   XII (360–83)
Oct. 1869:   XIII–XIX (490–511)
Nov. 1869:   XX–XXII (626–46)
Dec. 1869:   XXIII–XXVII
                (761–80)
Jan. 1870:   XXVIII–XXIX
                (53–75)
Feb. 1870:   XXX–XXXII
                (149–69)
March 1870:   XXXIII–XXXVII
                (295–320)
April 1870:   XXXVIII–XXXIX
                (439–65)
May 1870:   XL–XLI (583–98)

June 1870: XLII–XLIV
(731–49)
July 1870: XLV–XLVIII
(77–96)

□

A Simpleton: A Story of the Day
Harper's New Monthly Magazine,
Vols. 45–47
Aug. 1872: I–II (450–57)
Sept. 1872: III (609–16)
Oct. 1872: IV (771–78)
Nov. 1872: V–VI (933–38)
". . . to twice their
value under
hammer."
Dec. 1872: VI, cont. (98–103)
"Rosa got flushed,
and her eye . . ."
Jan. 1873: VII (258–70)
Feb. 1873: VIII–IX (418–28)
". . . 'You have
deceived both.' "
March 1873: IX, cont.–XI
(577–85)
"I suspect Dr.
Staines . . ."
April 1873: XII (741–51)
May 1873: XIII (897–906)
June 1873: XIV–XVII (45–59)
July 1873: XVIII–XXI (202–14)
Aug. 1873: XXII–XXIII
(371–82)
Sept. 1873: XXIV–XXV
(560–67)
Oct. 1873: XXVI–XXVIII
(728–40)

□

A Woman–Hater
Harper's New Monthly Magazine,
Vols. 53–55
July 1876: I–II (226–38)
Aug. 1876: III–V (408–20)
" '. . . coming, but
she is alone.' "
Sept. 1876: V, cont.–VII
(569–81)
"The next moment
Fanny . . ."
Oct. 1876: VIII–X (727–40)
" '. . . I'll shut the
carriage door.' "
Nov. 1876: X, cont.–XII
(848–59)
"Ina smiled at his
ingenuity . . . "
Dec. 1876: XIII–XIV (82–97)
Jan. 1877: XV–XVI (272–84)
Feb. 1877: XVII–XVIII
(431–45)
March 1877: XIX (529–43)
April 1877: XX–XXI (711–22)
May 1877: XXII–XXIII
(837–48)
June 1877: XXIV–XXVI
(111–22)
July 1877: XXVII–XXXII
(205–24)

□

The Picture
Harper's New Monthly Magazine,
Vol. 68
March 1884: I–II (625–37)
". . . 'as he would
a wild boar.' "
April 1884: III (680–87)
" 'What I took to
be . . .' "

□   □   □   □   □   □

Simms, William Gilmore

The Bride of the Battle
Graham's Magazine, Vol. 37
July 1850:   I–III (23–29)
Aug. 1850:   IV–VII (89–91)
Sept. 1850:   VIII–XI (163–69)

□

The Pirate Hoard
Graham's Magazine, Vol. 48
Jan. 1856:   I–III (54–59)
Feb. 1856:   IV–VIII (124–31)
March 1856:   IX–XI (224–29)
April 1856:   XII–XV (344–51)

□   □   □   □   □

Spofford, Harriet Elizabeth Prescott

The Amber Gods
The Atlantic Monthly, Vol. 5
Jan. 1860:   "Story First"
                (7–18)
                " '. . . did you
                ever know such
                insolence.' "
Feb. 1860:   [Part II] I–III
                (170–85)
                "Papa made Mr.
                Dudley stay and
                dine, . . ."

□

Midsummer and May
The Atlantic Monthly, Vols. 6–7
Nov. 1860:   I (544–71)
                ". . . 'You are mis-
                taken, as I said.' "

Dec. 1860:   II (674–92)
                "When Miss Kent,
                the maternal
                grandaunt . . ."
Jan. 1861:   III (9–27)

□

Fauntleroy Verrain's Fate
Knickerbocker Magazine, Vol. 57
Jan. 1861:   I (57–70)
Feb. 1861:   II (186–94)
                ". . . had fulfilled
                their mission and
                left America."
March 1861:   II, cont. (278–85)
                "Two years
                slipped away
                now . . ."
April 1861:   III (388–98)
May 1861:   IV (465–74)

□

The South Breaker
The Atlantic Monthly, Vol. 9
May 1862:   Part I (557–70)
                ". . . any day un-
                der sunshine and
                a south wall."
June 1862:   Part II (687–700)
                "Blue-fish were
                about done
                with . . ."

□

Madeleine Schaeffer
Harper's New Monthly Magazine,
Vol. 25
June 1862:   I–II (37–52)

Oct. 1862: III–VI (651–60)
Nov. 1862: VII–IX (753–64)

□

Rosemary: In Three Parts
Harper's New Monthly Magazine,
Vols. 26–27
May 1863: Part I (803–09)
"... his so lately
beautiful darling!"
June 1863: Part II (41–52)
"April showers
bring forth ..."
"... forest screen
of shadow and
coolness."
July 1863: Part III (195–200)
"The long deli-
cious twilight ..."

□

The Rim
The Atlantic Monthly, Vols. 13–14
May 1864: Part I (605–15)
"... as a feint to-
wards the other."
June 1864: Part II (701–13)
"Affairs went
smoothly and
noiselessly ..."
"... 'Life is
best!' "
July 1864: Part III, Conclusion (63–73)
"The boat went
cutting
through ..."

□

Flotsam and Jetsam
The Atlantic Monthly, Vol. 21
Jan. 1868: Part I (7–16)
"... 'but he
knows it by
name!' "
Feb. 1868: Part II (186–98)
"Joey stood
silent ..."
"... inferences of
the evening paper
ceased."
March 1868: Part III (313–25)
"I folded up the
sheet ..."

□

Ordronnaux
Scribner's Monthly (later *Century*),
Vol. 8
Sept. 1874: Part I (611–19)
"... a whole row
of Japan lilies as
he walked away."
Oct. 1874: Part II (734–44)
"In the letter of
cordial
thanks ..."

□ □ □ □ □

Stevenson, Robert Louis

The Silverado Squatters: Sketches
from a California Mountain
The Century Magazine, Vol. 27;
n.s. 5
Nov. 1883: [Part I] (27–39)
"... planted un-
der the overhang-
ing rock."

Stevenson, Robert Louis (continued)

Dec. 1883: [Part II] (183–93)
"There is quite a
large race or
class . . ."

□

The Master of Ballantrae
Scribner's Magazine, Vols. 4–6
Nov. 1888: "Summary of
Events During the
Master's Wander-
ings" [I] (570–81)
Dec. 1888: II (697–706)
Jan. 1889: III (49–57)
Feb. 1889: IV (152–62)
March 1889: V (278–86)
April 1889: VI (413–23)
May 1889: VII (624–35)
June 1889: VIII (749–59)
July 1889: IX (93–101)
Aug. 1889: X (145–54)
Sept. 1889: XI (351–62)
Oct. 1889: XII (407–14)

□ □ □ □ □

Stevenson, Robert Louis, and Lloyd Osborne

The Wrecker
Scribner's Magazine, Vols. 10–12
Aug. 1891: Prologue, I–III
(171–94)
Sept. 1891: IV–VI (287–307)
Oct. 1891: VII–IX (418–42)
Nov. 1891: X–XI (575–93)
Dec. 1891: XII–XIII (723–36)
Jan. 1892: XIV–XV (85–97)
Feb. 1892: XVI–XVII (155–68)

March 1892: XVIII–XIX (315–33)
April 1892: XX–XXI (471–81)
May 1892: XXII (598–610)
June 1892: XXIII (777–88)
July 1892: XXIV–XXV; Epi-
logue (57–76)

□ □ □ □ □

Stevenson, Robert Louis, and Lloyd Osborne

The Ebb Tide
McClure's Magazine, Vols. 2–3
Feb. 1894: Part I, I–III
(243–59)
March 1894: IV–VI (371–90)
April 1894: Part II, VII–IX
(489–504)
" '. . . not which,
of course,' said
Attwater."
May 1894: IX,cont.–X
(593–600)
"As the boy was
filling Huish's
glass . . ."
". . . 'Oh, yes, it
is,' said Huish."
June 1894: X, cont.–XI (89–96)
" 'Come, come!'
said the
Captain . . ."
". . . 'fythful ser-
vant, John
Dyvis.' "
July 1894: XI, cont.–XII
(186–92)
"Huish read the
letter . . ."

□

Stevenson, Robert Louis

*St. Ives: The Adventures of a French
Prisoner in England*
McClure's Magazine, Vols. 6–8
March 1896:   I–II (393–401)
April 1896:   III–IV (493–500)
May 1896:   V–VII (586–96)
June 1896:   VIII–XI (668–84)
July 1896:   XII–XV (778–92)
   ". . . 'going to fol-
   low me?' "
Aug. 1896:   XV,cont.–XVI
   (896–903)
   "I was scarce clear
   of . . ."
Sept. 1896:   XVII–XXII (975–99)
Oct. 1896:   XXIII–XXVIII
   (1061–84)
   ". . . on the com-
   mand of temper."
Nov. 1896:   XXVIII, cont.–XXX
   (33–44)
   "It is a strange
   thing how . . ."

□ □ □ □ □

Stowe, Harriet Beecher

The Minister's Wooing
The Atlantic Monthly, Vols. 2–4
Dec. 1858:   I–III (870–89)
Jan. 1859:   IV–V (97–111)
Feb. 1859:   VI–VII (219–29)
March 1859:   VIII–IX (375–86)
April 1859:   X–XI (504–13)
May 1859:   XII–XIII (620–31)
June 1859:   XIV–XV (749–59)
July 1859:   XVI–XVII (106–19)
Aug. 1859:   XVIII–XXI
   (196–207)

Sept. 1859:   XXII–XXIV
   (305–20)
Oct. 1859:   XXV–XXIX
   (421–42)
Nov. 1859:   XXX–XXXIV
   (541–61)
Dec. 1859:   XXXV–XLII (667–
   88)

□

Agnes of Sorrento
The Atlantic Monthly, Vols. 7–9
May 1861:   I–IV (513–25)
June 1861:   V–VI (641–54)
July 1861:   VII–VIII (2–13)
Aug. 1861:   IX (215–26)
Sept. 1861:   X–XI (311–22)
Oct. 1861:   XII–XIII (449–63)
Nov. 1861:   XIV–XV (558–71)
Dec. 1861:   XVI–XVII (682–96)
Jan. 1862:   XVIII–XIX (14–27)
Feb. 1862:   XX–XXII (146–61)
March 1862:   XXIII–XXVI
   (306–27)
April 1862:   XXVII–XXXII
   (474–92)

□

*House and Home Papers, by Chris-
topher Crowfield*
The Altantic Monthly, Vols. 13–14
Jan. 1864:   I (40–47)
Feb. 1864:   II (201–9)
March 1864:   III (353–63)
April 1864:   IV (458–65)
May 1864:   V (621–29)
June 1864:   VI (754–61)
July 1864:   VII (93–98)
Aug. 1864:   VIII (230–40)

Stowe, Harriet Beecher (continued)

Oct. 1864:   IX (434–43)
Nov. 1864:   X (565–79)
Dec. 1864:   XI (689–702)

□

The Chimney-Corner, by Christopher Crowfield
The Atlantic Monthly, Vols. 15–18
Jan. 1865:   I (109–15)
Feb. 1865:   II "Little Foxes"
                    (221–32)
March 1865:   III "Little Foxes"—
                    Part II (353–62)
April 1865:   IV "Little Foxes,"
                    III (490–500)
May 1865:   V "Little Foxes,"
                    IV (602–12)
June 1865:   VI "Little Foxes,"
                    V (732–42)
July 1865:   VII "Little Foxes,"
                    VI (100–107)
Aug. 1865:   VIII (232–37)
Sept. 1865:   IX "Little Foxes,"
                    VII (347–56)
Nov. 1865:   X (567–75)
Dec. 1865:   XI (672–83)

□

The Chimney-Corner for 1866.
Jan. 1866:   I (88–100)
Feb. 1866:   II (215–20)
March 1866:   III (345–52)
April 1866:   IV (490–99)
May 1866:   V (577–85)
June 1866:   VI (737–43)
July 1866:   VII (85–93)
Aug. 1866:   VIII (197–203)
Sept. 1866:   IX (338–43)

□

Oldtime Fireside Stories
The Atlantic Monthly, Vols. 25–26
June 1870:   "The Ghost in the
                    Mill" (688–94)
July 1870:   "The Widow's
                    Bandbox" (63–68)
Aug. 1870:   "Mis' Elderkin's
                    Pitcher" (157–61)
Oct. 1870:   "Colonel EPH's
                    Shoe-Buckles"
                    (424–29)
Nov. 1870:   "Captain Kidd's
                    Money" (522–27)
Dec. 1870:   "The Ghost in the
                    Cap'n Brown
                    House" (654–59)

□   □   □   □   □

Tarkington, Booth

The Gentleman from Indiana
McClure's Magazine, Vol. 13
May 1899:   I–III (84–96)
June 1899:   IV–V (130–42)
July 1899:   VI–VII (235–47)
Aug. 1899:   VIII–IX (334–44)
Sept. 1899:   X–XII (411–25)
                    " '. . . where I
                    shall not find you.'
                    John Harkless."
Oct. 1899:   XII,cont.–XIV
                    (566–76)
                    "Very early in the
                    morning . . ."

□   □   □   □   □

Taylor, Bayard

Joseph and His Friend
The Altantic Monthly, Vols. 25–26
Jan. 1870:   I–III (30–43)
Feb. 1870:   IV–VI (128–44)
March 1870:   VII–VIII (262–72)
April 1870:   IX–X (385–95)
May 1870:   XI–XIII (513–25)
June 1870:   XIV–XVI (641–56)
July 1870:   XVII–XIX (41–53)
Aug. 1870:   XX–XXII (129–44)
Sept. 1870:   XXIII–XXIV
     (274–85)
     ": . . . She was
     dead."
Oct. 1870:   XXIV [sic]–XXV
     (403–12)
     " 'It cannot be!' "
Nov. 1870:   XXVI–XXIX
     (571–90)
Dec. 1870:   XXX–XXXII
     (665–76)

☐ ☐ ☐ ☐ ☐

Thackeray, William Makepeace

The Newcomes. Memoires of a Most
Respectable Family
Harper's New Monthly Magazine,
Vols. 7–11
Nov. 1853:   I–III (815–30)
Dec. 1853:   IV–VI (104–18)
Jan. 1854:   VII–IX (178–94)
Feb. 1854:   X–XII (351–65)
April 1854:   XIII–XVI (637–54)
May 1854:   XVII–XX (780–96)
June 1854:   XXI–XXIII (57–73)
July 1854:   XXIV–XXVI
     (201–18)

Aug. 1854:   XXVII–XXIX
     (348–66)
Sept. 1854:   XXX–XXXII
     (492–509)
Oct. 1854:   XXXIII–XXXV
     (618–34)
Nov. 1854:   XXXVI–XXXVIII
     (782–96)
Dec. 1854:   XXXIX–XLI (61–78)
Jan. 1855:   XLII–XLIV
     (222–39)
Feb. 1855:   XLV–XVLII
     (353–71)
March 1855:   XLVIII–LI (511–27)
April 1855:   LII–LIV (653–70)
May 1855:   LV–LVII (799–816)
June 1855:   LVIII–LXI (47–64)
July 1855:   LXII–LXV (205–21)
Aug. 1855:   LXVI–LXIX
     (335–52)
Sept. 1855:   LXX–LXXIII
     (479–95)
Oct. 1855:   LXXIV–LXXX
     (622–49)

☐

The Virginians
Harper's New Monthly Magazine,
Vols. 16–19
Dec. 1857:   I–IV (92–108)
Jan. 1858:   V–VIII (240–57)
Feb. 1858:   IX–XII (381–98)
March 1858:   XIII–XVI (525–41)
April 1858:   XVII–XX (670–87)
May 1858:   XXI–XXIV (813–30)
June 1858:   XXV–XXVIII
     (95–112)
July 1858:   XXIX–XXXII
     (239–56)

Thackeray, William Makepeace
(continued)

Aug. 1858:	XXXIII–XXXVI (384–401)
Sept. 1858:	XXXVII–XL (525–42)
Oct. 1858:	XLI–XLIV (669–87)
Nov. 1858:	XLV–XLVIII (813–29)
Dec. 1858:	XLIX–LII (95–113)
Jan. 1859:	LIII–LVI (237–54)
Feb. 1859:	LVII–LX (381–99)
March 1859:	LXI–LXIII (525–43)
April 1859:	LXIV–LXVII (670–86)
May 1859:	LXVIII–LXXI (816–33)
June 1859:	LXXII–LXXV (101–18)
July 1859:	LXXVI–LXXIX (240–55)
Aug. 1859:	LXXX–LXXXIII (381–98)
Sept. 1859:	LXXXIV–LXXXVI (537–54)
Oct. 1859:	LXXXVII–XC (677–94)
Nov. 1859:	XCI–XCII (818–30)

□

Lovel the Widower
Harper's New Monthly Magazine,
Vols. 20–21

Feb. 1860:	I (383–92)
March 1860:	II (525–34)
April 1860:	III (680–88)
May 1860:	IV (813–24)
June 1860:	V (99–107)
July 1860:	VI (238–47)

□

The Adventures of Philip
Harper's New Monthly Magazine,
Vols. 22–25

Feb. 1861:	I–III (381–93)
March 1861:	IV–V (529–42)
April 1861:	VI–VII (669–82)
May 1861:	VIII–X (815–27)
June 1861:	XI–XII (90–105)
July 1861:	XIII–XIV (233–46)
Aug. 1861:	XV–XVI (381–94)
Sept. 1861:	XVII–XVIII (524–37)
Oct. 1861:	XIX–XX (689–702)
Nov. 1861:	XXI–XXII (819–32)
Dec. 1861:	XXIII–XXIV (90–102)
Jan. 1862:	XXV–XXVI (233–45)
Feb. 1862:	XXVII–XXVIII (379–92)
March 1862:	XXIX–XXX (522–35)
April 1862:	XXXI–XXXII (684–96)
May 1862:	XXXIII–XXXIV (823–35)
June 1862:	XXXV–XXXVI (99–112)
July 1862:	XXXVII–XXXVIII (237–49)
Aug. 1862:	XXXIX–XL (404–16)
Sept. 1862:	XLI–XLII (533–45)

□

Denis Duval
Harper's New Monthly Magazine,
Vols. 28–29

April 1864:	I–III (675–92)
May 1864:	IV–V (815–28)
July 1864:	VI–VII (213–26)

Aug. 1864:   VIII–Note by the
              Editor (358–71)

□   □   □   □   □

Thoreau, Henry David

Chesuncook
The Altantic Monthly, Vol. 2
June 1855:   [Part I] (1–12)
              ". . . All the rest
              of the pines had
              been driven off."
July 1855:   [Part II] (224–33)
              "How far men go
              for the material of
              their houses . . ."
              ". . . any that went
              to the Mexican
              war."
Aug. 1855:   [Part III] (305–17)
              "Early the next
              morning . . ."

□   □   □   □   □

Trollope, Anthony

Orley Farm
Harper's New Monthly Magazine,
Vols. 22–26
May 1861:   I–IV (793–809)
June 1861:   V–VIII (36–52)
July 1861:   IX–XII (204–20)
Aug. 1861:   XIII–XVI (331–47)
Sept. 1861:   XVII–XX (491–507)
Oct. 1861:   XXI–XXIV (617–34)
Nov. 1861:   XXV–XXVIII
              (793–810)
Dec. 1861:   XXIX–XXXII
              (60–77)

Jan. 1862:   XXXIII–XXXVI
              (202–18)
Feb. 1862:   XXXVII–XL
              (325–42)
March 1862:   XLI–XLIV (473–90)
April 1862:   XLV–XLVIII
              (639–56)
May 1862:   XLIX–LII (785–801)
June 1862:   LIII–LVI (77–93)
July 1862:   LVII–LX (201–17)
Aug. 1862:   LXI–LXIV (341–57)
Sept. 1862:   LXV–LXVIII
              (506–22)
Oct. 1862:   LXIX–LXXII
              (634–50)
Nov. 1862:   LXXIII–LXXVI
              (785–804)
Dec. 1862:   LXXVII–LXXX
              (80–97)

□

The Small House at Allington
Harper's New Monthly Magazine,
Vols. 25–29
Oct. 1862:   I–III (691–704)
Nov. 1862:   IV–VI (815–28)
Dec. 1862:   VII–VIII (117–26)
Jan. 1863:   IX–XII (248–66)
Feb. 1863:   XIII–XV (385–97)
March 1863:   XVI–XVIII
              (544–56)
May 1863:   XIX–XXI (775–89)
June 1863:   XXII–XXIV
              (90–104)
July 1863:   XXV–XXVII
              (234–47)
Aug. 1863:   XXVIII–XXX
              (374–88)
Sept. 1863:   XXXI–XXXIII
              (514–27)

Trollope, Anthony (continued)

Oct. 1863:	XXXIV–XXXVI (634–47)
Nov. 1863:	XXXVII–XXXIX (788–801)
Dec. 1863:	XL–XLII (80–93)
Jan. 1864:	XLIII–XLV (222–35)
Feb. 1864:	XLVI–XLVIII (321–34)
March 1864:	XLIX–LI (480–94)
April 1864:	LII–LIV (623–36)
May 1864:	LV–LVII (782–94)
June 1864:	LVIII–LX (41–53)

□

The Vicar of Bullhamptom
Lippincott's Magazine, Vols. 4–5

July 1869:	I–IX (5–43)
Aug. 1869:	X–XVIII (129–64)
Sept. 1869:	XIX–XXVI (241–71)
Oct. 1869:	XXVII–XXXIV (353–83)
Nov. 1869:	XXXV–XLI (465–91)
Dec. 1869:	XLII–XLVII (577–604)
Jan. 1870:	XLVIII–LII (9–26)
Feb. 1870:	LIII–LVI (129–48)
March 1870:	LVII–LXIII (241–64)
April 1870:	LXIV–LXIX (353–81)
May 1870:	LXX–LXXIII (532–44)

□

Sir Harry Hotspur of Humbleth-
waite: A Novel
Lippincott's Magazine, Vols. 5–6

May 1870:	I–III (465–77)
June 1870:	IV–VI (633–45)
July 1870:	VII–IX (77–89)
Aug. 1870:	X–XII (160–72)
Sept. 1870:	XIII–XV (270–82)
Oct. 1870:	XVI–XVIII (427–39)
Nov. 1870:	XIX–XXI (539–51)
Dec. 1870:	XXII–XXIV (651–63)

□

The Eustace Diamonds
The Galaxy, Vols. 12–15

Sept. 1871:	I–VI (395–421)
Oct. 1871:	VII–XI (535–56)
Nov. 1871:	XII–XV (651–68)
Dec. 1871:	XVI–XVIII (804–16)
Jan. 1872:	XIX–XXII (61–76)
Feb. 1872:	XXIII–XXVI (212–28)
March 1872:	XXVII–XXX (359–75)
April 1872:	XXXI–XXXIV (504–20)
May 1872:	XXXV–XXXVIII (635–55)
June 1872:	XXXIX–XLIV (787–807)
July 1872:	XLV–XLIX (49–70)
Aug. 1872:	L–LVI (192–220)
Sept. 1872:	LVII–LXI (355–78)
Oct. 1872:	LXII–LXV (495–509)
Nov. 1872:	LXVI–LXIX (645–63)
Dec. 1872:	LXX–LXXV (798–821)
Jan. 1873:	LXXVI–LXXX (92–114)

□

The Golden Lion of Granpere
Harper's New Monthly Magazine,
Vols. 44–45
Feb. 1872:   I–III (420–34)
March 1872:   IV–V (581–89)
April 1872:   VI–VIII (740–50)
May 1872:   IX–XI (881–91)
June 1872:   XII–XIII (84–94)
July 1872:   XIV–XVI (245–55)
Aug. 1872:   XVII–XVIII
              (362–72)
Sept. 1872:   XIX–XXI (546–56)

□   □   □   □   □

Twain, Mark

Old Times on the Mississippi
The Altantic Monthly, Vol. 35
Jan. 1875:   I (69–73)
Feb. 1875:   II, "A 'Cub' Pilot's
              Experience; or,
              Learning the
              River" (217–24)
March 1875:   III, "The Contin-
              ued Perplexities of
              'Cub' Piloting"
              (283–89)
April 1875:   IV, "The 'Cub' Pi-
              lot's Education
              Nearly
              Completed"
              (446–52)
May 1875:   V, " 'Sounding.'
              Faculties Peculiarly
              Necessary to a Pi-
              lot" (567–574)
June 1875:   VI, "Official Rank
              and Dignity of a
              Pilot. The Rise and
              Decadence of the

              Pilot's Associa-
              tion" (721–30)
July 1875:   VII, "Leaving Port:
              Shortening of the
              River by Cut-Offs:
              'Stephen's' Plan of
              'Resumption' "
              (190–96)

□

Some Rambling Notes of an Idle
Excursion
The Atlantic Monthly, Vols. 40–41
Oct. 1877:   I (443–47)
              ". . . 'the chro-
              nometer of
              God?' "
Nov. 1877:   II (586–92)
              "At dinner, six
              o'clock, . . ."
              ". . . with inno-
              cent, sympathetic
              interest."
Dec. 1877:   III (718–24)
              "So the Reverend
              and I had . . ."
              ". . . to size the
              country again."
Jan. 1878:   IV (12–19)
              "The early twi-
              light of a Sunday
              evening . . ."

□

An Adventure with Huckleberry
Finn: With an Account of the Fa-
mous Grangerford-Shepherdson Feud
The Century Magazine, Vols. 29;
n.s. 7

Twain, Mark (continued)

Dec. 1884: [Part I] (268–78)
"Here is the way
we put in the
time. It was a
monstrous big
river down
there . . ."
". . . You feel
mighty free and
easy and comfort-
able on a raft."

Jan. 1885: [Part II] "Jim's Investments and
King Sollermun"
(456–58)
"Jim knowed all
kinds of
signs . . . "
". . . Sollermun,
dad fetch him!"

Feb. 1885: [Part III] "Royalty
on the
Mississippi"
(544–67)
"Soon as it was
night, out she
shoved . . ."
". . . how the peo-
ple yelled, and
laughed, and kept
it up!"

□

Pudd'nhead Wilson
The Century Magazine, Vols. 47–
48; n.s. 25–26
Dec. 1893: I–III (233–40)
Jan. 1894: IV–VIII (329–40)
Feb. 1894: IX–XI (549–57)

March 1894: XII–XIV (772–81)
April 1894: XV–XVII (817–22)
May 1894: XVIII–XIX (17–24)
June 1894: XX–XXI (232–40)

□

Personal Recollections of Joan of
Arc, by Sieur Louis de Conte
Harpers' New Monthly Magazine,
Vols. 90–92
April 1895: Preface, Part I, I–V
(683–99)
May 1895: VI–IX (845–58)
June 1895: Part II, I–IV
(82–94)
July 1898: V–VII (227–39)
Aug. 1895: VIII–XI (456–67)
Sept. 1895: XII–XV (543–55)
Oct. 1895: XVI–XIX (743–53)
Nov. 1895: XX–XXIII (879–94)
Dec. 1895: Book II, I–VI
(135–50)
Jan. 1896: VII–XIII (288–306)
Feb. 1896: XIV–XVIII
(432–45)
March 1896: Book III, I–VI
(585–97)
April 1896: VII–XIII (655–71)

□

Tom Sawyer, Detective: As Told by
Huck Finn
Harper's New Monthly Magazine,
Vol. 93
Aug. 1896: I–VII (344–61)
". . . I warn't ever
so down on a
corpse before."

Sept. 1896: VIII–XI (519–37)
"It warn't very
cheerful at break-
fast . . ."

☐ ☐ ☐ ☐ ☐

Verne, Jules

The Mysterious Island
Scribner's Monthly (later *Century*),
Vols. 7–11
April 1874: I–III (722–34)
May 1874: IV (49–54)
June 1874: V–VI (204–13)
July 1874: VII–VIII (284–94)
Aug. 1874: IX–X (412–22)
Sept. 1874: XI (574–79)
Oct. 1874: XII (669–74)
Nov. 1874: XIII–XIV (61–70)
Dec. 1874: XV–XVI (158–66)
Jan. 1875: XVII–XXII (342–53)
Feb. 1875: Part II, I–III
(439–48)
March 1875: IV–VI (597–606)
April 1875: VII (711–13)
May 1875: VIII–X (46–52)
June 1875: XI (149–50)
Aug. 1875: XII (470–71)
Sept. 1875: XIII (552–54)
Oct. 1875: XIV–XX (770–77)
March 1876: Part III, I–V
(703–12)
April 1876: VI–XII (866–71)

☐ ☐ ☐ ☐ ☐

Ward, Mrs. Humphrey

The Story of Bessie Costrell
Scribner's Magazine, Vols. 17–18
May 1895: Scenes I–III
(548–64)

June 1895: Scene IV (680–89)
July 1895: Scene V (25–32)

☐

Sir George Tressady
The Century Magazine, Vols. 51–
52; n.s. 29–30
Nov. 1895: I–II (137–50)
Dec. 1895: III–IV (177–92)
Jan. 1896: V–VI (397–408)
Feb. 1896: VII–VIII (570–86)
March 1896: IX (658–68)
April 1896: X–XII (817–46)
May 1896: XIII–XIV (28–47)
June 1896: XV–XVI (179–97)
July 1896: XVII–XVIII
(423–41)
Aug. 1896: XIX–XX (507–22)
Sept. 1896: XXI–XXII (722–33)
Oct. 1896: XXIII–XXIV
(934–53)

☐ ☐ ☐ ☐ ☐

Warner, Charles Dudley

Baddeck and That Sort of Thing
The Atlantic Monthly, Vol. 33
Jan. 1874: I (36–44)
Feb. 1874: II (183–93)
March 1874: III (301–11)
April 1874: IV (453–62)
May 1874: V (576–85)

☐

The Adirondacks Verified
The Atlantic Monthly, Vol. 41
Jan. 1878: I (63–67)

□ □ □ □ □

Woolson, Constance

Feb. 1882:   XXIX–XXXI
                (415–28)
March 1882: XXXII–XXXIV
                (592–607)
April 1882:   XXXV–XXXVII
                (752–60)
May 1882:   XXXVIII–XLI
                (902–18)

□

The Street of the Hyacinth
The Century Magazine, Vol. 24;
n.s. 2
May 1882:   Part I (134–44)
                ". . . The next day
                he went to Paris."
June 1882:   Part II (177–84)
                "The events of
                Raymond Noel's
                life . . ."

□

For the Major
Harper's New Monthly Magazine,
Vols. 65–66
Nov. 1882:   I (907–17)
Dec. 1882:   II–III (93–105)
Jan. 1883:   IV (243–50)
Feb. 1883:   V (405–14)
March 1883: VI (564–71)
April 1883:   VII–IX (749–64)

□

At Mentone
Harper's New Monthly Magazine,
Vol. 68
Jan. 1884:   I (189–216)

                ". . . But wait thy
                summons on the
                sunny shore."
Feb. 1884:   II (367–91)
                " 'So having rung
                that bell once too
                often . . .' "

□

East Angels
Harper's New Monthly Magazine,
Vols. 70–72
Jan. 1885:   I (246–64)
Feb. 1885:   II–III (466–83)
March 1885: IV–V (613–31)
April 1885:   VI (781–99)
May 1885:   VII (879–96)
June 1885:   VIII (102–21)
July 1885:   IX–X (284–304)
Aug. 1885:   XI–XIII (451–73)
Sept. 1885: XIV–XV (522–46)
Oct. 1885:   XVI–XVIII
                (691–713)
Nov. 1885:   XIX (901–8)
Dec. 1885:   XX (115–27)
Jan. 1886:   XXI–XXIII
                (188–210)
Feb. 1886:   XXIV–XXV
                (382–404)
March 1886: XXVI–XXVIII
                (527–45)
April 1886:   XXIX (774–88)
May 1886:   XXX–XXXII
                (949–68)

□

Jupiter Lights
Harper's New Monthly Magazine,
Vols. 78–79
Jan. 1889:   I–IV (240–55)
Feb. 1889:   V–VIII (435–52)

221

Woolson, Constance (continued)

March 1889:	IX–XII (598–610)
April 1889:	XIII–XVI (703–22)
May 1889:	XVII–XVIII (951–58)
June 1889:	XIX–XXI (114–23)
July 1889:	XXII–XXVI (265–82)
Aug. 1889:	XXVII–XXX (415–31)
Sept. 1889:	XXXI–XXXV (583–99)

□

Horace Chase
Harper's New Monthly Magazine,
Vols. 86–87

Jan. 1893:	I–II (198–211)
Feb. 1893:	III–IV (438–54)
March 1893:	V–VII (596–613)
April 1893:	VIII–IX (753–70)
May 1893:	X–XII (882–97)
June 1893:	XIII–XIV (140–49)
July 1893:	XV–XVII (276–86)
Aug. 1893:	XVIII–XIX (414–23)
Sept. 1893:	XX–XXI (595–602)
Oct. 1893:	XXII–XXIV (755–70)

Index

For authors of nineteenth-century serial works, see also **Works of Serial Fiction** (151–222), arranged alphabetically.